Responsible Finance India Report 2016

Thank you for choosing a SAGE product!
If you have any comment, observation or feedback,
I would like to personally hear from you.
Please write to me at **contactceo@sagepub.in**

Vivek Mehra, Managing Director and CEO, SAGE India.

Bulk Sales

SAGE India offers special discounts
for purchase of books in bulk.
We also make available special imprints
and excerpts from our books on demand.

For orders and enquiries, write to us at

Marketing Department
SAGE Publications India Pvt Ltd
B1/I-1, Mohan Cooperative Industrial Area
Mathura Road, Post Bag 7
New Delhi 110044, India

E-mail us at **marketing@sagepub.in**

Get to know more about SAGE

Be invited to SAGE events, get on our mailing list.
Write today to **marketing@sagepub.in**

Responsible Finance India Report 2016
Client First: Tracking Social Performance Practices

Alok Misra

Los Angeles | London | New Delhi
Singapore | Washington DC | Melbourne

First published in 2017 by

 SAGE Publications India Pvt Ltd
B1/I-1 Mohan Cooperative Industrial Area
Mathura Road, New Delhi 110 044, India
www.sagepub.in

SAGE Publications Inc
2455 Teller Road
Thousand Oaks, California 91320, USA

SAGE Publications Ltd
1 Oliver's Yard, 55 City Road
London EC1Y 1SP, United Kingdom

SAGE Publications Asia-Pacific Pte Ltd
3 Church Street
#10-04 Samsung Hub
Singapore 049483

ACCESS Development Services
28, Hauz Khas Village
New Delhi 110 016
www.accessdev.org

Published by Vivek Mehra for SAGE Publications India Pvt Ltd, Phototypeset in 10/13 pt Minion Pro by Diligent Typesetter India Pvt Ltd, Delhi and printed at Sai Print-o-Pack, New Delhi.

Library of Congress Cataloging-in-Publication Data Available

ISBN: 978-93-860-6220-8 (PB)

SAGE Team: Rajesh Dey, Vandana Gupta, Shobana Paul and Rajinder Kaur

Disclaimer: The views expressed in this publication are those of the authors and do not necessarily reflect the views and policies of ACCESS Development Services.

Cover photograph courtesy: ACCESS.

Sponsors & Partners

 WORLD BANK GROUP

Maanaveeya Development
& Finance Private Limited

Contents

List of Tables, Figures, Boxes, Annexures, and Abbreviations

Tables

Figures

Boxes

Annexures

Abbreviations

AKMI	Association of Karnataka Microfinance Institutions
AP	Andhra Pradesh
APY	Atal Pension Yojana
BC	Business Correspondents
BFIL	Bharat Financial Inclusion Limited
BM	Bank Mitra
BMM	Block Mission Manager
BMZ	Federal Ministry for Economic Cooperation and Development
BOP	Bottom of Pyramid
BPL	Below Poverty Line
BSR	Basic Statistical Returns
CAR	Capacity Assessment Rating
CB	Credit Bureau
CDF	Credit & Development Forum
CDFIs	Community Development Financial Institutions
CGAP	Consultative Group to Assist the Poor
CGR	Client Grievance Redressal
CGT	Compulsory Group Training
CIBIL	Credit Information Bureau (India) Limited
CICs	Credit Information Companies
CIF	Community Investment Fund
CIR	Credit Information Report
CoC	Code of Conduct
CoCA	Code of Conduct Assessment
CPP	Client Protection Principles
CSR	Corporate Social Responsibility
DBT	Direct Benefit Transfer
DFS	Digital Financial Services
DMM	District Mission Manager
DRDAs	District Rural Development Agencies
ESAF	Evangelical Social Action Forum
EC	Enforcement Committee
FGDs	Focus Group Discussions
FLCC	Financial Literacy and Counselling Centres
FPC	Fair Practices Code
FWWB	Friends of Women's World Banking
GIIRS	Global Impact Investing Rating System
GPFI	Global Partnership for Financial Inclusion
GRM	Grievance Redressal Mechanism
GRO	Grievance Redressal Officer
HDI	Human Development Index
HO	Head Office
IA	Internal Audit
IC Index	Industry Compliance Index
IFAD	International Fund for Agricultural Development
IFC	International Finance Corporation
IHHL	Individual Household Latrine

IKP	Indira Kranthi Patham
IMEF	India Microfinance Equity Fund
IMFP	India Microfinance Platform
IMPS	Immediate Payment Service
IoI	Incidence of Indebtedness
IPO	Initial Public Offer
IRDP	Integrated Rural Development Programme
IRP	Internal Rules of Procedure
ITU	International Telecommunication Union
JAM	Jan Dhan, Aadhaar, and Mobile phone
JLG	Joint Liability Group
KAMFI	Kerala Association of Microfinance Institutions
KYC	Know Your Customer
LU	Loan Utilization
MAS	Mahila Abhivruddhi Society
MFDEF	Microfinance Development Equity Fund
MFIs	Microfinance Institutions
MFIN	Microfinance Institutions Network
MIS	Management Information System
MIX	Microfinance Information Exchange
MP	Madhya Pradesh
MUDRA	Micro Units Development & Refinance Agency Ltd
NABARD	National Bank for Agriculture and Rural Development
NAFSCOB	National Federation of State Cooperative Banks
NBFCs	Non Banking Finance Companies
NCD	Nonconvertible Debenture
NPAs	Non Performing Assets
NPCI	National Payments Corporation of India
NRLM	National Rural Livelihoods Mission
OD	Overdraft
OID	Overindebtedness
P2P	Peer-to-peer
PACS	Primary Agricultural Credit Societies
PBs	Payment Banks
PIDA	Protection of Depositors' Act
PMJDY	Pradhan Mantri Jan Dhan Yojana
PMJJY	Prime Minister Jeevan Jyoti Yojana
PMMY	Pradhan Mantri Mudra Yojana
POS	Point of Sale
PPI	Progress out of Poverty Index
PPP	Purchasing Power Parity
PSIG	Poorest State Inclusive Growth Programme
RBI	Reserve Bank of India
RF	Revolving Fund
RFF	Responsible Finance Forum
ROE	Return on Equity
RRBs	Regional Rural Banks
SAMN	South Asian Micro-entrepreneurs Network
SBLP	SHG-Bank Linkage Programme

SERP	Society for Elimination of Rural Poverty
SFBs	Small Finance Banks
SGSY	Swarnjayanti Gram Swarozgar Yojana
SHG	Self-help Group
SHPA	Self-help Promoting Agency
SIDBI	Small Industries Development Bank of India
SIM	Subscriber Identity Module
SME	Small and Medium Enterprises
SOP	Standard Operating Procedure
SPM	Social Performance Management
SPM	Social Performance Measurement
SPTF	Social Performance Task Force
SROs	Self-regulatory Organizations
TPE	Third-party Evaluation
TPP	Third-party Products
UCoC	Unified Code of Conduct
UID	Unique Identification
UP	Uttar Pradesh
UPI	Unified Payments Interface
UPMA	Uttar Pradesh Microfinance Association
USSPM	Universal Standards for Social Performance Management
VARs	Voluntary Advance Receipts
VOCs	Voice of Customers
VRF	Vulnerability Reduction Fund
WASH	Water, Sanitation and Hygiene

Foreword

The slew of government programs focused on financial inclusion launched over the last two-and-a half years—starting with near-universal coverage of bank accounts followed by offering risk protection and old age security through insurance and pension schemes and enterprise loans through MUDRA—were designed to enable comprehensive access of financial services till the last mile and to the unreached. The delivery of government programs continues to be channeled through mainstream banks and their business correspondents (BCs). While the viability of the BC model has been in discussion so far, there have now been some initial deliberations and studies on the need for code of conduct or client protection standards for the BC channel. With over 240 million bank accounts (by August 2016), access to formal banking through Jan Dhan Yojana (JDY) and their Aadhaar seeding can be transformative by reducing leakage in government payments, promoting electronic payments, and progressively reducing the use of cash. However, the recent news of banks themselves putting money into JDY accounts under pressure to make the zero balance accounts 'active' raises concerns about ethics, accuracy of data, and potential for misuse.

In parallel, RBI has been working toward setting up of differentiated banks, at a fast pace, resulting in small finance banks and payments banks getting ready to be operational in the next few months. RBI is also expected to release guidelines for peer-to-peer (P2P) lending, providing legitimacy to another channel that would potentially offer services to the unbanked and low-income segments as well. Several non-banking finance companies (NBFCs) and FinTechs are actively developing technology-led models for credit assessment and delivery, which could scale up in the coming years. While all these initiatives and policies will positively create a dynamic landscape of institutions and delivery models for financial inclusion, the efforts of enabling client education and ensuring client protection to keep pace with these developments will need proactive and concurrent attention of all stakeholders.

Meanwhile, the existing microfinance channels—microfinance institution (MFI) and self-help group (SHG) bank linkage—continue to provide services to this client segment, albeit with much different growth rates. Gross MFI loan portfolio grew by 84% over the last FY with growth in client outreach of 44% and an increase of 65% in the amount of loan disbursed during the year (*MFIN MicroMeter*). SHG channel in comparison showed an increase of 23% in loans disbursed and 4% in the number of SHGs with bank loans. A significant policy direction of the RBI this year has been the requirement for banks to report SHG credit data to credit bureaus; the progress on this front, however, is yet to be seen since there are gaps in member-level data available with banks. A fast emerging channel of credit to microfinance clients is lending by banks through BCs in addition to bulk loans to MFIs. Concerns on high MFI growth rates have been raised along with risks associated with (sole) reliance on credit bureau for credit decision owing to possibility of gaps in bureau data. Incidences of client distress in some districts of Madhya Pradesh and Uttar Pradesh point to the need for greater vigil on part of institutions in credit policies and processes. The MFI sector, nevertheless, deserves credit for showing progress on embracing responsible practices, which is evident from examples and best practices incrementally shared across editions of the *Responsible Finance India Report*.

So, while the *Responsible Finance India Report* in its earlier avatar largely tracked social performance-related issues for about 20 million MFI clients, it now needs to expand its sweep to 240 million, maybe more, clients from low-income households that have been integrated into the mainstream financial ecosystem through efforts under the Pradhan Mantri Jan Dhan Yojana. How comprehensively this will be done, will remain a challenge, at least in the short run.

The transition of *Microfinance India: Social Performance Management (SPM) Report* to broader coverage of channels beyond microfinance (MFIs and SHGs) was initiated in spirit in 2014 with inclusion of themes on BCs and (micro) insurance, and in 2015 the report was rechristened to *Responsible Finance India Report*. Since SPM is a term not commonly understood and used by stakeholders outside the MFI space, the group of advisors supported the idea of 'responsible finance' as an appropriate term that could cover all channels, mainstream, and alternate, reaching out to the low-income and poor clients. The challenge, however, of fully transitioning from microfinance to responsible inclusive finance is still distant because of continued limitations of availability of relevant performance data beyond outreach numbers for channels others than MFIs. It is our endeavor to exhort stakeholders to undertake institutional analysis and assessments and sector-level research to plug the gaps in information on performance of financial inclusion efforts to cover issues of client protection and depth and quality of services delivered to clients.

We are fortunate that Dr Alok Misra accepted the challenge of authoring the report for another year. We are deeply grateful for his efforts in progressively expanding the ambit of the report beyond MFIs while working under the limitations of data availability, and for bringing together a well-structured and researched document. With transition in the team at Inclusive Finance India Secretariat, Dr Misra had to manage with limited support this year. We are thankful to all the contributors, individuals, and institutions that responded to requests from Dr Misra for interviews, insights, data, and studies. We particularly appreciate that Dr Kshatrapati Shivaji, CMD, SIDBI, provided his time and shared insights for the report. Teams at CRIF High Mark and MFIN were generous with their inputs. We must acknowledge the support from Department for International Development (DFID) and SIDBI for supporting two client-level studies as part of the Poorest States Inclusive Growth Programme—one on 'indebtedness level of clients' and second on 'microfinance client voices'. The studies provided important field-level inputs for this year's report. I am thankful to the board of directors and the Inclusive Finance India group of advisors for their guidance on the structuring of the report.

ASSIST is fortunate to receive consistent support from the key sponsors SIDBI and the World Bank Group (Finance and Markets) since the inception of this annual document in 2011. We also thank the teams of Maanaveeya and Dia Vikas for their support to the *Responsible Finance India Report*. While Standard Chartered Bank, the original lead supporter of this report, is not a sponsor this year, we appreciate Balaji at StanC for being a friend and well-wisher and for his continued interest in this initiative. I would like to thank the team at SAGE Publications for their patience and perseverance with tight schedules in bringing out the report and hope for much wider dissemination of the publication in India and globally. I am grateful for Vipin Sharma's leadership and guidance to the new and small team at ACCESS ASSIST in managing this sectoral initiative. I must appreciate Keerti's efforts in coordinating with the publisher and author, Sivani for leading on the overall management, and Lalitha for ably supporting with the logistics.

I am happy that the sixth edition of *Responsible Finance India Report* will be released at the inaugural of the Inclusive Finance India Summit in December 2016. With greater mainstreaming and diversity of financial service providers and intermediaries, a progressive and enabling policy environment, and the potential offered through disruptive technology, these are exceptionally exciting times for financial inclusion in India. I hope the *Responsible Finance India Report* will continue to track performance of existing and emerging channels, document and share good practices, raise flags and highlight gaps in policy and practice, and offer recommendations for promoting ethics, transparency, and client centricity in financial inclusion.

Radhika Agashe
Executive Director
ACCESS ASSIST

Preface

This is the second year of my authoring the Responsible Finance report. The report was rechristened last year from its earlier name, Social Performance Management. This was done to broaden the coverage of the report beyond microfinance institutions (MFIs) as responsible finance has become a key theme in financial sector policy globally. It has been realized that full potential of financial inclusion can be reaped only with integrating responsible lens in financial sector and responsibility can be broadly defined as matching clients' needs and preferences. India's financial inclusion landscape has never looked more promising as in current times. Last two–three years have ushered in paradigm changes. The policy has shifted from being bank-led to channel-neutral, and new initiatives in the form of Pradhan Mantri Jan Dhan Yojana (PMJDY), small finance banks (SFBs), payment banks (PBs), Micro Units Development & Refinance Agency Ltd (MUDRA), and banking correspondents (BCs) have been added to the existing canvas of commercial banks, regional rural banks (RRBs), cooperative banks, and microfinance (MFIs and SHG–Bank Linkage Programme [SBLP]). The impact has been instantaneous in cases like PMJDY, wherein the scheme has enabled universal savings inclusion by opening ~0.25 billion accounts in 18 months. The policy initiatives have been backed by advances in ecosystem with Jan Dhan, Aadhaar, and Mobile (JAM) trinity coverage covering almost all and opening up possibilities of robust e-KYC-based infrastructure and mobile phone-based financial services. In my 26 years of association with the journey of India's financial sector to reach the unbanked, the possibility of universal financial inclusion to ensure inclusive growth has never looked more achievable. I am thankful that I was asked to author this report by Vipin Sharma, CEO, ACCESS Development Services, in current interesting times. I deeply value the opportunity.

As the criticality of 'Responsible Finance' is being increasingly recognized, it is important that in the wave of new initiatives, clients' needs and preferences are accorded primacy in the delivery of financial services and mistakes of earlier top–down model are avoided. This is more so when the client segment belongs to bottom of pyramid and is vulnerable on account of its credit needs. While the new initiatives will take some time to show results, at present the bottom of pyramid (BOP) segment financial services space continues to be dominated by microfinance, cooperative banks, and small borrowal accounts of commercial banks. Microfinance sector in India accounts for an outreach of nearly 100 million clients and plays a vital role in financial inclusion of the excluded. Commercial banks have ~20 million small borrowal accounts and cooperatives banks have an equally high outreach—data available for cooperatives is dated. However, the report focuses on MFIs, SBLP, commercial banks through BCs and PMJDY, and MUDRA on account of twin factors. First, there is enough granular data available for these channels and second, availability of information/studies on double-bottom-line performance. Also, these channels play a major role in financial inclusion of the poor and excluded and are also witnessing high growth. The report analyzes their double-bottom-line performance, analyzes risks to their client-centricity model, and suggests policy and operational suggestions for strengthening the responsible finance agenda. The unifying thread of the report is that all initiatives and channels have to be evaluated on the touchstone of client centricity—growth without this is of little use in meeting the inclusion challenge. It is hoped that in near future, the stakeholders will be able to evolve responsible finance metrics for all channels; this report can serve as defining the broad contours of responsible finance.

A sector report of this type requires cooperation and sharing of information from several stakeholders. I have a lot of people and organizations to thank for providing data, sparing time for discussions, sharing study findings and reports, and pointing toward useful sources of information.

The chapters on MFIs have benefited immensely from the insights shared by MFI heads and senior management (Udaya Kumar and Gururaj of Grameen Financial Services Pvt. Ltd [GFSPL], Radhakrishnan of Janalakshmi, M.R. Rao and Ritesh Chatterjee of Bharat Financial Inclusion Limited [BFIL], Devesh Sachdev of Fusion, and Sandhya Suresh of EMFIL), Ratna Vishwanathan, CEO of Microfinance Institutions Network (MFIN), bankers and donors (Manoj Mittal and Prakash Kumar of SIDBI, Jiji Mammen, CEO, MUDRA, and Ragini Chaudhary from DFID), technical agencies (Manoj Sharma, Director, MicroSave and Isabelle Barres, Hema, and Tanwi from Smart Campaign), and global platforms (Leah from Social Performance Task Force [SPTF]). Equally significant was the contribution of 24 MFIs who responded to the data request. It was my good fortune that these senior functionaries spared time to provide valuable insights and data. The data provided by Parijat Garg, CRIF High Mark Credit Information Services, has been valuable in analyzing risks in Chapter 5. Special thanks is due to Dr Kshatrapati Shivaji, CMD, Small Industries Development Bank of India (SIDBI), for being generous in providing substantial time to share his sector insights and agree for an interview. The chapter on role of self-regulatory organizations (SROs) would not have been possible but for Ratna Vishwanathan, CEO, MFIN, cheerfully agreeing to provide details requested by me at short notice and agreeing to point out factual errors in the chapter. Thanks is also due to Sugandh, Pallavi, and Devika in MFIN. ACCESS was instrumental in commissioning two client-level studies by IFMR and M2i; Chapter 4 capturing client perspective comes from these studies especially M2i study. Deepak of M2i also wrote major parts of Chapter 4.

The credit for chapter on SBLP is due to Dr H.K. Bhanwala (Chairman, NABARD), G.C. Chintala (CGM, NABARD), and C.S. Reddy (CEO of APMAS). Dr Bhanwala agreed to meet at a short notice and shared his unique perspective on issues pertaining to SBLP and National Rural Livelihoods Mission (NRLM). C.S. Reddy on account of his long association with SHG movement enlightened me on various historical issues and current challenges. I cannot thank him enough for sharing the draft report of multi-state SBLP assessment conducted in 2016.

I am thankful to Radhika and Keerti from Access Assist for their help throughout the assignment and Raja Banerjee for help with data entry. The list can go on and on but considering the length limitation, I seek apology from those whose names I have missed. This report would not have been possible but for the generous help of all stakeholders.

Much has been done in advancing responsible financial inclusion and I hope that the report provides enough thinking and action points for improving the performance of MFIs, SBLP, BCs, and MUDRA to meet the needs of BOP clients. Action on the policy and operational suggestions in the last chapter will strengthen the cause of responsible finance for the excluded by the existing and emerging institutions.

Alok Misra

Inclusive Finance at the Cusp: Keeping Clients at the Core

1

Chapter

1.1 GOAL IN SIGHT; DIVERSIFIED FINANCIAL SECTOR TAKES SHAPE

The quest for universal financial inclusion has been a central objective of India's development policy since independence but its achievement never seemed so near. While the erstwhile minister of state for finance declared the task complete with the implementation of Pradhan Mantri Jan Dhan Yojana (PMJDY)[1] and exhorted the financial sector to move to the next stage—of deepening access—the task is far from over. Real universal financial inclusion would require going beyond the opening of bank accounts, to ensuring functional access points, availability of varied financial services beyond savings accounts, to credit, insurance, and remittances, and above all, seeing that the services are 'demand driven' and 'responsible'. Being responsible, which is the focus of this report, requires keeping clients at the core of service delivery and avoiding a top-down approach, as well as focusing on outreach numbers as outcome measures. The crucial aspect of 'client centricity' will avoid the mistakes of a supply-driven past and be meaningful to those for whom it is intended. Despite this, it is undeniable that in terms of policy, technology, infrastructure, or institutions, the situation has never seemed so full of promise.

The past year under review saw a phase of grounding of new institutions and programs announced in the previous two to three years. The flagship financial inclusion program of the government—PMJDY—aimed at ensuring that each household in the country has access to a basic bank account, clocked an impressive outreach of 22.37 crore bank accounts by July 2016[2]. These impressive numbers in a record time won the PMJDY an entry into the Guinness Book of World Records. PMJDY is supplemented by pension and insurance schemes to provide holistic financial inclusion. However, the outreach under these add-on schemes does not match PMJDY numbers, with Prime Minister Jeevan Jyoti Yojana (PMJJY, an insurance scheme) reaching an enrollment of 3.07 crore by July 2016. MUDRA was launched in 2015 with the slogan of "funding the unfunded," which implied that MUDRA will provide loans to the small entrepreneur segment hitherto considered too small by banks and too big by microfinance institutions (MFIs). MUDRA claims to have funded through banks 34 million small entrepreneurs during the financial year 2015–16 with a sanctioned loan amount of ₹137,449 crore under Pradhan Mantri Mudra Yojana (PMMY)[3].

The two new universal banks given licenses in 2014 (Bandhan and IDFC) have started banking operations, adopting different strategies. While Bandhan rides on its prebank avatar infrastructure of branches and clients, IDFC has adopted the route of acquisition of MFIs to cater to the low-income segment[4]. Of the 10 entities given in-principle licenses as small finance banks (SFBs) in 2015, 8 were MFIs; moreover, the year 2016 saw a lot of subsequent activity on this front. While the smaller-sized MFIs are still working out their transformation strategy as the 18-month in-principle phase ends early 2017, Equitas and Ujjivan recently concluded their initial public offer (IPO) to boost their domestic shareholding, for complying with norms. Both IPOs received massive responses, being oversubscribed 17 and 40 times, respectively, for the two institutions. This reflects the confidence of institutional as well as retail investors in their business model. Equitas and Ujjivan are expected to commence operations as SFBs late 2016.

Janalakshmi, another large MFI, also plans to commence operations late 2016.

The wave of policies and institutions launched in 2014 and 2015 also included payment banks (PBs), a concept quite new to the financial sector. The objective of PBs as stated in the guidelines[5] is to ensure cost-effective services, greater proximity, access to remittances, and small savings. PBs were seen as a graduation model for prepaid issuers and mobile network operators (MNOs) similar to SFBs, providing a graduation model for MFIs. However, even at the time of drafting guidelines, it was felt by experts that by not allowing PBs to lend, there will be viability issues. The year 2016 has validated some of that apprehension, with 3 out of 11 in-principle license awardees deciding not to go ahead[6]. The Reserve Bank of India (RBI) governor opined that those withdrawing did not think through while applying, and added that the model suits those who have an existing infrastructure, such as MNOs and prepaid issuers. There is merit in that, as even in the case of universal banks, Bandhan with its established network has forged ahead of other players. Similarly, India Post, which is one of the entities granted a PB license, is being wooed by investors and banks because of its deep pan-India reach through nearly 150,000 outlets. However, the issue of the lack of a business model cannot be overlooked, as it has been accentuated with almost universal coverage of bank accounts and a wide network of banking correspondents. By the end of 2016, a few PBs will become operational, adding to the mosaic of financial intermediaries.

The year also saw a move from the Central Bank in another innovative sphere—peer-to-peer (P2P) lending—which has seen quite a bit of traction in the past few years in India (discussed in Chapter 7). RBI released a discussion paper on P2P lending in April 2016. The discussion paper attempts to assess the various P2P models prevalent in India as well as internationally, and the legal and regulatory framework for their operation. It is expected that the formulation of guidelines on P2P lending will provide legitimacy and fillip to the operations of existing P2P lenders in India.

1.1.1 JAM to Provide the Backbone for Financial Inclusion

While the financial sector has become diverse as never before with functional specialization, the most significant change that will provide the backbone for financial access is the implementation of

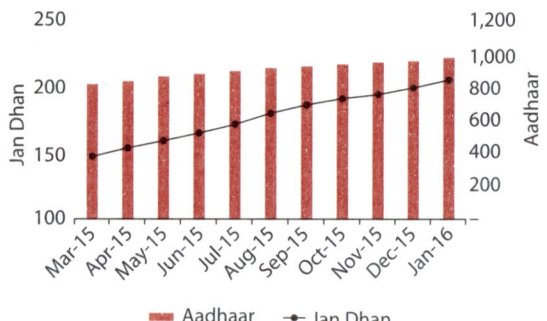

Figure 1.1 The Thickening of JAM–Jan Dhan, Aadhaar, and Mobile Phone—Coverage over Time
Source: Economic Survey, 2016–17.

the JAM trinity (Jan Dhan, Aadhaar, and mobile phone). The identity issue is addressed by Aadhaar, which based on a unique number and biometrics, and has the capability to authenticate identity electronically. Despite initial skepticism, the coverage of 1,020 million people and its potential to be the base on which other financial services can be built is now being acknowledged by all. The genius of the concept lies in its use being limited to authentication rather than the normal practice of bundling authentication with entitlements. Its potential has been realized through the opening of Jan Dhan accounts (Figure 1.1), adoption of Aadhaar as Know Your Customer (KYC) by MFIs, and also the recent move by few MFIs to use biometric-based authentication of Aadhaar. The ubiquitous nature of Aadhaar lends it for use in multiple requirements of the citizen, be it bank account, loans, mobile phone connections, or cooking gas connections as well as social assistance programs. Aadhaar's utility of online authentication provides a common platform that can be used across programs and institutions. The platform of biometric-based unique ID, high penetration of mobile phones, and universal coverage of bank accounts (JAM) provide robust bedrock on which multiple financial inclusion efforts can be built further. Delivery of financial services through mobile phones has already decreased costs, and the Aadhaar-based authentication adds to risk mitigation strategies. Seeding of all loan and savings accounts with Aadhaar in the near future could enhance the reliability of credit bureau checks.

The potential of the JAM trinity to further financial inclusion and be cost effective has been further enhanced by advances in the payments system. The launch of the unified payments interface (UPI) by the National Payments Corporation of India (NPCI)

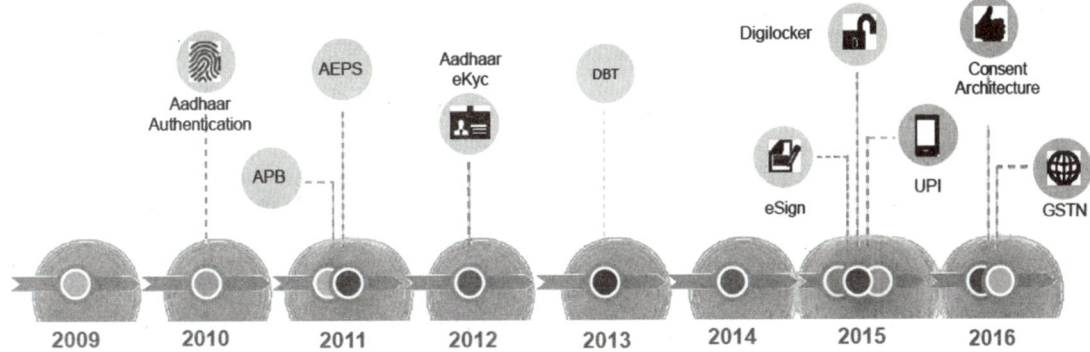

Figure 1.2 The Evolution of the India Stack—Built on JAM

Source: Ericsson Mobility Report.

in April 2016 has further bolstered the ecosystem for financial inclusion as well as India's movement toward a cashless economy. The UPI is an advance over the immediate payment service (IMPS) as payments up to ₹100,000 lakh can be made through an Aadhaar number, a mobile number or a virtual address through SMS, obviating the need for an IFSC code, or a bank account number. The UPI is interoperable across banks. Nandan Nilekani, the architect of Aadhaar, said that this is leapfrogging of the payments system and added that "Payments have evolved in different ways. You had a card system, mobile money, Internet e-wallets. But completely mobile interoperable person-to-person instant real time with push and pull really didn't exist anywhere"[7]. It is hoped that the UPI, by providing a phone-based real-time payment system through the banking network, will lead to the elimination of e-wallets.

The evolution of the JAM trinity and its application is nicely captured in Figure 1.2.

The India stack has already achieved key milestones such as direct benefit transfer (DBT) to bank accounts and electronic Aadhaar-based KYC, and its future components include e-signature, digital locker, and UPI. Financial institutions can access these features and database to know about the customer and customer history, and based on that take lending decisions.

These technological, ecosystem innovations, coupled with a vibrant financial sector landscape, have brought the promise of universal financial inclusion through responsible financial services within a striking distance. At the cost of repetition, it is worth stressing that if the financial services do not adopt a client-centric approach, the achievement of

numbers will not optimize the potential of inclusion. *The Responsible Finance India Report, 2015*[8] brought out the link between financial access and growth, as empirical studies have shown a strong positive correlation between deeper financial system and economic growth. Global agencies like the World Bank also enunciate this view, and critically say that it is the poor who benefit greatly from using basic payments, savings and insurance services, stressing that financial inclusion can be a powerful accelerator of economic growth, helping achieve the goals of eliminating extreme poverty and building shared prosperity. At the same time, it is also important to note that unless the financial services are client-centric and cater to the special needs of the poor such as small amounts, frequent transactions, physical proximity, and cost sensitivity, the link between financial access and development diminishes.

India is at a tipping point in financial inclusion, and it is imperative that past lessons from supply-led and subsidized approach to inclusion are avoided and at the same time excesses of the market are not allowed to be passed on to the poor. A fine balance between sustainability and affordability is a key to the approach, wherein clients come first and are protected against unscrupulous practices, profiteering, and indebtedness.

1.2 FINANCIAL SECTOR PLAYERS AND LEVEL OF INCLUSION

As discussed in the previous section, the financial sector has become diverse, with specialized institutions and some institutions focusing exclusively on the BOP segment while others catering to the entire spectrum (Figure 1.3).

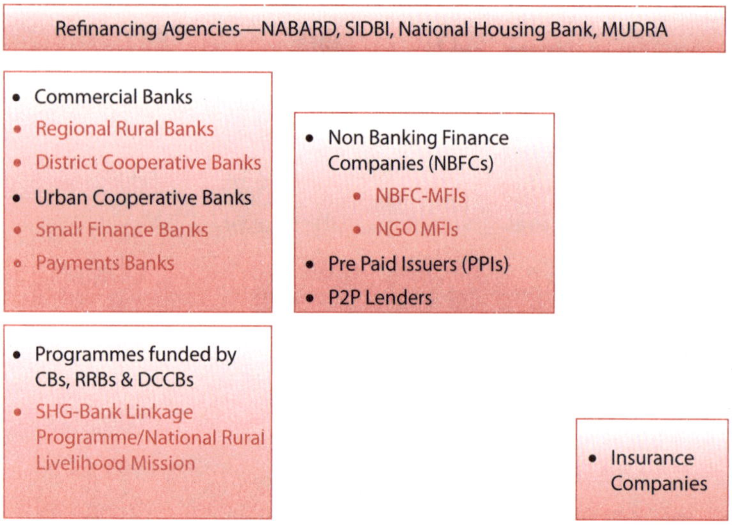

Refinancing Agencies—NABARD, SIDBI, National Housing Bank, MUDRA

- Commercial Banks
- Regional Rural Banks
- District Cooperative Banks
- Urban Cooperative Banks
- Small Finance Banks
- Payments Banks

- Non Banking Finance Companies (NBFCs)
  - NBFC-MFIs
  - NGO MFIs
- Pre Paid Issuers (PPIs)
- P2P Lenders

- Programmes funded by CBs, RRBs & DCCBs
- SHG-Bank Linkage Programme/National Rural Livelihood Mission

- Insurance Companies

Figure 1.3 Refinancing Agencies

Source: Author.

Note: Red font indicates exclusive BoP focus.

The landscape is enriched with the presence of 126,000 banking correspondents, who are enabling the banking system to tackle the last mile. In addition to individual bank BCs, there is a trend of MFIs increasingly adopting the BC model to build their portfolio as it obviates capital requirement and partly offsets credit risk.

Financial inclusion data relating to the BOP segment are not available readily, as outreach is not mapped to the poverty profile, and even the limited available data are in silos. The Global Findex dataset released in 2015 is the second round of data under the Global Findex initiative, and that captured the overall financial access scenario in India in 2014. The dataset has become out-of-date in a short time primarily because of new initiatives like PMJDY and MUDRA. As the topic of responsible finance is primarily concerned with the BOP segment, it is useful to look at financial exclusion in this segment. It is not possible to have estimates for savings exclusion, as the numbers of bank accounts do not provide insights into the account holders' socio-economic status. The RBI data[9] on deposits for scheduled commercial banks (which includes RRBs) provide area-wise (rural, semi-urban, urban) and gender-wise breakdown, but does not go beyond that. However, considering that PMJDY has achieved coverage of nearly 22 crore deposit accounts and was directed at the financially excluded segment, it can be roughly estimated that the deposit side inclusion at household level is almost universal. This is a broad estimate, as there is no way to know whether accounts opened under PMJDY are new accounts, or additional accounts of existing customers, and which segment they belong to.

A more accurate estimate can be made in respect of the credit-side exclusion of the BOP segment by using a proxy indicator of the loan size for bank lending, while it can be safely assumed that the entire microfinance lending through the SHG-Bank Linkage Programme (SBLP) as well as MFIs is exclusively for the BOP segment. For scheduled banks, the outreach under two loan sizes can be seen (loans less than ₹25,000 and loans less than ₹200,000), assuming that typically loans to the BOP segment would not be above this limit. In case of cooperative banks, the data published by National Federation of State Cooperative Banks (NAFSCOB) on number of borrowers of primary agricultural credit societies (PACS) belonging to scheduled caste, scheduled tribe, small farmer, and rural artisans categories can be taken on a conservative side for analyzing the outreach under the BOP segment, though all the PACS borrowers typically belong to this segment. The size of the BOP segment can be derived from the poverty percentage data. The Indian government's definition of the poverty line can be taken for this, which corresponds to the World Bank's $1.90 at the purchasing power parity (2011 Prices) poverty line. This analysis is neither decimal-perfect nor exhaustive. This is because a few institutions such as non banking finance companies (NBFCs) and urban cooperative banks are not included, as their outreach is not focused on the BOP; however, they also lend a part of their portfolio to the BOP. Further, the date of various datasets is not consistent and cases of overlap of the same client sourcing loans from two different sources limit the accuracy. However, this does provide us a good picture of credit penetration among the BOP segment (Table 1.1).

The outreach based on this analysis seems quite flattering, with a 60% coverage. The exemplary contribution of microfinance (both SHGs and MFIs) is evident from the fact that both contribute about 60% share in the BOP segment, while banks account for a mere 20% share. However, the ground-level situation shows a very different picture, with both sectoral and regional disparities. Evidence for this comes from the recently concluded FinScope survey[10], which shows that a total of 23% households in four states (i.e., Uttar Pradesh, Madhya Pradesh, Odisha, and Jharkhand) avail credit. Of this, only

Table 1.1 **Estimate of Credit Penetration at Bottom of Pyramid**

S. No.	Particulars	Number/Percentage
a.	Population 2011	1,210,854,977
b.	Poverty percentage as per government	21.9%
c.	BOP segment (a)*(b)	254,279,545
d.	Outreach of scheduled banks as on 31.3.2015 (loans less than ₹25,000)#	29,858,230
e.	MFI outreach as on 31.3.2016	32,500,000
f.	SHG outreach as on 31.3.2016 (assuming 13 members per SHG)	60,744,073
g.	PACS outreach to SC/ST/small farmers/artisans as on 31.3.2014	29,302,000
h.	Total BOP outreach	152,404,303
i.	Percentage coverage at BOP level (h/c)	59.94%

Sources: https://rbi.org.in/Scripts/AnnualPublications.aspx?head=Basic%20Statistical%20Returns; http://nafscob.org/pacs_f.htm, accessed on September 23, 2016; Micrometer (data as on March 31, 2016, MFIN; NABARD; Economic Survey 2016–17 (Table 9.3); Census of India, 2011.

7% access credit through banks and 3% through other formal (non-bank) sources. Despite the policy emphasis on formal channels, 13% continue to seek credit from informal sources. Moreover, the FinScope dataset does not focus exclusively on the BOP segment. This underlies the fact that despite impressive gains, much of which are regionally skewed, a lot of work needs to be done on credit-side inclusion in deprived areas (Figure 1.4).

On the savings side, the FinScope study does validate the assumption of near universal coverage reporting 92% coverage even in these four poorest states (Figure 1.5).

The underlying implications of the analysis is that while savings side access has become almost universal, credit-side inclusion has a lot of spatial

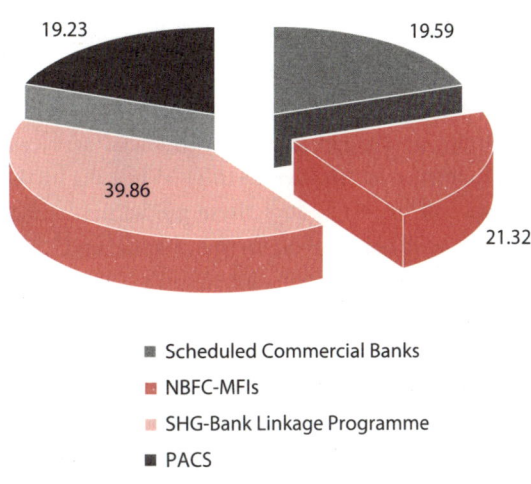

- ■ Scheduled Commercial Banks
- ■ NBFC-MFIs
- ■ SHG-Bank Linkage Programme
- ■ PACS

Figure 1.4 Percentage Share of Agencies in BOP Coverage

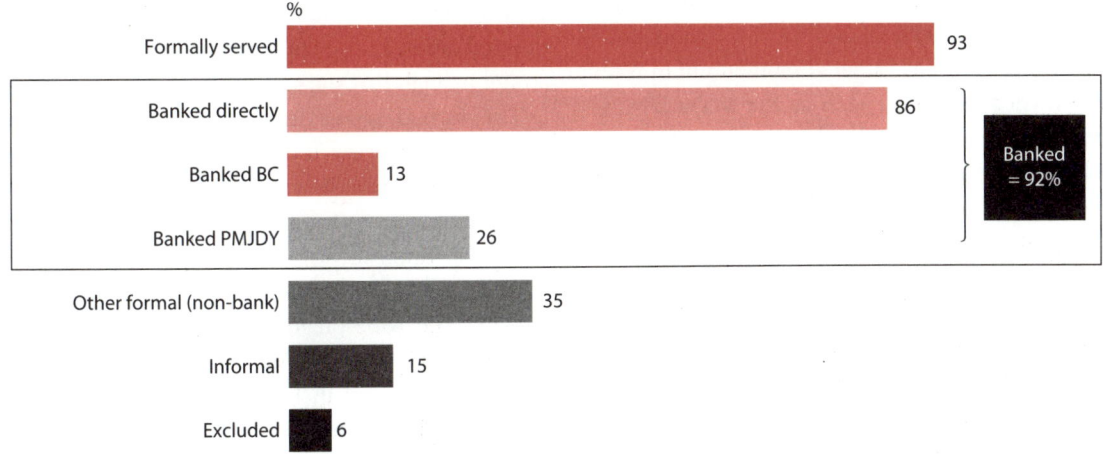

Figure 1.5 Percentage of Households Having Access to Financial Services in PSIG States

Source: FINSCOPE. 2015. *Consumer Survey under the Poorest States Inclusive Growth Programme,* Figure, 24.

gaps, and the situation worsens in the case of insurance and pension. While on the savings side the need of the hour is to back the access with efforts, to see traction in the accounts, on the credit side, the spatial gaps need to be filled by moving away from saturated areas (Chapter 5). The other implication is that microfinance plays an important role in credit-side inclusion, especially for the BOP segment, and it needs to be ensured that lending to this segment is 'responsible'—lending that is cost efficient, tailored to client needs, avoids over-indebting clients, and is delivered transparently. The advances in the ecosystem by way of JAM, UPI, and specialized institutions need to be harnessed to achieve this. Digital and Fin-Tech are the catch phrases now. While BCs rely on them for transactions, and MFIs are increasingly adopting features such as tab-based record keeping and card-based and cashless disbursements, how the clients perceive these technological advances is the key question. Globally, efforts are on to ensure consumer protection in digital financial services (the following section details this). While the institutions will need to adopt these guidelines, some pointers have emerged on the BC channel and have critical lessons for responsible finance (Chapter 7).

1.3 RESPONSIBLE FINANCE FRAMEWORK: NEW INITIATIVES

Last year's *Responsible Finance Report* brought out the international initiatives in financial inclusion, showing as to how it has become the policy pivot of governments and multilateral institutions, based on the premise that financial depth in an economy leads to growth and inclusive development. This focus coincided with the advent of microfinance in early 1990s, and has gathered momentum in recent years. Global accords, such as the Maya Declaration in 2011[11] followed by the Sasana Accord, G20 adopting the Financial Inclusion Action Plan, and creating the G20 Global Partnership for Financial Inclusion (GPFI) reflect the global urgency in achieving financial inclusion. The global financial crisis of 2008 followed by crisis in microfinance sector in various countries such as India (the Andhra Pradesh crisis), Bosnia, Nicaragua, Morocco, and Pakistan nudged the global discourse to 'responsible finance' from financial inclusion. Responsible finance has been defined by various agencies and networks such as the International Finance Corporation

(IFC) and Consultative Group to Assist the Poor (CGAP), but the common thread that runs through these definitions is that financial services need to be client centric. The Responsible Finance Forum (RFF)[12], in its enunciation of responsible finance captures the essence nicely by saying, "One of the critical dimensions of financial sector responsibility is fair treatment of clients and acting in ways that protect clients' social and economic welfare."

It is only natural that inasmuch as microfinance deals with vulnerable sections of the society, the focus of responsible finance in terms of developing specific metrics has remained on microfinance. Microfinance has seen both global initiatives such as the Social Performance Task Force (SPTF) and the Smart Campaign, and national initiatives such as the Industry Code of Conduct and detailed regulatory guidelines by the RBI in India[13]. The development of a framework for responsible finance in microfinance has been backed by assessment, be it through client protection principles (CPP) certification, Universal Standards for Social Performance Management (USSPM) evaluation, or social ratings. However, in case of mainstream sector, the focus has been limited to disclosures/transparency and grievance handling, and not much attention has been paid to double bottom-line performance, governance, design of appropriate products, prevention of over-indebtedness, and responsible pricing, with market discipline and prudential regulation providing the architecture for rules of the game. In such a scenario, assessing responsible finance performance of formal sector, that is, banks, and the channels used by them, like business correspondents, is contingent on one-off studies. This limitation was pointed out in last year's report, as it acts as a constraint in analyzing the formal sector performance.

The formal sector in India and elsewhere is increasingly moving toward digital financial services, and alternate channels, in catering to the low-income segment as the cost structure of brick and mortar institutions, as well as cash handling, has been found to be unsuitable for low-value transactions. The widespread reach of banking correspondents in India, mobile wallets, and the future of JAM–UPI based inclusion in India are important examples of this shift. Fortunately, there has been forward movement on developing responsible finance metrics for digital and alternate delivery channels, and it is hoped that its mainstreaming will throw useful insights into responsible performance of the formal sector.

1.3.1 Digital Finance: Building Responsible Framework

The International Telecommunication Union (ITU), a specialized agency of the United Nations has set up a focus group on 'digital financial services' (DFS), bringing together experts from the telco and financial services sectors, to collaborate on making digital and mobile technology accessible and affordable for everyone. It started work in June 2014 and has the support of over 60 organizations from 30 countries from around the world, across both public and private sectors. The formation of the focus group by ITU is based on the belief that digital financial services reduce the costs associated with basic, low-value payment transactions, and enable providers to deliver right-sized financial services that are affordable and also address the issue of reaching people living in rural areas. As such, scaling mobile money could be the catalyst to the proliferation of vital digital financial services that benefit the lives of the poor.

As the development of a DFS ecosystem critically depends on the underlying regulatory framework, development of appropriate regulation is a key factor being addressed by the focus group on DFS. The importance of the regulatory framework has increased on account of an increased variety of non-traditional players in DFS. The focus group, through its wider participation, aims to bridge the gap between the telecommunications and financial services regulators, and between the private and public sectors.

The objectives of the group are[14]:

- Study and identify the technology trends in digital financial services over the coming years, and how the role of various stakeholders in this ecosystem will evolve
- Understand where there are challenges and issues, where there is overlapping, and gaps that need to be filled
- Identify best practices for a digital financial services toolkit for regulators
- Develop a roadmap for interoperable products, networks, and services
- Establish liaisons and relationships with other organizations, which could contribute to the standardization activities of digital financial services

- Identify successful use cases for implementation of secure digital financial services, including developing countries, with a particular focus on the benefits for women
- Work toward the creation of an enabling framework for digital financial services
- Ensure that consumer protection is a critical part of financial inclusion, particularly in the case of fraud

To achieve these objectives, the group will develop a series of toolkits, principles, and guidelines to help national policymakers and regulatory authorities, to fast-track policy reforms, and to stimulate the offering and adoption of DFS. The group's work is being handled through four working groups (Box 1.1), and importantly, consumer protection is one of them, reflecting the importance being attached to client centricity. The consumer protection group is tasked with,

developing guidelines and principles, to mitigate the different risks, for consumer protection and quality of service, and experience related to digital financial services. Additionally it will study the consumer protection, legal and policy framework in DFS markets, and quality of services issues of mobile networks in developing countries, which can affect the availability of DFS.

Box 1.1 Four Working Groups of ITU

- DFS Ecosystem
- Interoperability
- Technology, Innovation, and Competition
- Consumer experience and Protection

Source: www.itu.int

CGAP is also involved with ITU's initiative, though CGAP on its own is also working on responsible digital financial services, seeking, "[T]o build the evidence base and menu of industry and policy solutions, to address evolving consumer risks, ensuring strong trust, and high levels of uptake and usage." CGAP's work in this area include a deep dive in four markets to understand consumer risks. These CGAP studies have pointed various risks, such as unreliable networks and DFS services, complex customer interfaces leading to over-the-counter transactions, agent misconduct, and inadequate complaints handling mechanism. Building on its work, CGAP rightly highlights the issue of consumer centricity by enunciating the

---

Box 1.2 Agent Network and Client Protection Issues

Client Protection Principle	Key Potential Risks[16]
Appropriate Product Design and Delivery	• Inability to transact due to network/service downtime • Insufficient agent liquidity or float, which also affects ability to transact • User interfaces that many find complex and confusing
Transparency	• Nontransparent fees and other terms • Clients do not make informed decisions due to inadequate information from providers
Responsible Pricing	• Nontransparent fees and other terms • Unauthorized fees, abusive prices charged to clients
Fair and Respectful Treatment of Clients	• Fraud that targets customers • Agent's misconduct against clients
Privacy of Client Data	• Inadequate data privacy and protection
Mechanism for Complaints Resolution	• Inadequate or lack of client care channel/recourse mechanism (e.g., client support, client helpdesk, dispute resolution, and complaint mechanisms)

---

core issues in DFS, by saying "What risks do customers perceive and experience with DFS, what are the consequences of those risks for consumers, providers, and financial inclusion outcomes, and how can those risks be addressed?"[15]

It is encouraging that the global focus on responsible finance is being embedded in DFS in the early stages, and in the near future there will be a framework for evaluation of DFS providers. India stands to gain immensely by incorporating these frameworks as the DFS ecosystem is still a work in progress. Changing operational framework after growth of DFS channels will be a difficult task and, hence, the necessity to adopt global best practices at the start.

Alternate Delivery Channel of Banking Correspondents—Smart Initiative for Client Protection

During the last year (2015–16), the Smart Campaign, which mainstreamed CPP standards and certifications for the microfinance institutions, rightly focused attention on applicability of CPPs to agent network. Rightly, because there is an increased thrust on last-mile delivery of financial services, using the agent network. The Smart Campaign, in collaboration with Accion, carried out research in India to map its CPPs and standards against various agent models, to develop a deeper understanding of the client protection risks, as well as effective mitigating steps for agent managers. The research used a variety of techniques such as mystery shopping visits across India, group discussions with customers, and discussion with BC management.

This Smart Campaign study has been timely, as BCs lend to a segment similar to microfinance institutions and, as previously noted, there are growing concerns on client protection in service delivery by BCs. The main risks captured by the study and mapped across seven client protection principles are summarized in Box 1.2.

The research found that while network managers already have many policies and procedures on their books regarding appropriate agent behavior, training, oversight, and monitoring systems, these procedures were not sufficiently robust and policies were often applied inconsistently across geographies and languages. The policy inconsistency especially related to transparency, products and product features, pricing, training, and customer support. The Smart Campaign intends to leverage the insights from India to conduct similar mappings in other geographies, Africa in particular. In the longer term, and with knowledge from additional mappings and industry consultations, the Smart Campaign plans to move from risk mapping and suggestions of good practices to more concrete recommendations and standards, and potentially, even a CPC module for agent networks[17].

These initiatives (the ITU Focus group and Smart Campaign's work on agent networks) will hopefully come up with a framework in the near future that will allow application of the responsible finance lens in assessment of DFS and agent network.

1.3.2 Initiatives to Strengthen Responsible Finance Framework During Last Year[18]

Last year's edition of this report highlighted the role of (a) SPTF[19] through its USSPM and (b) Smart Campaign[20] through its CPP standards as two major global initiatives, shaping the responsible finance agenda of microfinance institutions. Both initiatives took significant steps forward during last one year by way of new work, refinement of existing frameworks/standards, and establishment of funding mechanisms. These initiatives are worth mentioning, inasmuch as they provide the architecture for responsible practices by microfinance institutions and analysis in this report.

Review of USSPM

To ensure that the Universal Standards stay updated, relevant, in line with the advancement of related standards, and in accordance with global best practices for standard-setting organizations, the SPTF set up the Technical Review Committee (TRC) in 2015. The TRC is a body composed of SPTF board members, leaders from relevant responsible finance initiatives (such as microfinance information exchange [MIX], CERISE, and The Smart Campaign), as well as representatives from frontier initiatives (such as environment and digital financial services), and practitioners. Over the past year, the TRC reviewed the comments submitted by SPTF members and the public, discussed them, and provided expert commentary on the proposed revisions to the Universal Standards. They also offered strategic direction on how to include three frontier initiatives into the Universal Standards—digital financial services, microinsurance, and green microfinance. The SPTF, Smart Campaign, and CERISE have committed to updating their respective standards and tools on a synchronized schedule, meaning that all three sets of materials will be completely aligned at all times.

The updates in the new version of the Universal Standards are aimed at *simplifying the existing content,* plus adding some *new content, that reflects the evolution of the industry.* Examples of new content include standards on monitoring the risks associated with agents/third parties, protecting clients who use microinsurance, and aligning pricing with client interests.

Country Mapping on USSPM

During last year, SPTF's Responsible Inclusive Finance (RIF) group created a framework for mapping regulation in various countries to the Universal Standards. It has till date mapped regulatory efforts in six countries around the world that are supporting social performance regulation. India has still not been covered, and it is hoped that it will be covered this year. The regulatory architecture put in place by the RBI and industry's self-evolved code of conduct can provide useful insights to other countries in shaping their responsible finance agenda.

Smart Campaign's CPP Standards Version 2.0[21]

Based on experience gained through CPP certifications carried out in last three years, the client protection standards (the basis for the certification program) have been revised with the purpose of making them clearer and easier to understand. The other critical objective of the revision was to address institutions that offer forward-looking products and services, such as savings, insurance, and alternative delivery channels to their clients. The Smart Campaign solicited public feedback on the standards through online surveys, webinars, and field pilots and the feedback has been incorporated. After receiving and analyzing feedback from over 150 stakeholders, the campaign has finalized the Standards 2.0.

Smart Campaign's Model Legal Framework for Consumer Protection

As regulators around the world work to install stronger client protection regimes, the Smart Campaign developed an important new tool, the Consumer Protection Model Legal Framework and Commentary. The model legal framework creates a regulatory template for financial consumer protection, based on the client protection principles. The model legal framework was developed by a team of experienced model legislation developers, and the team drew on a broad survey of experts and relevant scholarship, along with existing laws and regulations from countries across the globe.

The model legal framework is an excellent focal point for dialogue among regulators and providers. It can serve as: (a) a template for developing legislation or regulation, (b) a tool to assess a given jurisdiction's client protection regulatory regime, or (c) a resource for the development of codes of conduct and guidelines, for any group or industry association.

These developments strengthen the responsible finance discourse, promote the adaption of the existing tools and frameworks by microfinance institutions, to incorporate new products and technology, and more importantly, are setting ground for inclusion of the formal sector financial inclusion efforts. The expansion of responsible finance framework to cover the formal sector is very encouraging, as it will not only strengthen client centricity across channels, but also allow comparison of the performance of different channels on a common framework.

1.4 REPORT STRUCTURE

The earlier annual social performance report published since 2011 was renamed 'Responsible Finance', to cover all players involved in providing financial services to the poor, and not just MFIs. Even though the tenets of social performance are in complete sync with responsible finance, responsible finance is a broader term and is now globally used. This chapter shows that financial inclusion space in India has become varied, and the right ecosystem has been developed to harness various channels specializing in their domain to achieve financial inclusion. It also details the initiatives being taken to develop a client-centric responsible approach for DFS and alternate channels—the channels being used by formal sector players to reach the excluded segment. However, as it is still a work in progress, assessment of the formal sector (banks and BCs) has to rely on study reports, wherever available. In case of microfinance institutions, the framework of responsible finance has been well ingrained through regulations and industry efforts, and this accounts for focus in this report on microfinance.

Last year's report presented the various initiatives at both national and global level, which drive MFIs toward responsible finance and used the analytical frame of USSPM to analyze the performance of Indian MFIs on responsible finance. The USSPM framework was used as it encompasses the tenets of other initiatives such as CPP, RBI regulations and the Industry Code of Conduct. Chapter 2 presents the various initiatives taken by MFIs to bolster their client centricity and the narrative is based on the six dimensions of USSPM framework like last year. Unlike last year, this year there has been no sector wide study report and, hence, the information source has been the author's personal interviews and the information submitted by the MFIs in response to the questionnaire circulated for this report. As MFIs play a key role in financial inclusion, and the Small Industries Development Bank of India (SIDBI) has played a leadership role in this space, the chapter also has an interview with the SIDBI CMD covering the current issues and the future, as well as the role of MUDRA.

Chapter 3 examines the role of self-regulatory organizations (SROs) in promoting responsible finance. Since 2010, SROs, especially Microfinance Institutions Network (MFIN) has played a key role in formulating code of conduct for the industry, monitoring compliance, mainstreaming best practices in grievance redressal, and supplementing the efforts of the RBI in ensuring orderly growth of the sector. The chapter starts with examining the concept of self-regulation and related international experiences, followed by presenting the role of MFIN in promoting responsible finance.

The essence of responsible finance is customer delight, and while institutional reports and other secondary level information provide insights, there is no better way than to get the response directly from the client. With the frenetic pace of activity in financial inclusion space, institutions, technology, and programs, what do the clients feel is the litmus test. Chapter 4 is based on two client-level studies, commissioned by ACCESS ASSIST for this report. One study focusses on client-level indebtedness, and the other captures client voices. The findings provide pointers for future work by both policy makers and practitioners.

Last year, a separate chapter was devoted to analyzing the emerging risks in the microfinance sector. Considering the positive feedback, and the growing worry that the sector is again growing at a scorching pace, Chapter 5 analyses the growth factors and the associated risks. Based on credit bureau data, and the narrative seen in hot spots during last year, it analyses whether regulations are able to instill credit discipline and if areas of credit saturation are emerging. The industry needs to be ever vigilant, as poverty lending will always be subject to greater scrutiny, and it must realize that regulations cannot be a substitute for institutional intent.

Chapter 6 is devoted to the other major player in microfinance, that is, and attempts to flag the gaps in the SHG—Bank Linkage Programme—from the responsible finance angle. The advent of NRLM, rising non performing assets (NPAs), mono product, and regional skew are affecting the program, while the initiative on the digitization of SHG records is a positive step that has the potential to revive the program as well as enable better credit assessment of SHG clients.

Chapter 7 starts with an analysis of the new initiatives of MUDRA and PMJDY, and their possible impact on the national agenda of meeting the financial needs of the excluded poor. The RBI has recently circulated draft guidelines on P2P lending, and in keeping with the policy recognition of P2P lenders, the chapter presents the current model of two prominent P2P lenders in microfinance, using the responsible finance lens. The concluding part of the chapter, building on the previous chapters, provides a summary and lists out areas requiring action on the part of policymakers, MFIs, and other stakeholders to strengthen the responsible finance agenda of microfinance. It is heartening that quite a few action points mentioned in the last report have been acted on. The focus of the report is on documenting the positive steps taken to reach the unserved and poorer sections of the society with financial services, as well as to flag issues that need to be addressed to ensure sustained growth.

NOTES AND REFERENCES

1. Shri Jayant Sinha, speaking at Inclusive Finance India conclave in December 2015.
2. http://www.pmjdy.gov.in/account, accessed on July 16, 2016.
3. http://www.mudra.org.in, accessed on July14, 2016.
4. http://www.vccircle.com/news/micro-finance/2016/07/12/idfc-bank-acquire-vc-backed-microlender-grama-vidiyal, accessed on July16, 2016.
5. https://rbi.org.in/scripts/BS_PressReleaseDisplay.aspx?prid=32615, accessed on September 23, 2016.
6. http://www.livemint.com/Opinion/AkQRSzB-KVC1DmiZN31W9DN/Payments-banks-How-many-more-will-call-it-quits.html, accessed on July 25, 2016.
7. http://www.livemint.com/Industry/BTgri6AXT-bue3WFPyp6dEN/Unified-payments-interface-new-banks-signal-revolution-in-b.html, accessed on September 23, 2016.
8. https://us.sagepub.com/en-us/nam/responsible-finance-india-report-2015/book251469, accessed on September 23, 2016.
9. Basic Statistical Returns (BSR).
10. FinScope. 2015. Consumer Survey under the Poorest States Inclusive Growth Programme.
11. http://www.afi-global.org/sites/default/files/publications/Maya%20Declaration_2011.pdf, accessed on September 23, 2016.
12. Responsible Finance Forum was founded in 2010 as a global initiative by the German Federal Ministry for Economic Cooperation and Development (BMZ), the Ministry of Foreign Affairs of the Netherlands, the Consultative Group to Assist the Poor (CGAP), and the International Finance Corporation (IFC).
13. For a detailed description of these initiatives refer to Chapters 1 and 2 of Alok Misra. 2015. *Responsible Finance India Report.* New Delhi: SAGE Publications.
14. http://www.itu.int/net/pressoffice/backgrounders/itu-t/DFS_Media-briefing.pdf, accessed on September 23, 2016.
15. http://www.cgap.org/topics/responsible-digital-finance, accessed on September 23, 2016.
16. CGAP. 2015. "Doing Digital Finance Right: The Case for Stronger Mitigation on Customer Risks." Available at: http://www.cgap.org/sites/default/files/Focus-Note-Doing-Digital-Finance-Right-Jun-2015.pdf, accessed on September 23, 2016.; Smart Campaign. 2014. "Potential Risks to Clients When Using Digital Financial Services: An Analysis Report to Inform the Evolution of the Client Protection Standards." Available at: http://www.smartcampaign.org/storage/documents/Tools_and_Resources/EoS_Risk_identification_and_analysis_vSA_AR_LT.pdf, accessed on September 23, 2016.
17. Inputs from Smart Campaign team.
18. Inputs from Leah Nedderman Wardle, SPTF, and Alexandra Rizzi, Smart Campaign.
19. http://sptf.info
20. http://www.smartcampaign.org
21. http://www.smartcampaign.org/about/smart-microfinance-and-the-client-protection-principles, accessed on September 23, 2016.

MFIs and Responsible Finance: The Journey Continues

The concept of responsible finance and keeping clients at the core of operations is natural to MFIs, given that microfinance emerged from the failure of the formal sector to be client-centric. Except the new-generation institutions, most MFIs have transformed from a development sector background. The service delivery of MFIs is rooted in creating a positive impact in the lives of their clients who have been bypassed by the financial sector. As such, the double-bottom-line concept is integral to the concept of microfinance as well as MFIs. In such a scenario, it would have been logical for MFIs to pursue client centricity on their own, as part of their mission and vision, and not require external guidelines and regulations to keep them focused on clients. It was hence ironical that MFIs drifted from this approach to start chasing profitability in the period of 2005–10, and it took the 2010 crisis to nudge rethink of their strategy. The reasons for the drift and the fallout have been discussed at length in various reports and papers, especially the State of Sector reports. Post 2010, the sector started rediscovering its original DNA and was guided in this by the RBI guidelines, Industry Code of Conduct, and global initiatives such as the SPTF and Smart Campaign. The last year's responsible finance report detailed these initiatives and also mapped them to show the commonality across them.

During the year 2015–16, there have been both positive action from MFIs, and regulation in the push toward responsible finance, as well as the emergence of concerns[1]. Last year's responsible finance report had listed issues requiring action on part of the RBI, which seemed to constrain MFIs from broadening their service offering, in line with the needs of the clients. It is heartening that the RBI has acted on a few of them and furthered the cause of responsible financial inclusion.

RBI's Action on Regulations Furthering Responsible Finance

Since the last report, the RBI has taken positive steps on loan-amount-linked repayment tenure and expansion of the scope of CB reporting. In order to prevent indebtedness of clients, the RBI in its first set of guidelines in 2011 had prescribed that the loan size be restricted to ₹35,000 in the first cycle and ₹50,000 in subsequent cycles. Additionally, it stipulated that the tenure of the loan should not be less than 24 months for any loan amount in excess of ₹15,000. In April 2015, the RBI revised the annual household income limit for eligible microfinance clients and[2] hiked loan ceilings to ₹60,000 for the first cycle and ₹100,000 for subsequent cycles. However, it did not change the loan-size-linked repayment tenure, and it was pointed that this stipulation stifles demand-driven loans, leads to unsavory practices like accelerated loan repayments, and has become obsolete with the raising of household income criteria. The RBI in November 2015[3] raised the limit of the loan amount, for which the tenure of the loan shall not be less than 24 months, to ₹30,000. This is a positive step, but it will allow NBFC-MFIs to offer shorter tenure loans of less than ₹30,000 to their clients, depending on the needs of the clients. However, to achieve the full potential of diversified loan products, it is necessary to give freedom to the institutions to decide the tenure based on needs of the clients. Many clients involved in the retail trade want a shorter repayment time, even with a higher loan size, and this is more so with clients in urban and semi-urban areas, who have faster inventory turnover. The situation has become more pressing, with the sector gradually drifting toward urban areas, and it is hoped the regulations will take this factor into account. Since responsible finance is all about client centricity and regulation, it needs to focus on transparency and ethical behavior, and product design should be linked to client needs.

The other favorable policy action during the year has been the move to include SHG lending details in CBs. The last year's report showed that the states with higher MFI penetration also have higher SBLP penetration. In such a scenario, the CB checks conducted by MFIs do not provide the correct estimate of borrowers' creditworthiness, as loans from SHGs are not captured by CBs. The issue was flagged by the Aditya Puri Committee[4], which suggested that lenders should consider prior borrowings from SBLP and MFIs, and hence, banks were needed to capture and provide the credit-related information of individual borrowers within an SHG to CBs. As banks capture only group-level records at present, the committee recommended that banks may be required within a reasonable period of, say, 18 months, to arrange for capturing the required data from SHGs for reporting to CICs. Considering the enormity of the task, as well as the view of SHG purists that SHGs are meant for collective decision-making and individual tracking goes against the grain of the concept, the RBI's earlier policy directive to banks in 2014 did not see much traction. The issue was reexamined by a working group, and based on its recommendations, the RBI issued a fresh policy directive to banks in January 2016[5], requiring them to capture SHG lending details in two phases, one starting from July 2016 and the other from July 2017, with the depth of information increasing in the second phase. Inter-loaning among members has been excluded as of now. This is a very positive step and as SBLP and MFI borrowers are homogeneous, it will allow MFIs to have a correct assessment of a client's indebtedness. Avoiding client indebtedness is a key component of responsible finance, and the implementation of this directive along with Aadhaar-based KYC will address the problem of indebtedness to a very large extent.

Initiatives Shaping the Responsible Finance of MFIs

Broadly, while the RBI regulations and the Industry Code of Conduct, being mandatory, are the major influencers for NBFC-MFI responsible business practices, the global initiatives of SPTF and Smart Campaign also play a critical role in providing an overarching framework, as well as in showcasing global best practices. The commonality among all these initiatives was detailed in the last year's report and a snapshot of it is provided for reference in Annexure 2.1.

During the year, the Industry Code of Conduct applicable to MFIs was reviewed by two industry associations (MFIN and Sa-Dhan) through a working group and a revised code[6] was formulated. The key changes made in the code are encouraging as they reinforce the credo that microfinance is a double-bottom-line industry and needs to keep clients at the center of its operations. Table 2.1 shows the key changes effected in the CoC.

While most of the changes are related to detailing the earlier prescriptions, the insertion of social performance and its measurement, as a core value of microfinance, is a step to remind the sector that it is

Table 2.1 Key Changes in the Industry Code of Conduct (Changes in Red)

Part I: Core Values of Microfinance	Earlier Code of Conduct	Revised Code of Conduct
Integrating social values into operations	To ensure high standards of governance and management.	To ensure high standards of governance and management (management focused on not only financial performance but also social impact of business). To assess the social performance and social relevance of the institution from time to time.
Feedback and grievance redressal mechanism	To provide a formal grievance redressal mechanism for clients.	To provide a formal and easy-to-access grievance redressal mechanism for clients.

Part II: Code of Conduct	Earlier Code of Conduct	Revised Code of Conduct
Integrity & Ethical Behavior	MFIs must design appropriate policies and operating guidelines to treat clients and employees with dignity.	MFIs must design appropriate, board-approved policies and operating guidelines to treat clients and employees with fairness and dignity. The incentive structure for the staff should aim at promoting good business and service practices toward customers.
Transparency	MFIs must disclose all terms and conditions to the client for all services offered.	MFIs must disclose all terms and conditions, in a form and manner that is understandable, to the client for all services offered.
Client Protection: Fair Practices	Products should not be bundled. The only exceptions to bundling may be made with respect to credit life, life insurance, and live-stock insurance products, which are typically offered bundled with loans.	Products should not be bundled. (Bundling in this context means purchase of a product or service conditional to the provision of another product or service.) The only exceptions to bundling may be made with respect to credit life, life insurance, and live-stock insurance products, which are typically offered bundled with loans.
Client Protection: Avoiding Over-indebtedness		Added the following to existing provisions of two-lender limit and CB check: MFIs should check the efficacy of their processes relating to avoiding over-indebtedness through additional CB reports on a select sample of clients after loan disbursement. The result of this verification should be reviewed by the board periodically.
Client protection: Grievance redressal mechanism	MFIs must establish dedicated feedback and grievance redressal mechanisms to correct any error and handle/receive complaints speedily and efficiently.	Added The minimum standards required of the GRM are (a) an easy procedure for recording a complaint over phone, (b) a staff-assisted procedure at the branch for recording complaints, (c) acknowledgement for the receipt of a complaint, (d) a time limit for resolution, and (e) a clear appeal procedure in cases where the customer is not satisfied with the solution and assurance to customers that they will be treated fairly despite the complaint/grievance being registered.

Source: Author.

a double-bottom-line industry. The changes are not limited to what is captured in Table 2.1, which only highlights the key aspects related to client centricity. The adoption of the revised code is expected to strengthen the responsible finance agenda of MFIs.

Client Protection Principles (CPP) Certification of Indian MFIs

Globally, CPP certification is seen by investors as a reassurance that clients of the certified institutions are not being harmed. Investors accord high importance to CPP certification which is based on global best practices in client protection. CPP certification entails an examination of MFIs' adherence to these seven principles and nearly 100 indicators.

On meeting all indicators, the CPP certificate is awarded by the Smart Campaign and the certification agency. The certification status is valid for four years, with a renewal required two years from the date of issuance. It is a matter of pride that out of 61 organizations which have achieved the certification, 11 organizations are from India[7]. What is more noteworthy is that in the list of top-10 NBFC-MFIs by gross loan portfolio, 7 are CPP certified, and the top 5 are all certified. Between them, they account for nearly 60% of NBFC-MFIs portfolio as on end March 2016. Cashpor, which is a section-8 company and not an NBFC-MFI, is the biggest MFI in NGO-MFI category.

Box 2.1 CPP Certified MFIs in India

- Bharat Financial Inclusion Ltd.
- Ujjivan
- Grameen Financial Services
- Janalakshmi
- Equitas
- CASHPOR
- Swadhar
- Arohan
- Sonata
- Utkarsh
- Satin Creditcare
- Annapurna Microfinance

Source: Compiled by Author from SMART website.

This achievement, coupled with the mandatory compliance to the RBI guidelines and CoC, can be seen as a testimony to the good practices of the microfinance sector in India.

2.1 RESPONSIBLE FINANCE: MFIs PERFORMANCE ACROSS USSPM DIMENSIONS

Guided by these external push factors, as also the reexamination of their original mission, the microfinance sector has, over the last six years, adopted many client-centric practices, as well as refined earlier policies, to fit in with the changing requirements. This section captures few of these practices and, like last year, the description is organized according to USSPM dimensions, with the caveat that some dimensions could not be covered due to lack of information. Unlike the last year, during the past year under review, there has been no sector-wide study capturing responsible finance practices and the number of CoC assessments commissioned by SIDBI has also reduced substantially. As such, this narrative is based on the author's interviews with MFIs, data reported by MFIs in response to the questionnaire circulated for this report, and, wherever available, relevant studies and reports.

2.1.1 Social Goals and Governance: Progress Needs to be Strengthened with Information Related to Social Goals

Under these parameters, there are two broad aspects. One relates to quality of governance, its focus on social performance, and balancing it with financial performance. The other relates to formulation of

well-defined and measurable social goals. The governance structure of NBFC-MFIs in particular has strengthened significantly post-2010, and this has been brought out in the study on governance practices by MicroSave[8]. The improvement has occurred across both aspects, that is, quality of board composition and information being reviewed by the board, as well as social goals. The report showed that 61% of the sampled MFIs boards had at least, or more than, 1/3rd of independent members and, more significantly, it showed that 24% of sampled MFIs had majority independent members. This could be seen as a very significant progress from the phase of promoter-driven governance structures. The higher share of independent members is supposed to provide a balanced perspective, bring market perspective, and ensure that the institution grows on a sustainable business model. The revised CoC formulated by both industry organizations (MFIN and Sa-Dhan) has retained the provision, and the revised code says: "MFIs will endeavor to have independent directors to the extent of 1/3rd of the governing board".

While board composition has improved significantly across the sector, the focus on social performance has also gone up. MicroSave's Pan-India report clearly showed that the majority of boards do review social performance data (Figure 2.1), with 84% MFIs scoring 'average' or 'high' under this parameter. A review of social performance data being submitted to the board across MFIs shows varying levels of depth and breadth.

Arohan has the practice of documenting its social performance on a quarterly basis, and presenting it to its board. The social performance data is captured across five dimensions—social goals, client protection principles, customer satisfaction, staff satisfaction, client outreach, and gender. While the data is comprehensive, the monitoring of social goals is through indicators which are easy to capture, but are not necessarily a true measure of the progress on social goals. To illustrate, one of

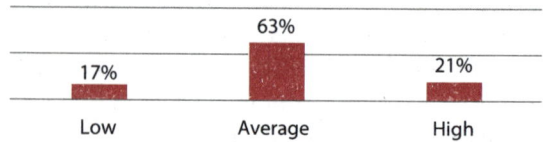

Figure 2.1 Review Level of Social Performance Data by Boards

Source: Governance Practices among MFIs in India, MicroSave.

Arohan's social goals is "financial empowerment through diversification of Arohan's financial products," and the progress on this is seen through the number of products available to the clients, average number of accounts per customer, and share of total customers who have more than one account. Similarly, client satisfaction is monitored through turnaround time for disbursement, insurance claim settlement, and effective rate of interest. ESAF's quarterly social performance report to its board's sub-committee includes progress in achievement of social targets related to poverty outreach, outreach to backward communities and so on, reasons for client exit, grievances resolved, and internal audit (IA) reports on social performance checklist. Annapurna microfinance strengthened its social governance by forming a social performance sub-committee of the board. The board of Annapurna reviews information pertaining to progress out of poverty index, client feedback, grievance redressal, water and sanitation awareness drive, and financial literacy training drive. Grameen financial provides regular information to the board on client satisfaction, target clientele, client protection practices, grievance practices, social and development activities, and compliance on CoC as well as fair practices code (FPC).

While most of the MFIs do report similar data on social performance to the board, there are also examples of a more minimalist approach. Fincare provides the board with updates on 'operations, financial performance, and business performance results', not including social performance as a separate information piece. Bharat Financial Inclusion Limited (BFIL) reporting to board on social performance includes initiatives taken to strengthen client protection, financial literacy training to clients, and skill-building program initiated with business partners to develop skills of clients.

> Almost all MFIs report data on social performance to the board with varying levels of detail

The varying approaches on the range of social goals/performance-related data to the MFI boards show a few significant aspects. First, almost all MFIs report social performance-related data to the board. Second, the depth and scope of data/information is strongly correlated to the articulation of social goals in the mission statement, that is, MFIs with well-defined social goals have a more comprehensive

report. Finally, the critical issue flagged in the last report continues to persist, and that relates to clear enunciation of social goals based on the mission, backing it up with SMART objectives and establishing a continuous monitoring mechanism. In absence of this, the tendency is to rely more on indicators of outreach and proxy indicators for aspects like client level outcomes rather than a systematic tracking of achievements. If the social goals are not well defined and embedded in service delivery, it is natural that monitoring mechanisms would fail to comprehensively capture progress on mission achievement.

The sector has achieved good progress on strengthening governance and tracking social performance. However, there is work to be done, in terms of clear articulation of social goals, having specific and measurable targets, and incorporation of these in the regular MIS. Now that social performance has been added explicitly as a core value of microfinance in the revised CoC, it is hoped that the sector will devote higher attention to this aspect. In the absence of a streamlined reporting framework, much of the positive work in social performance by the microfinance sector goes unnoticed.

Poverty Outreach: Partial Data Shows Good Depth

As most MFIs define their target population as 'excluded, poor, and disadvantaged', it is useful to see the performance on this count. Though some of the MFIs use terms like 'unserved' and 'excluded', it is common knowledge that it is the poor who are normally excluded. Data on poverty outreach is not available, and the datasets published by MFIN and Sa-Dhan also do not provide this information. The last year's report used Grameen foundation's study of the poverty outreach of MFIs in the states of UP, Odisha, and Madhya Pradesh under the PSIG program. The report showed that the outreach of MFIs is more toward borderline poor, rather than very poor and poor categories, as the MFIs matched the state poverty incidence on $2.5 and $1.88 poverty line, but lagged under $1.25 and national poverty line definition.

Dia Vikas, the Indian arm of Opportunity International, is a social investor and works through its MFI partners who are focused on social goals. Dia Vikas's social performance report[9] shows the poverty outreach of its seven partners (Figure 2.2) and the results show that the majority of clients are below the international poverty line of $1.88.

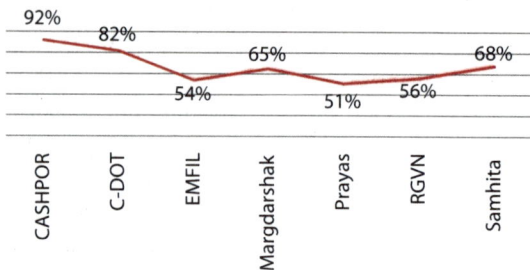

Figure 2.2 Poverty Outreach at $1.88 Poverty Line of Dia Vikas Partners

Source: See Note 9.

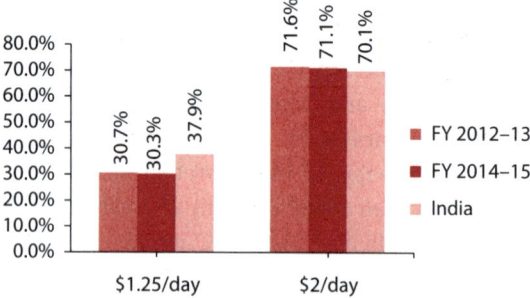

Figure 2.3 Poverty Concentration (All New Clients) Grameen Koota Compared to Poverty Rates

Source: Social rating report of GFSPL.

Although the figures for these seven institutions have a positive bias, on account of Dia Vikas being proactive in furthering social mission, seen with the last year's Grameen foundations study, they corroborate the fact that the majority of MFI clients belong to the segment below $2 poverty line. Social ratings are another source of credible data on poverty outreach; however, during the last year only one social rating was conducted. The poverty outreach data of GFSPL as per the rating report shows good poverty outreach and validates the assumption of microfinance institutions outreach depth (Figure 2.3). In the discussion of microfinance, this contribution is often lost sight of. This aspect needs to be highlighted as, despite policy push, formal sector banks could not reach this segment. Even under PMJDY, the inclusion has happened on the savings side and the real test will come in extending credit facilities.

The national level studies relating to debt and investment clearly show that exclusion is highest at the bottom of the pyramid, and this is where MFIs have built their client base. The All India Debt and Investment Survey (70th round)[10] looked at the borrowing level based on household asset size. The households in the lowest decile of the sample had average assets of ₹25,071 in rural areas, and mere ₹291 in urban areas—these are the typical clients of microfinance institutions. The incidence of indebtedness (IoI), which is households having any debt in the lowest decile, was 19.62% in rural areas and 9.34% in urban areas, reflecting severe exclusion in the segment. The role of MFIs in providing credit facilities to this segment needs to be seen and appreciated in this macro context. It will be useful if the industry reports data on this consistently, after sample verification by external agencies, to showcase its contribution to financial inclusion of the poor.

CSR to Shared Value: Need of the Hour

Though the practice of reporting social performance to the board has become common place, there still exist gaps in having measurable social goals in alignment with the mission and linking social performance reporting to these goals. The other trend seen is the conflation of social goals with Corporate Social Responsibility (CSR). Two factors account for this. The Companies Act, 2013 has mandated CSR provisions for companies meeting any of the three conditions—annual turnover of 1,000 crore, or net worth of 500 crore, or net profit before taxes of 5 crore: Companies meeting these criteria have to allocate 2% of the average profit of the last three years for CSR activities. Most NBFC-MFIs meet one of these criteria and have to mandatorily allocate funds for CSR activities. While this is an external imposition which has to be complied with, there is also a lack of clarity between social performance management and CSR.

Many MFIs do CSR activities (whether mandated by law or otherwise) more actively than social performance management, and often the answer to social performance comes in the form of medical camps, relief material distribution, and donations to charities. Social performance management relates to setting social goals aligned to mission, setting measurable targets, and integrating these in business planning. While MFIs not obligated by CSR provisions of the Companies Act can fine tune their social performance metrics, companies falling under the purview of CSR provisions have to take the additional role of social performance management (SPM), plus CSR, to ensure that CSR activities do not substitute SPM. It must be mentioned that even under CSR, a lot of socially useful work has been done, and quite a few MFIs have upped the ceiling. Equitas has gone beyond mandatory

Table 2.2 Outreach Under Equitas' CSR Activities

Social Activity	FY 2014–15	FY 2015–16	Growth	Cumulative
Health screening	845,205	864,384	2%	37,45,109
Skill training	44,462	41,268	−7%	4,09,489
Health help line	2,153	1,616	−25%	20,642
Equitas Bird's Nest (Upliftment of platform dwellers)	199	362	82%	711
Placement services	15,869	26,320	66%	59,629
Sugam Clinic	0	13	0	13

Source: Equitas.

provisions and, setting a policy for allocating 5% of profits for CSR activities, has also appointed one exclusive CSR staff for every 10 branches. Equitas' achievements under CSR are also equally impressive (Table 2.2). Grameen Financial also has a policy of earmarking 5% of its surplus for CSR, and provides this surplus to its foundation, "Navya Disha Trust" for CSR.

BFIL did the following activities under its CSR spending last year:

- Jagruti Se Unnati, wherein the attendees were made aware of various welfare schemes of state and central governments.
- Under CSR Project 'Drishti', free cataract surgery camps were organized in the states of Odisha, Jharkhand, and Bihar.
- Individual Household Latrine (IHHL) in which people in rural areas were motivated to construct toilets, and avail the benefits of the scheme.
- Animal wellness camps conducted in rural areas with the objective of providing primary and emergency veterinary services to the animals.

The domination of CSR speak, nudged by regulations, begets an important question for policymakers. CSR as a concept has been conceived for the commercial industry and services sector, which has been blamed for social, environmental and economic problems, so as to ensure that companies chasing profits share part of the profits for restoring the social, ecological, and economical balance. The concept is based on the principle of redistribution or giving back part of the gains to the community for ensuring sustainable development. However, it does not seem to fit in with the operating paradigm of social businesses such as microfinance. Michael Porter and Mark Krammer[11] have espoused the concept of shared value in place of CSR even for commercial sector, stressing that it is the only way forward for sustainable development. The main idea behind shared value relates to creating economic value in such a way that it also creates value for the society by addressing its needs and challenges. Shared value can be created in three distinct ways by companies: by reconceiving products and markets, by recalibrating value chain productivity, and by addressing gaps in the cluster where it operates. As against the redistributive approach of CSR, the shared value concept takes co-creation approach, creating a win-win paradigm for the society as well as the corporation. It junks the conventional logic that for larger society to benefit, economic expectations of corporates have to be blurred.

Microfinance institutions are a perfect example of shared value approach. The institutions' business model is built on addressing a fundamental societal problem of lack of financial access for poorer segments of the society. Thus, they have redefined the market for financial services, and their low-cost operational model is an example of reworking the value chain, to ensure low-cost doorstep delivery of financial services. Excess profitability in their operations is frowned upon, and the basic approach is to be sustainable, and pass on the benefits of higher profitability to the clients. It can be argued that for the MFIs, the policy should look at shared value approach rather than impose CSR guidelines. This will lead to a more focused approach on mission-aligned social goals, and also enable microfinance clients to benefit from it. The challenge with the implementation of shared value matrix by policy relates to setting clear and measurable social goals, but this does not apply in the case of microfinance, as there are well established matrices for capturing social goals, and the same can be quantified also. To illustrate it further, if an MFI sets a social goal of reaching the excluded segment in hilly areas, to do so, it will incur additional operational costs, as compared to operating in a densely populated or urban area. The incremental cost can be captured as part of social value creation by the MFI. Similarly, the efforts of MFIs to do credit plus activities, such as livelihood training, financial literacy training, and health awareness can be quantified in terms of cost as well as benefits to its clients. Such an approach, if adopted, can check the not-so-focused spend on CSR and instead be used for generating value for its clients, in sync with the institutional social goals. Most MFI CEOs in their discussion with the author found this approach novel and felt that this framework can add value to their operations.

> *We do create shared value and it will be nice to have a framework which captures our value creation for customers in alignment with institutional objective.* —M.R. Rao, CEO, BFIL

If the policy can recognize this approach, and make it applicable to MFIs, the sector will think more concretely about social goals, monitoring and reporting them, and it will translate into higher value creation for its clients. This approach is in complete alignment with social performance management, and it does not restrict institutions who want to go beyond it and do CSR also.

2.1.2 Products, Services, Channels That Meet Client's Needs and Preferences: Still to Scale

The MFIs in India have regulatory limitations on what products they can offer, as well as guidelines relating to loan size and tenure, in the case of eligible products. MFIs cannot on their own accept deposits or provide insurance and pension services, though they can offer these services as a banking correspondent and through insurance companies. The credit side is hemmed in by regulations on loan size linked tenure, maximum loan size, and target clientele, defined by income as well as total indebtedness. To add to these, till the last year, for meeting the eligibility conditions for qualifying assets, MFIs had to ensure that the loans were used for income generating purposes. However, based on industry demand and realizing the value of loans for education, housing, and sanitation, the RBI in April, 2015 relaxed the norm of loans to be exclusively used for income generation.

The new guidelines[12] stipulate that other purposes such as housing repairs, education, medical, and other emergencies can constitute up to 50% of the portfolio. Even though the MFIs have been criticized for negligible product innovation, this was attributed to easier scale-up with a plain vanilla one-year loan product as it obviated the necessity of investing in staff training and changes in operational systems.

Despite these microregulations, and recent enabling changes in regulation, the sector has seen quite a bit of action on new products. There is no comprehensive sector-wide data on share of diversity of loan products and its relative share in loan portfolio. Industry associations do not publish data on product diversity. However, the information submitted by MFIs for this report as well as information on institution's websites shows that almost all MFIs have diversified beyond typical one-year/two-year income generating loan. This assertion is substantiated by the review of CoC assessments commissioned by SIDBI. According to the study done by MicroSave[13], while 40% MFIs had higher-sized individual loans, 21% had housing and water/sanitation loans, 19% had education loans, and 11% had emergency loans. Dia Vikas's SPM report of its partners also shows a healthy diversification of loan products (Table 2.3).

The two reports, despite being dated, show a healthy diversification of loan products even before the regulatory relaxations. Currently, the field situation is more dynamic, with almost all MFIs having loan products, in addition to the basic JLG income generation loan. Besides the diversification, the other significant change taking place is in processes, with MFIs moving toward cashless disbursements and repayments.

Broadly, the following categories of loan products are in vogue, which cover quite a wide gamut

1. Water, Sanitation, and Energy
2. Micro-Housing
3. Livelihood based
4. Education and Emergency Loans

A few examples of the above broad category of products are:

Arohan, a MFI headquartered in Kolkata has traditionally been offering group loans (Saral) and loans for urban vendors (Bazaar), and had built its portfolio around these products. Last year, it added

Table 2.3 Credit Products of Dia Vikas' Partners as on March 31, 2015

MFI	Income Loan	Sanitation Loan	Water Loan	Education Loan	Agri Loan	Energy Loan	Housing Loan	Health Loan
Adhikar	Yes	Yes	Yes			Yes		
Annapurna	Yes			Yes			Yes	
Cashpor	Yes	Yes	Yes			Yes		Yes
C-DOT	Yes	Yes	Yes	Yes		Yes		
EMFIL	Yes	Yes	Yes	Yes		Yes	Yes	
Go-Finance	Yes						Yes	
Margdarshak	Yes					Yes		
Prayas	Yes	Yes		Yes				
RGVN	Yes	Yes	Yes	Yes	Yes			
Sambandh	Yes	Yes	Yes					
Samhita	Yes							
Shikhar	Yes							

Source: Transforming Lives, Dia Vikas Social Performance Report, 2015.

loans for purchase of solar lanterns to existing customers. The loan amount is capped at ₹1,950, which is the price of solar lantern and is repayable in monthly installments. Sonata, based in Eastern UP, has been focused on Grameen style lending, but has now started offering loans for solar as well as other consumer durables, under the loan product called 'utility loan'. The loan has a higher maximum ceiling of ₹20,000, and the repayment tenure ranges from 3 to 18 months. Future Financial Services also offer solar loans as also the facility of outright purchase, and the amount ranges from ₹699 to ₹1,299. Evangelical Social Action Forum (ESAF) has also introduced a similar loan product named Suryajyothi loan for existing customers. The loan amount ranges from ₹1,000 to ₹10,000, and is payable in six months for loan amounts up to ₹3,000, and in one year for loans ranging from ₹3,000 to ₹10,000. In addition to it, it has another energy loan product (Table 2.4). Financing for solar lanterns has seen quite a bit of traction.

In addition to the above, many other MFIs have also ventured into energy financing. The outreach numbers are not available for most but in the case of ESAF, solar loan had an outreach of 34,204 customers, and Grihajyothi loan had an outreach of 7,681 customers as on March 31, 2015. Field interactions of the author with MFIs show that the outreach is significant in all MFIs, with some large ones touching a customer range of 200,000.

Table 2.4 ESAF's Grihjyothi Loan

S. No.	Product Attributes	Description/Details
1	Purpose	For promoting energy-efficient cooking stoves
2	Loan Amount	From ₹1,000 to ₹10,000
3	Rate of Interest	24.92% on diminishing basis
4	Processing fee	1% of the loan amount + service tax
5	Loan Period	For loans up to ₹3,000, 26 weeks/6 months
		For loans above ₹3,000, 52 weeks/12 months
6	Repayment Frequency	Weekly/Fortnightly/Monthly
7	Moratorium Period	1 week/2 weeks/1 month, according to repayment frequency
8	CB Verification	Nonmandatory
Eligibility: Any Sangam member having credit worthiness and part of a Sangam having active IGL/GL		

Source: ESAF.

In contrast, to solar and utility loans, water and sanitation loans have not grown that much. Guardian, an NGO-MFI, is one example of an MFI which is solely focused on water and sanitation. Guardian's focus is evident in its mission statement: "Guardian envisions poorer societies to have easy access to household water and sanitation facilities through micro credit." At present, it offers six types of water, sanitation and hygiene (WASH) loans to its clients, and has an impressive client outreach of 89,797 borrowers as of June 2016. It is a shining example of socially-focused MFI, which has not been able to scale up, as under the earlier regulations, its loans were not considered as 'qualifying asset', and hence banks were not willing to fund it.

Box 2.2 Guardian's WASH Products Range

- Water connection loan
- Toilet construction loan
- Renovation loan
- Water Purifier loan
- Biogas loan
- Rainwater harvesting

Source: www.Guardianmfi.org.

Micro-housing is another area which has seen product offerings from MFIs. Belstar offers a home improvement loan of ₹25,000 to its existing clients, and the loan is repayable in 25 months. The start of home improvement loans in the industry saw conservative loan sizes, but over the years the loan amount has started inching up. ESAF offers a home improvement loan with a maximum amount of ₹75,000, while Annapurna's microfinance's loan size under home improvement goes up to ₹120,000, with an extended loan repayment period of four years. Ujjivan's home improvement loans have a maximum loan size of ₹150,000, and the maximum repayment duration is three years. It is heartening to see that MFIs are catering to the key housing needs of the clients, and offering higher repayment period to reduce the burden on clients. Under housing, there is also a need for disaster risk mitigation. Low income households in disaster prone areas are often vulnerable to natural disasters, trapping them in vicious cycle of poverty, as disasters deplete their assets and negatively affect their earning capacity. Habitat for Humanity is piloting a disaster insurance product, that provides asset and property coverage against a wide range of natural and man-made perils, including storms, typhoon, earthquakes, fire, riots and malicious damage, in partnership with HDFC Ergo. The pilot will throw learnings on the feasibility of such an insurance product, and if it succeeds, it will be worthwhile for MFIs to offer this insurance product in tandem with home loans.

The other category of loans relate to livelihood based loans, termed according to the activity, such as agriculture loan, dairy loan, and micro-enterprise loans. While most have similar features, there are a few interesting examples. Janalakshmi has piloted an agriculture loan in group mode called 'Jana Kisan loan'. Under this, a small batch loan is provided to individuals in a group comprising a minimum of 4 and a maximum of 10 engaged in agricultural activity residing in the same village, where each guarantees the other. After completion of each, a customer can borrow the same amount or move to the next level. The loan amount is minimum ₹25,000 and maximum ₹60,000 for the first loan cycle. The loan tenure is of 24 months. The product has two variants—dairy and mixed farming—aimed to cater to all kinds of farmers and their specific monetary needs. Annapurna microfinance has an agriculture loan targeted exclusively for small and marginal farmers, and, more importantly, has flexible repayment options.

Box 2.3 Annapurna's Agriculture Loan

- For Small/Marginal Farmer
- Max loan amount ₹25,000 based on crop cultivated
- Flexible repayment—bimonthly, quarterly, once in 4 months, half yearly
- Loan tenure- 12 months
- Current Outreach- 175

Source: Annapurna Microfinance.

ESAF has an interesting livelihood loan which is typical of the area it is offered. The loan product is called MELU-Microenterprise Loan for umbrella making. The umbrella-making kit is provided by ESAF Retails through loan support from ESAF Microfinance. Umbrellas are in huge demand in Kerala, especially due to a rainy season that lasts for over five months. Considering the seasonality of umbrella making, this loan product is only offered during the months of December–April. The loan amount is capped at ₹10,000.

Grameen Koota Financial Services (GFSPL) is an interesting case of offering multiple loans to its clients in group mode, and it defines its product diversity to its life-cycle approach. Like other MFIs, it started offering its customers income generation loans. Over a period of time, GFSPL has devised various products along with income generation loans to provide financial assistance to customers' during their time of need. The main objective of this was not only to help customers for their needs, but also to make sure that they do not fall into to trap of local money lenders who charge exorbitant interest rates. Through constant interactions and feedback from customers, GFSPL devised products that help the customers to meet their needs at various stages of their life, under its conceptualization of clients' life-cycle needs (Figure 2.4).

Based on this life cycle approach, GFSPL at present offers four broad categories of loans (Figure 2.5).

Under these broad categories, are various types of loans. For example, under the head "family welfare loans", it provides three types of loans.

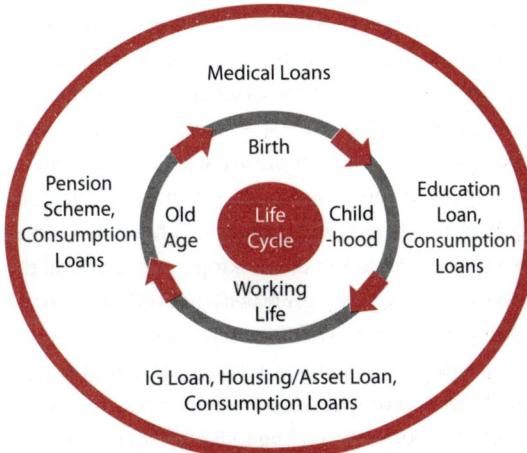

Figure 2.4 Life Cycle–based Product Line of GFSPL

Source: Grameen Financial Services Pvt Ltd.

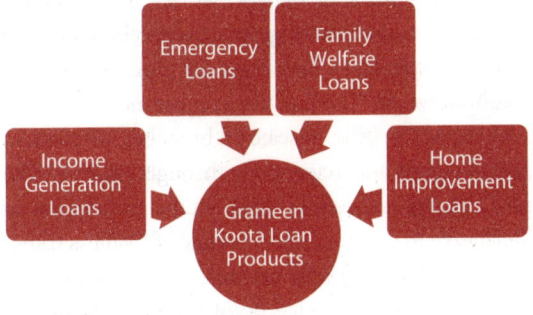

Figure 2.5 Product Line of GFSPL

Source: Grameen Financial Services Pvt Ltd.

Festival Loan: In order to cater these ad-hoc expense requirements during festivals, customers are provided with festival loans. Customers are allowed to avail this loan to celebrate any festival. Customers can avail up to ₹2,000 as festival loan.

Medical Loan: For health issues, which require medical attention and treatment, customers can avail this loan for basic medical facilities by providing medical loans. Medical loans range from ₹500 up to ₹2,000, based on the requirement.

Education Loan: Customers can avail this loan for up to two children in respect of school education expenses with loan assistance for each child capped at ₹5,000. These loans are available to customers only during the start of the school season.

This is a novel approach, and its fit with client needs is reflected in the high outreach under this loans. During FY 2015–16, 1.8 million clients availed emergency loans, 49,576 availed medical loan and 296,925 clients availed education loans. These are impressive numbers and bear testimony to the effectiveness of this approach.

Thus, it is seen that the MFIs are increasingly diversifying their loan products within the regulatory ambit. At present, the outreach of many MFIs under these diversified products is not so significant, and it is hoped that in future these will scale up. Product diversification is a welcome step but, based on field interactions with clients and practitioners, two things emerge which have to be guarded against. First, any of the products should not be bundled with another product. Doing this increases the cost for the client, and forces him/her to take a product which he/she does not want. Second, at present, there is less of innovation on terms and conditions, and more emphasis is on loan size based on activity. For these loans to be truly beneficial to the clients, these loans, especially the livelihood loans repayment, has to be made in sync with the cash flow generation pattern of the activity.

The diversification has also touched products which cannot be directly offered by the MFIs, but are extremely useful for the clients. Pension product is a case in example. Despite the changes to the Swalamban pension scheme, which was renamed as Atal Pension Yojana (APY), with critical feature changes affecting MFIs, the pension enrollment by NBFC-MFIs has increased (Figure 2.6). The amount of subscription by March 2016 has gone up to ₹161 crore. Under APY, only banks can become

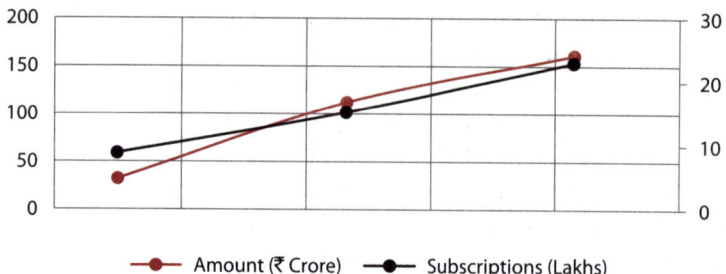

Figure 2.6 Pension Coverage by NBFC-MFIs over Last 3 Years

Source: MFIN, Micrometer Issue 17.

aggregators for APY. The change adversely affected MFIs acting as aggregators under the earlier scheme, as not only because their commission got halved but also on account of the fact that availability of bank branches in many rural areas is limited. A representation has been made to Pension Fund Regulatory Development Authorit by MFIs, and the issue was raised in the international conference held in March 2016, by South Asian Micro-entrepreneurs Network (SAMN) and MFIN. During the conference, Secretary, Department of Financial Services, hinted toward a rethink on the issue[14] and hopefully the issue will be resolved, allowing MFIs to increase the pension outreach.

Processes—Move Toward Cashless in Sync with Digital India

The Digital India program of the Government of India is aimed at broadbasing the use of information technology (IT) in business and governance. Backed by JAM trinity, it also supports wider use of cashless transactions. MFIs processes in India have seen integration of IT and cashless processes on a wide scale over the last one–two years. The innovations range from tab-based operations at the field level, cashless disbursements and repayments, and card-based loans, as well as moving toward Aadhaar-based e-KYC. These steps are well in sync with the broader national agenda of digital transformation. Although the last year's report mentioned a few of such initiatives, it is worthwhile to describe a few of these initiatives in detail, to show the extent of changes taking place.

Equitas Micro Finance, which is now in the process of transforming as an SFB, places strong emphasis on digitization. It has provided tablet PCs (tab) to its field staff, and with the use of the tabs, its member declaration form is being captured digitally across all the branches. The tab-based application at

Equitas also has a provision for capturing signature or biometric details of the member. One important feature of this tab relates to integrating it with CB, so that CB checks can be made instantly in the field. The near future vision of Equitas is to implement the mobile-based application for the loan application process. Some of the other MFIs which have moved toward tab-based field processes are GFSPL (in pilot), Janalakshmi, and BFIL. Ujjivan started the process of cashless disbursement through bank accounts, and now several medium-sized MFIs such as Belstar (pilot), Annapurna, and Fincare have also started doing so. This is a welcome trend and has been helped by the penetration of bank accounts under PMJDY. Arohan is exploring options with digital wallet/potential payment bank entities to offer mobile money options to customers, so as to reach an end-stage where disbursement and collections are facilitated though cashless mode.

BFIL has been undertaking a measured journey toward digitization for the last three years. The journey started with providing its field officers (called Sangam managers—SMs) with tabs. Besides empowering SMs digitally with custom-built applications (e.g., SKS Smart) that are essential to perform field tasks, considering the poor connectivity in field areas, BFIL has built an offline solution, wherein all the policies enforcement and application installation/updates are shared via a gateway machine. As soon as an SM syncs his tab to the desktop in a branch, all the relevant data of a user get transferred offline from the desktop to the tab. The SM then goes to the centers along with the tab, enters relevant details in it during center meetings, and on his return resyncs the tab with the desktop. According to BFIL, this has enabled it to increase SM productivity from handling 675 clients to 800 clients, and has also reduced the time of center meetings from 45 minutes to 30 minutes on account of elimination of paper work. Client feedback on shorter center meetings has also been positive as it enables clients to save time for their household/livelihood work. The last year's report mentioned the pilot started by BFIL in selected branches for cashless disbursement and repayment through M-Pesa. The pilot did not succeed, so BFIL is now looking for an alternative to continue this journey of cashless transactions and is exploring options, including building its own customer service points (CSPs). According to BFIL, the reasons for the M-Pesa experiment not working out related to both clients and the M-Pesa interface. At the client level, the issue faced was that clients often removed the subscriber identity module (SIM) cards and during transactions handed over the SIM cards to agents for transactions as the interface was being seen as too complicated to operate. M-Pesa could not change the interface architecture locally. The other challenge related to cash maintenance by agents, as in the case of nonavailability of cash for withdrawal, it was leading to client dissatisfaction. The cost structure related to commission was also high for BFIL to continue this partnership.

Like Equitas, BFIL has also started integrating CB checks with the tab, and importantly, gone ahead with the e-KYC functionality in tabs. The e-KYC, done based on thumb impression captured in the Aadhaar database, will go a long way in establishing identity, de-duping with CB, and reducing credit risk. Going ahead, it is planning to use tabs for financial literacy.

As a part of Arohan's banking correspondent arrangement with IDBI Bank (started in March 2016), a joint partnership was started between MUDRA, Arohan, and IDBI Bank in order to offer MUDRA's cash credit facility to Arohan's customers. This facility works similar to an overdraft facility; however, for this product, MUDRA also offers a debit-cum-ATM Rupay card to customers through which cash withdrawals and payments at point of sale (POS) locations can be made by the customer. Currently, Arohan offers a cash credit limit of ₹5,000–10,000 to customers who are active-term loan customers of IDBI Bank (provided the cash credit limit is not more than 20% of the sanctioned term loan amount). Repayment by the customer is done by way of monthly payments to Arohan staff to service any interest amount, and the principal or remaining amount is to be paid in a lump sum directly to IDBI Bank. As on June 30, 2016, Arohan had 229 cash credit customers.

Janalakshmi is another institution that places strong emphasis on digital, with complete digital operations. Janalakshmi's digital inclusion model has three pillars. First is a transactional platform, which includes an open-loop prepaid card issuing platform. All loans are disbursed via prepaid cards. It has issued 5.2 million cards till date, and every month over 0.4 million new cards are added. It is supplemented with a mobility solution that serves as a technology platform both for self-initiated transactions (mobile wallet) and assisted services via agency banking. Both the

mobile wallet and prepaid card are linked and allow seamless transfer of funds between the platforms. The platforms have been enabled for a wide range of basic financial services, including cash deposits and withdrawals, remittances, bill payments, mobile/DTH recharge, and so on, which meet the requirements of Janalakshmi's primarily urban/semi-urban clients. The second pillar is agency banking through Jana Cash points. These agents are equipped with mobile phones, and their biometric readers provide a wide range of assisted basic financial services. Additionally, these cash points also serve as cash deposit points where Jana collection executives deposit cash collected from customers toward loan installments. The digital ecosystem is supported through the third pillar of device and biometrics. These include client/agent mobile phones on which the customer app (Jana Cash wallet) or agent app (Jana Mitra wallet) is downloaded from the Apple/Google Play store. The other is a handheld biometric reader through which the customer and transaction are authenticated. The mobile phone and biometric reader are paired via Bluetooth. Janalakshmi Financial Services has also been certified by unique identification (UID) for e-KYC like BFIL, which paves the way for digital customer enrollment.

SONATA Finance is doing a pilot on digital repayments. Grameen Foundation India, through funding by Citi Foundation under their 'India Innovation Grant Program', has formed a partnership with SONATA Finance Pvt. Ltd and a payment service provider, Oxigen Services India Pvt Ltd., for a pilot project on digital financial inclusion[15]. The project applies a human-centered design approach to deliver mobile banking services and education to female borrowers in the northern state of Uttar Pradesh. The aim of the pilot is to educate women clients of SONATA from rural areas to use mobile phones as a channel for their loan repayments. It is expected that as they become comfortable with mobile phone usage for financial transactions, the usage will be expanded to include an extensive suite of products, including airtime top-up, remittances, financial education, and savings among others. Being a pilot, Grameen Foundation India has also trained customers of SONATA to become mobile money agents, providing them with an additional source of business income.

The project has been conceptualized to ensure that each partner benefits from the arrangement

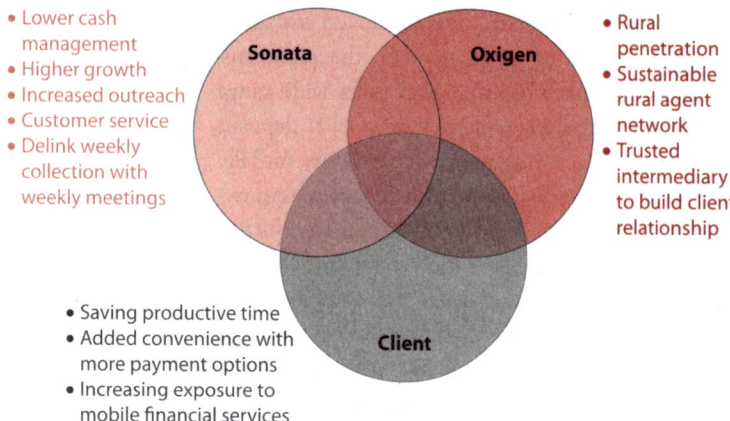

- Lower cash management
- Higher growth
- Increased outreach
- Customer service
- Delink weekly collection with weekly meetings

- Rural penetration
- Sustainable rural agent network
- Trusted intermediary to build client relationship

- Saving productive time
- Added convenience with more payment options
- Increasing exposure to mobile financial services

Figure 2.7 Sonata's Digital Repayments Pilot—Benefits to Stakeholders

Source: SEEP Network.

(Figure 2.7), and importantly from the client perspective, it provides a payment channel option for them closer to their homes, avoiding the need to repay by cash every week at a center or branch.

Till May 2016, this program had reached out to over 23,222 clients, to train them on mobile financial services, of which 7,000 clients had been enrolled. This payment option had been introduced at over 18 branches at SONATA, and transactions had started coming in and till May 2016 transactions worth ₹1.1 crore had been routed through Oxigen.

The microfinance sector's move toward digital and cashless is gaining ground, and as a concept, it seems to be a win-win situation for both the client and MFIs. MFIs have been facing law and order problems relating to cash disbursement and collection, and going cashless helps solve the issue as well as lower costs—those of moving cash. For clients, it is also useful in inculcating familiarity with digital financial services that seem to be the future, as well as creating awareness about banking and other financial services. However, based on field reports, there are two issues related to cashless and mobile phone/POS/card-based transactions, which can erode its client centricity. First issue relates to introducing these processes without client training, and this can result in an increase in assisted transactions, which are open to misuse. Clients accustomed to paper records also find it difficult to be comfortable with the digital confirmation of transactions. While this can be addressed by adequate training before the introduction of new technology, the other aspect relates to costs and inconvenience. A few prepaid cards are issued at a cost, which create a negative value for the client and more so as the

card-based disbursement is not based on the client's demand. MFIs need to ensure that the costs associated with these cards are kept to minimum. Related to this are issues like the availability of transaction points, liquidity with agents, and freedom to withdraw the amount. Few and far-off transaction points and lack of liquidity with agents to ensure withdrawal of the card amount create a negative value for clients. MFIs going this route need to ensure that these two aspects are addressed, before launching digital services, in order to be responsible to the needs of clients.

2.1.3 Transparency and Grievance Redressal— Good Standards Established

As noted in the last year's report, aided by microfinance regulation and CoC, transparency and grievance redressals have seen a lot of strengthening. On transparency, sector good practices relate to clear communication of terms and conditions initially in group trainings and later in loan pass book, interest rate declaration on declining basis, full disclosure of other charges like processing fee and insurance fee, and in many cases providing clients with a copy of the loan contract. As an example, a snapshot of Fusion's loan pass book in Figure 2.8 shows the typical level of transparency achieved by the sector. Similarly, grievance redressal system has also strengthened across institutions. All institutions provide multiple grievance redressal channels to the clients in the form of complaint box, toll-free number, and industry association help line number, and these are mentioned in the clients' pass books. MFIN's work in this area with Smart Campaign in designing a comprehensive grievance redressal framework will further strengthen the system (see more details in the next chapter). Filing of complaints is one aspect of it, while resolution is the other. A perusal of CPP-certified MFIs shows that the resolution is being accorded priority, and MFIN, through its surveillance activity, monitors the complaint resolution mechanism of NBFC-MFIs.

Staff behavior with clients has been another area which has seen strengthening with MFIs, including checks on staff behavior as part of their internal control mechanism. At Satin Creditcare, the IA unit verifies the customer perspective on staff behavior during their center visits. Supervisory staff also regularly monitors staff behavior. Customer service and communication with clients have, respectively, 10% and 5% weights on performance appraisal of

Loan Type (ऋण प्रकार)	IGLM26-20000-KL-S@25.75%
Loan Amount (ऋण राशि)	₹20,000/-
Reducing Rate of Int. (घटत क्रम ब्याज दर)	25.75%
Annual Percentage Rate (वार्षिक प्रतिशत)	27.23%
Loan Period (ऋण अवधि)	दो साल
No. of Installment (किस्त हर 28 दिन पर)	26
Installment Amount (किस्त की राशि)	₹1,400/-
LPF (ऋण कार्यवाही शुल्क (1%) सेवा कर (15%) सहित)	₹230/-
Insurance (बीमा कार्यवाही शुल्क सेवा कर सहित)	₹428/-
फयूजन निशुल्क ग्राहक सेवा न0: 1800 1037 808	
पंजीकृत कार्यालय एवं प्रधान कार्यालयः C-3 कम्युनिटी सेन्टर, नारायणा विहार, नई दिल्ली–110028 फोनः 011–46646600	
ग्राहक हस्ताक्षर	

Figure 2.8 Loan Card of Fusion

Source: Fusion Microfinance.

the staff. IA's interactions with clients include their experience with staff, behavior and communication mannerisms of the customer service officer, awareness of the grievance redressal mechanisms (GRMs), and other aspects of CoC. The IA team of the MFIs also checks the awareness of the customers about grievance redressal and right to complain. BFIL conducts CPP training for staff and members on an annual basis. All staff members have been trained, and detailed CPP training has been done in more than 100,000 centers to strengthen the awareness levels of clients. The IA team covers client awareness during their monthly audit, and during the last financial year 90,000 clients were covered.

2.1.4 Responsible Pricing: Steep Decline in Rates but What Are the Dynamics?

During the Andhra Pradesh (AP) crisis of 2010, one of the major concerns with MFI operations was the high interest rates, and these were contrasted with low rates under the SHG—Bank Linkage Programme. Although the logic and facts of this assertion have been debated both ways, it can be safely said that the truth lies somewhere else. The issue has been discussed at length and does not merit another narrative[16]. However, this obsession with rates of interest has persisted and was recently seen in 2014 in the observations of the Parliamentary Standing Committee on Finance on Micro Finance Institutions (Development and Regulation) Bill, 2012, which said, "the committee notes with alarm that the rate of interest on individual loans by NBFC-MFIs may exceed 26 percent"[17]. Despite all

this, the fact remains that public policy and civil society will always be concerned about lending rates to the poor, and the sector needs to ensure that efficiency gains are passed on the clients, rather than bloating profitability.

It was, thus, natural that Malegam Committee[18] examined the cost structure of MFIs and prescribed certain norms relating to margin and profitability. It is worthwhile to see that, and it contrasts the earlier practice with the situation prevailing today. The committee examined the financials for the year ended March 31, 2010 of nine large MFIs, which collectively account for 70.4% of the clients and 63.6% of the loan portfolio of microfinance provided by all MFIs. For the same year, it also analyzed the financials of two smaller MFIs. It found out that in the case of larger MFIs, the effective interest rate calculated on the mean of the outstanding loan portfolio as on March 31, 2009 and March 31, 2010 ranged between 31.02% and 50.53%, with an average of 36.79%. For the smaller MFIs, the average was 28.73%. This was perceived to be high, and therefore interest rate cap was prescribed, which after subsequent modifications currently stands at interest cost plus a maximum margin of 10% for large NBFCs-MFIs and 12% for others.

Responsible pricing is also an integral part of responsible finance framework for financial services discussed in Chapter 1. CPP has 'Responsible Pricing' as one of the seven principles which an institution has to comply with in order to be certified. The essence of CPP certification standards under responsible pricing relates to pricing being market-driven, continuous analysis of cost factors, nondiscriminatory pricing, contribution to sustainable operations, and, importantly, the requirement for the institution to invest a portion of its profits to increase value to its customers, such as lowering interest rates or adding or improving products and services. The last part of the CPP framework is directly related to passing on the efficiency gains to the customers. Similarly, responsible pricing is also a part of USSPM framework of SPTF and of the sixth dimension[19] relating to balancing of financial and social performance. The essence under USSPM is also similar requiring institutions to ensure that the pursuit of profits does not undermine the client's well-being and has a double-bottom-line approach focusing on both financial and social performance.

NBFC-MFIs Have Reduced Lending Rates Substantially

The position in respect of NBFC-MFIs lending rates prevailing currently shows that post 2010, the rates have consistently come down with BFIL currently charging 19.75%[20] on its main group loan product. While leaders in pricing such as BFIL are not only operating under the prescribed margin cap but have also gone below That.

Data from MFIN's Micrometer[21] show that interest rates in the sector have come down across the board. The pricing data provided in the report show the pricing range across products of the institution as well as pricing on majority portfolio (Annexure 2.2). The pricing on majority portfolio across 56 members ranges from 19.8% to 27.2%, the higher end figure is inflated because of smaller MFIs, which have a higher operating cost and also generally get debt funding at a higher rate—which pushes up the cost

of lending. If the pricing data are seen in respect of top-10 NBFC-MFIs (which account for 71% of microfinance loan portfolio), the rates of interest are on the lower side of the range.

This is a very positive trend, and Figure 2.9 also demonstrates that rates of interest fall with an increase in loan portfolio, a logical trend, considering the efficiency gains. This story of Indian microfinance is often ignored: the change affected has been impressive—the average rate of interest in 2010 reported by Malegam Committee for large MFIs was 36.79%; it has reduced to being in a range of 19.8–26%.

> NBFC-MFIs have reduced their lending rates by a whopping 10% to 16% in six years since 2010.

Legal Form-based Regulation Allows for Unequal Playing Field

As NBFC-MFIs have continued to raise the bar and lower the interest rates, making Indian microfinance one of the most efficient markets in the world, the demonstrated business model is attracting new players to lend to the same segment. During the last two–three years, mainstream banks (mainly private sector banks) started lending through the banking correspondent route, using the MFIs as BCs, but have now also started lending directly. In addition, a few mainstream NBFCs have also built a significant portfolio in the sector, and Bandhan, which transformed as a universal bank from being an NBFC-MFI, has built its business model on its existing client base, that is, microfinance clients. The shift of private sector banks from lending through BCs to direct lending seems to be borne out of a desire for higher margin. While under the BC model the

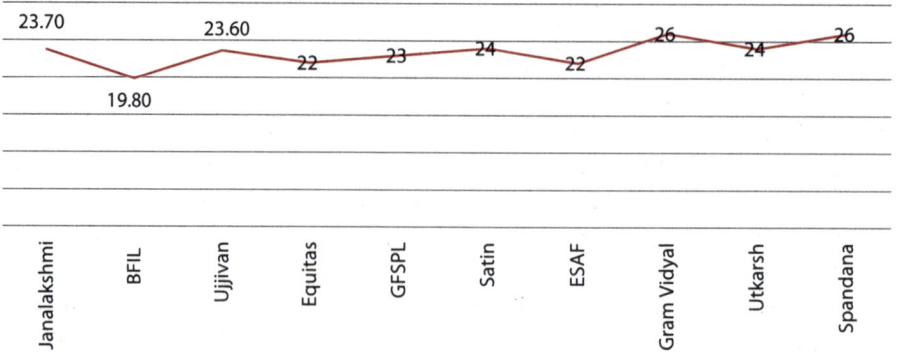

Figure 2.9 Rate of Interest of Top-10 NBFC-MFIs
Source: MFIN Micrometer.

Table 2.5 Interest Rate Being Charged by Banks and NBFCs

Institution	Rates of Interest	Source
Bandhan Bank	19.9%	http://www.business-standard.com/article/finance/bandhan-bank-reduces-microfinance-loan-rate-116071800513_1.html, accessed on September 30, 2016.
Private sector banks	26%	Field investigation by the author.
NBFCs	25.5–26.5	Field investigation by the author.

banks compensated the MFIs acting as a BC for their operating expenses and a small profit margin, under the direct model the entire spread accrues to the bank. The other argument espoused relates to having greater confidence in institution-generated portfolio, which is under direct supervision and control.

The presence of banks and mainstream NBFCs lending to microfinance clients is on one hand beneficial by way of greater competition, but on the other it has not-so positive outcomes. Banks and NBFCs are not subject to various regulations applicable to NBFC-MFIs by way of interest rate cap, loan limit ceiling, and tenure of loans linked to loan size. They are also not subject to two-lender limit for one client, and they can price their loans higher and give higher sized loans. This is creating an adverse situation at the client level, as the loans from banks and NBFCs are priced high (Table 2.5)

As the lending rates of banks and NBFCs are deregulated, there is no restriction on the interest rate charged. While under the extant regulations this is fine, from a responsible pricing lens the higher pricing of microfinance loans seems out of place, especially for banks, as their cost of funds is way below the cost of funds for NBFC-MFIs. Ideally, banks and NBFCs could have used the regulatory flexibility to provide diversified loan products meeting the client needs, but in reality the only change offered by them relates to higher loan size and interest rate. Even Bandhan Bank, which has the lowest rate amongst banks, is at the level of BFIL's rate of interest, though it was expected that with access to low-cost deposits it will lower its lending rate significantly.

The other negative associated with banks and NBFCs lending to microfinance segment relates to reemergence of features which create negative value to the clients. It is observed that tying deposits with loans is common, and a few have gone head and supplemented the initial deposit with recurrent deposits throughout the loan period—termed as voluntary advance receipts (VAR). These practices remind old timers of similar practices adopted by MFIs a decade back and were discontinued based on criticism of such unfair practices and regulation. The introduction of these practices in the microfinance market by mainstream lenders is a regressive step and needs to be addressed by the policy immediately. Although these institutions justify it by arguing that this is provision of real microfinance—both deposit and loans—field investigation shows that deposits are invariably tied to loans, acting more as a risk mitigation strategy, and entail higher costs for the clients.

> The entry of mainstream banks and NBFCs lending directly to microfinance clients has resulted in adverse practices such as deposits tied with loans and higher sized loans to microfinance clients at higher interest rates. Regulation needs to move to 'activity' from 'legal form'.

As the RBI is the regulator of banks and NBFCs, it needs to ensure that lending to microfinance clients remains entity-neutral with respect to compliance with various conditionalities imposed in the case of NBFC-MFIs. These conditionalities have created quite a positive impact for clients, and reintroduction of adverse practices by entities not bound by these rules is an unwelcome aspect, likely to contaminate the market. There is a pervasive argument in support of banks and NBFCs, observing that in competitive markets, if clients perceive NBFC-MFIs offering better terms and conditions, they are free to avail loans from them. The fact that there is a demand for credit from banks and other NBFCs shows that clients value these services. This is a flawed argument which is theoretical but does not stand the test of empiricism. Field reality shows that microfinance clients are cash deficient, and it is easy for them to fall for higher priced bigger loan over a smaller sized loan with better terms and conditions. After the AP crisis of 2010, lending discipline and client education have been painstakingly built through regulations as well as combined effort of the industry, and it is imperative that it is not allowed to wither away.

Dynamics of Interest Rate Reduction by NBFC-MFIs

It is heartening that lending rates of NBFC-MFIs have fallen significantly over the last six years creating positive gains for the clients, and it is worthwhile to examine as to what has led to interest rate reduction. By financial arithmetic, lending rates can come down either with reduction in cost of funds or improvement in efficiency or tolerance for lower profitability.

The Malegam Committee had worked out the cost structure for NBFC-MFIs in its report at existing levels to work out the lending cap. Table 2.6 shows the Malegam Report's calculations, and its comparison with current situation throws up insights into cost reduction dynamics.

As can be seen, operating expenses, return on equity, and cost of funds are the three variables used for calculating the lending rate. The cost of funds of MFIs on their borrowings during the year 2015–16 has been published by MFIN, which is another step toward transparency. Figure 2.10 shows that the cost of funds for all categories of NBFC-MFIs has gone up since 2010, with medium-sized MFIs (gross loan portfolio between ₹100 to 500 crore) having the highest average cost of funds at 15.40%. Thus, the cost of funds is not the factor driving the reduction in lending rates. Similarly, return on equity (ROE)

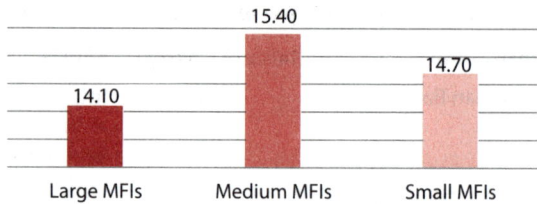

Figure 2.10 Average Cost of Funds of NBFC-MFIs (Including All Charges)
Source: MFIN Micrometer, Issue no. 17.

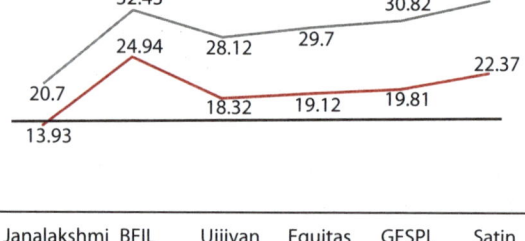

Figure 2.11 RoE of Top-six NBFC-MFIs during 2015–16
Source: Calculated by Author from Financial Statements available on respective websites.

(posttax) of NBFC-MFIs has also shown a surge in last two years, going beyond what was assumed by the Malegam Committee. Figure 2.11 presents the ROE (posttax and pretax) for top-six MFIs[22] by size during 2015–16. The calculations have been done based on audited financials, using average of year-end figures, which limits its accuracy but definitely provides a good measure of current profitability levels.

It is seen that, as against Malegam's assumption of 15% posttax ROE and 22.61% pretax ROE, the actual ROE of top-six MFIs, with the exception of Janalakshmi, is way above that. This analysis of cost of funds and profitability level of MFIs shows that the efficiency gains have come from the third variable, that is, staff costs and other overheads. How that has been achieved is discussed in greater detail in Chapter 5, but it needs to be stated that tweaking of loan repayment, higher loan size, and increased case load of loan officers have critical repercussions on basics of microfinance—the personal connect between the loan officers and the clients.

The sector needs to introspect the limitations of this approach which has achieved lower interest rates but has the potential to disrupt sustainability in the short to medium term. Any possible disruption, as seen in the case of AP crisis, is equally harmful

Table 2.6 Normative Cost Structure Worked Out by Malegam Committee

S. No.	Particulars	% of Loan Portfolio
1.	Staff costs	5
2.	Overheads (other than staff costs)	3
3.	Provision for loan losses	1
	Subtotal	9
4.	ROE (15% post tax, that is, 22.61 pretax on 15% of loan portfolio)	3.39
5.	Cost of funds 12% on 85% of loan portfolio	10.20
	Total of internal and external costs	22.59

Source: Malegam Committee, 2011.

to microfinance clients, eroding gains built through years. However, to be fair to the NBFC-MFIs, it needs to be reiterated that the Malegam Committee had also suggested setting up a 'domestic social capital fund' as a source of patient equity for NBFC-MFIs to temper the profitability chase. The issue was also flagged in the last year's report as a policy action point, but the same has not materialized, and NBFC-MFIs continue to rely on commercial private equity.

2.1.5 Client-level Outcomes: Positive Findings but Studies Need More Rigor

Considering that the focus of responsible finance is on client centricity, it is imperative to discuss client-level outcomes. The litmus test of positive steps taken on various aspects such as diversified products, transparency, rates of interest, and grievance redressal has to be based on the positive outcomes at client level. Although, according to best practices, under social performance management, institutions should have SMART goals, defined in alignment with their mission, the measurable aspect of the goals should be captured routinely through the MIS. As this practice is not so common even among MFIs, the evidence for client-level outcomes has to come from studies conducted on the subject. In the case of studies, the imperative of methodological rigor and avoiding positive bias can be met through external, credible third-party evaluations. During the last year, there has been a dearth of such robust impact/outcome studies, and the studies have tended to focus on client awareness, satisfaction, and outcomes of a specific initiative. A few such studies and their impact are discussed below, and these studies show a positive outcome at client level.

ESAF conducted an impact evaluation[23] of its clients, and the outcomes were compared with the counterfactual by having a control group of nonclients with similar profiles. The study was conducted in 10 districts of Madhya Pradesh, Maharashtra, and Chhattisgarh and covered 500 clients and nonclients respectively. In order for the impact to be captured, the selection of clients used the criteria of clients having availed three cycles of income-generation loans, as typically microfinance clients show positive outcomes after two–three years. Although the study shows improvement in clients' indicators in areas of quality of house, sanitation, and awareness over nonclients, the evidence in

Figure 2.12 Poverty Profile of ESAF Clients and Nonclients

Source: See Note 23.

the case of poverty profile and increase in household income is marginal. In the case of the poverty level based on international poverty lines (Figure 2.12), across all three poverty lines, the clients are marginally better off than nonclients. However, it also shows a critical point on poverty outreach of MFIs—discussed earlier in the report. ESAF has a good poverty outreach, even though these clients have been with the program for three years. The evidence on change in income over the last three years between clients and nonclients supports the poverty profile. While a very small proportion in the sample including nonclients saw a dip in income, surprisingly, a greater percentage of nonclients belong to the top category of income increase (Table 2.7).

As against marginal evidence on the economic side, the well-being indicators in the case of clients show a greater impact. Clients score over nonclients in terms of house quality, access to hospitals, and access to sanitation and potable water, as well as higher awareness of financial products.

GFSPL is one example of tracking the poverty profile of its clients through various loan cycles

Table 2.7 ESAF Study: Changes in Household Income over Past 24–36 Months

		Members	Total Response (%)	Nonmembers	Total Response (%)
I	Increased greatly	72	14	107	21
II	Increased	241	48	222	44
III	Remained constant	173	35	144	29
IV	Decreased	13	3	27	5
	Total	500	100	500	100

Source: See Note 23.

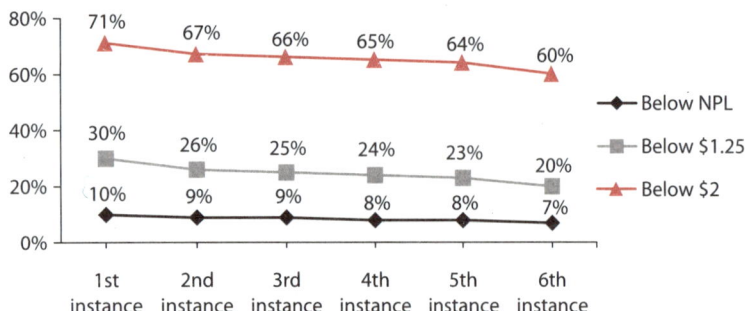

Figure 2.13 Poverty Likelihood of GFSPL Clients

Source: See Note 23.

Box 2.4 Impact Examples Inspired by Jagriti

Sanitation: Jagriti's messages about the ills of open defecation have resulted in a significant percentage of women taking loans to build toilets. Women have exhorted other women and the Gram Panchayat (GP)/local councillors to take action.

Financial Management: Women have opened or are in the process of opening bank accounts under PMJDY which ensures access to financial services (savings and deposit accounts, remittances, credit, insurance, pension, and so on). Women are also saving, are able to buy critical white goods for their families, and have become less dependent on moneylenders, as they are aware of other more viable sources of obtaining loans to meet their needs.

Source: Jagriti, An information tool to empower rural Indian women, summary report of impact created.

---

in order to measure the changes in their financial condition. According to the social rating report of GFSPL, the analysis of the data captured in the MIS shows a decline in poverty levels as clients mature (Figure 2.13). The poverty likelihood declines by one-third in the case of $1.25 poverty line and 14% in the case of $2 poverty line over six cycles. The findings, while based on self-reported data captured in the MIS, support the lower income and poverty impact in the case of SAF clients, as the study had the sample of clients with three loan cycles. Figures in both cases show that the impact on poverty level or economic condition takes a longer time to achieve.

GFSPL has been implementing an innovative financial literacy program called 'Jagriti' since 2011. It uses a fictitious character called Jagriti, who is portrayed as a knowledgeable, empathetic, fearless, and independent woman. She writes letters on issues affecting the everyday lives of women in simple and easy to understand stories. These letters are read out during the weekly meetings with women customers by the loan officers. The intention was to relate to the lives of women clients by having a character similar to them, narrating her experience and views on issues faced by them, and inspire them to follow in Jagriti's footsteps. The messages are simple, engaging, anecdotal, and cover a wide range of issues, including health, hygiene, nutrition, water and sanitation, financial literacy, and government schemes. At present, the program is functional in 263 branches of GFSPL across Karnataka and Maharashtra, covering approximately 863,000 women. In 2015, an assessment of the program was carried out by Phicus Social Solutions. The study found that women clients strongly relate to Jagriti, and actions taken after listening to messages have raised their self-esteem

and perception with others, acting as a strong factor for them to continue their relationship with GFSPL. Themes of sanitation, health, and financial management were most liked by the clients. Buoyed by the findings, GFSPL wants to strengthen the financial literacy initiative by introducing an audio version of the message, which will be disseminated through phone calls, and extending the concept to create a persona which can speak to children.

BFIL has a process of regular client feedback on its products and services through its initiative called 'Voice of Customers (VOC)'. Under VOC, BFIL conducts surveys with its members to understand their product satisfaction, awareness on CPP, satisfaction with grievance redressal, and few other aspects. Telephonic survey of approximately 9,000–10,000 randomly selected members from across the country is conducted every month, and, in 2015–16, a total of 105,550 customers were surveyed across the country. The results show a very positive situation, and BFIL tried to validate the findings through an external agency in 2015. The study conducted by a rating agency validates high customer satisfaction across different issues investigated (Table 2.8). With a coverage of 2,000 clients across different states and having been conducted by an external agency, the survey provides good evidence on customer satisfaction. The only area

Table 2.8 Satisfaction Levels of BFIL Clients across Different Operational Processes

Levels of Satisfaction	Lending Methodology (%)	Frequency of Meeting (%)	Loan Appraisal Process (%)	Loan Processing Time (%)	Loan Disbursement Process (%)	Collection Process (%)
Very satisfied	19.10	23.20	23	18.60	22.73	31.10
Satisfied	76.40	70.50	76.70	50.26	77.26	64.90
Dissatisfied	4.50	6.30	0.30	31.14	0.01	4

Source: VOC Study by BFIL.

where there is some dissatisfaction relates to loan processing time, which is natural, as clients expect quick disbursement sans the processes which need to be followed. BFIL feels that with integration of CB check in the tab provided to loan officers, even this should be taken care of.

Janalakshmi's customer focus been highlighted by CGAP in its report[24] and Janalakshmi's approach to understanding its clients' needs and designing an appropriate delivery mechanism have come for praise. In 2015, Janalakshmi got itself assessed on the Global Impact Investing Rating System (GIIRS). GIIRS is considered to be the gold standard in impact investment and provides an assessment of company's social and environmental impact. Janalakshmi got the highest (platinum) grade, and that demonstrates its social impact on a global methodology.

These positive evidences of client satisfaction and impact add credibility to the sector's journey toward responsible finance.

2.2 NEED TO CONTINUE BEING CLIENT-CENTRIC AND AVOID DRIFT

The MFIs as a sector have displayed good performance on various facets of responsible finance, especially the 'do no harm' aspects—of transparency, appropriate collection practices, GRM, and responsible pricing. The 'do good' agenda is also taking shape in the form of social goals, product diversity, and credit plus activities such as financial literacy, and the results of these initiatives are seen in various studies.

However, there is no room for complacency. As the sector surges ahead, old issues of growth versus client centricity, growing profitability and issues relating to reasonability of it, higher client attrition as well as newer challenges in the form of competition from new category of banks, higher levels of credit saturation in several pockets, moving away from traditional weekly model, and retailing of consumer durables are emerging. These issues seem different but in essence are interrelated inasmuch as any institution which places the clients' welfare at the center can avoid these, and any one of these issues has the potential to adversely affect the MFIs and their clients. These issues are discussed in detail in Chapter 5. It is hoped that the sector will be able to navigate through the emerging issues and come out even more responsive to clients. The role of industry networks, now also recognized as SROs, has been a strong factor in building responsible finance agenda of MFIs, and the next chapter examines the role of MFIN.

ANNEXURE 2.1
Universal Standards of Social Performance Mapped with Regulatory and Industry Guidelines

	USSPM	CPP	UCoC	RBI Guidelines	RBI FPC
Dimension	**DEFINE & MONITOR SOCIAL GOALS**				
Standards	The institution has a strategy to achieve social goals				
	The institution collects, reports, and ensures the accuracy of client-level data that are specific to the social goals				
Dimension	**ENSURE BOARD, MANAGEMENT, AND EMPLOYEE COMMITMENT TO SOCIAL GOALS**				
Standards	Members of the board of directors should hold the institution accountable to its mission and social goals	Partial			Partial
	Senior management oversees implementation of the institution's strategy for achieving its social goals				
	Employees are recruited, evaluated, and recognized based on both social and financial performance criteria	Full			Full
Dimension	**DESIGN PRODUCTS, SERVICES, DELIVERY MODELS, AND CHANNELS THAT MEET CLIENT'S NEEDS AND PREFERENCES**				
Standards	The institution understands the needs and preferences of different types of clients	Full			
	The institution's products, services, delivery models, and channels are designed to benefit clients in line with the institution's social goals	Full			Partial
Dimension	**TREAT CLIENTS RESPONSIBLY**				
Standards	Prevention of over-indebtedness	Full	Full	Full	Full
	Transparency	Full	Full	Full	Full
	Fair and respectful treatment of clients	Full	Full	Full	Full
	Privacy of client data	Full	Full	Full	Partial
	Mechanism for complaint resolution	Full	Full	Full	Full
Dimension	**TREAT EMPLOYEES RESPONSIBLY**				
Standards	The institution follows a written human resources policy that protects employees and creates a supportive working environment	Partial	Partial		Partial
	The institution communicates to all employees the terms of their employment and provides training for essential job functions	Full			Partial
	The institution monitors employee satisfaction and turnover				
Dimension	**BALANCE FINANCIAL AND SOCIAL PERFORMANCE**				
Standards	The institution sets and monitors growth rates that promote both financial sustainability and client well-being	Partial			
	Equity investors, lenders, board, and management are aligned on the institution's double bottom line and implement an appropriate financial structure in its mix of sources, terms, and desired returns				
	Pursuit of profits does not undermine the long-term sustainability of the institution or client well-being	Full		Partial	Full
	The institution offers compensation to senior managers that is appropriate to a double-bottom-line institution				

Partial Overlap
Full Overlap

ANNEXURE 2.2
Rate of Interest on Loans of NBFC-MFIs

S. No.	MFI	Category	Interest Rate Range	Majority Portfolio Pricing	Share of Portfolio
1	Janalakshmi	MFIs (large)	24%	24%	100%
2	Bharat Financial Inclusion Ltd.	MFIs (large)	19.6%–20.2%	20%	97.90%
3	Ujjivan	MFIs (large)	23–23.6	24%	
4	Equitas	MFIs (large)	22%	22%	100%
5	GK	MFIs (large)	20%–23%	23%	88%
6	Satin	MFIs (large)	24%	24%	
7	L&T	MFIs (large)	25.75%	26%	
8	ESAF	MFIs (large)	22%–22.99%	22%	94.40%
9	GV	MFIs (large)	26	26%	100%
10	Utkarsh	MFIs (large)	24%	24%	100%
11	Spandana	MFIs (large)	18%–27.92%	26%	76.50%
12	Suryoday	MFIs (large)	24%–25.1%	25%	76%
13	Sonata	MFIs (large)	22.14%–24.05%	23%	92%
14	SVCL	MFIs (large)	24.70%	25%	100%
15	Asirvad	MFIs (large)	24%–26%	25%	
16	Annapurna	MFIs (large)	18%–28%	28%	96%
17	FFSL	MFIs (large)	25.75%–26%	26%	89.44%
18	Arohan	MFIs (large)	22.99%	23%	99.27%
19	Muthoot	MFIs (large)	24%–24.15%	24%	99%
20	Fusion	MFIs (large)	26%–30%	26%	99%
21	Share	MFIs (large)	25%–26%	26%	96%
22	Madura	MFIs (large)	23.75%	24%	100%
23	BSS	MFIs (medium)	24%	24%	100%
24	Disha	MFIs (medium)	25.75%–26%	26%	93%
25	Intrepid	MFIs (medium)	26%	26%	100%
26	Belstar	MFIs (medium)	25%	25%	100%
26	VFS	MFIs (medium)	22.83%–24.58%	25%	72.94%
28	Chaitanya	MFIs (medium)	25%–26%	26%	100%
29	Saijja	MFIs (medium)	24%–25.98%	26%	96%
30	Margdarshak	MFIs (medium)	26%	26%	100%
31	Jagaran	MFIs (medium)	25.9%–29.5%, 12.5%–25.6%	27%	82.80%
32	Midland	MFIs (medium)	26%	26%	
33	Vedika	MFIs (medium)	25.4%–27.48%	27%	
34	Light	MFIs (medium)	25.99%	26%	100%
35	ASA	MFIs (medium)	27%	27%	99.30%
36	Samasta	MFIs (medium)	26%	26%	100%

(Continued)

(Continued)

S. No.	MFI	Category	Interest Rate Range	Majority Portfolio Pricing	Share of Portfolio
37	Svatantra	MFIs (medium)	22%	22%	100%
38	Namra	MFIs (medium)	26%	26%	100%
39	Mpower	MFIs (medium)	25.99%–28.5%	27%	100%
40	Hindusthan	MFIs (medium)	26%	26%	100%
41	Varam	MFIs (medium)	25%	25%	
42	Adhikar	MFIs (medium)	26%	26%	
43	Sambandh	MFIs (small)	26%	26%	100%
44	Uttarayan	MFIs (small)	26%	26%	100%
45	Navchetna	MFIs (small)	25.32%	25%	100%
46	Nirantara	MFIs (small)	26%	26%	
47	Svasti	MFIs (small)	25.96%	26%	100%
48	IDF	MFIs (small)	24%–26%	25%	100%
49	Shikhar	MFIs (small)	25.98%	26%	100%
59	Sahyog	MFIs (small)	26%	26%	100%
51	Sarvodaya Nano	MFIs (small)	25.3%–25.7%	26%	71.40%
52	MSM	MFIs (small)	26%	26%	100%
53	Nightingale	MFIs (small)	24%	23%	
54	Agora	MFIs (small)	26%	26%	100%

Source: MFIN Micrometer, May 2016.

Box 2.5 Interview of Dr Kshatrapati Shivaji, Chairman and Managing Director, Small Industries Development Bank of India, for *Responsible Finance Report 2016*

Dr Alok Misra: Globally, it is recognized that MF is a double bottom line business and must adopt responsible finance practices. Do you think RF agenda of Indian MFIs is well integrated or there are significant areas of concern?

Dr K Shivaji: Microfinance in recent times has transformed from an activity which was being done on a limited scale with elements of social service and marginal profit to commercial MFIs, albeit with a double bottom line focus. I agree that microfinance is a double bottom line business, as on one hand MFIs have to be viable and generate returns to their equity investors, and on the other hand they are answerable to their borrowers and stakeholders towards the value they have created while serving the bottom of the pyramid. I strongly agree that microfinance produces substantial, intangible value at the grassroots level than what can be seen through their financial statements.

Post the AP crises in 2010, the sector has become more sensitive towards client-related issues such as overindebtedness, transparency, fair recovery practices, grievance redressal, and so on. Responsible finance practices are reflected in MFIs' adherence to the code of conduct established by industry associations, CB referencing to avoid multiple lending, boards' increased roles in monitoring social performance, MFIs' practices as responsible employers, offering credit-plus services, and so on, as well as tracking these practices for both internal and external reporting.

SIDBI, as a development bank, had taken lead in integrating the responsible finance agenda in its MFI lending, even before the AP crisis. It included a set of responsible finance loan covenants in all the loan agreements, which are monitored from time to time. A code of conduct assessment (CoCA) by a third-party agency is a prerequisite for financial assistance to the MFIs by SIDBI. It has also extended grant support to incentivize MFIs to get the COCAs carried out through empaneled agencies. Supporting the India Microfinance Platform (IMFP) developed by MIX Market and pursuing with MFIs for sharing of financial and operational data on the platform to bring in the required transparency in the sector, creation of Lenders Forum to build a uniform approach toward financing and collectively drive the responsible finance agenda with MFIs are some of the other major initiatives by SIDBI, in this direction.

With responsible finance agenda getting integrated in the regulatory guidelines and fair practices code of RBI and SROs being set up to monitor the field level practices, I feel that the right regulatory prescription has already been put into place. There may be some occasional concerns reported, however, the system, in my opinion, is geared to address these.

Dr Alok Misra: I feel that much of RF agenda of Indian MFIs is driven by regulations and your answer also seems to suggest that. Do you agree or feel that MFIs have gone beyond regulations in promoting responsible MF? Any examples?

Dr K Shivaji: As mentioned earlier, the responsible finance practices are now being largely driven by the RBI regulations duly supported by the SROs. Since customer protection is one of the key goals to be achieved through RF, it is obvious that this can be more prudently achieved through regulation and supervision as in this way the basic minimum adherence to the agenda across the board is easier to ensure. However, even before the regulations, the industry has voluntarily adopted the Unified Code of Conduct issued by the two industry associations. Some of the MFIs had even gone beyond to adopt international best practices such as CPP of Smart Campaign, Social Performance Measurement (SPM) assessments, governance ratings, and so on.

I thus feel that the sector has taken proactive steps on its own also while being governed by regulatory requirements.

Dr Alok Misra: While interest rates have come down substantially in past few years, the growth rate is causing alarms with loan portfolio of NBFC-MFIs growing by 84% in 2015–16. Do you see a cause for alarm, especially when the majority of districts are in agrarian distress due to drought?

Dr K Shivaji: The ongoing growth in the microfinance sector has to be seen in emerging perspective. There is a huge demand-supply gap in this segment as brought out from various statistics. With a scalable low-cost model backed by technology, the MFIs have been able to reach out to a large segment of borrowers and post impressive growth rates. Growth rates are also a reflection of increased loan limits per client and income limits stipulated by the RBI. The increasing income levels as well as the substantial awareness created through the PMJDY and PMMY campaigns of GOI, the demand side of microfinance has got a significant boost. Since, the sector is now more regulated, more responsive, and better governed, concerns with the growth rates may not be an issue. Some aberrations of high growth and other related issues observed in certain pockets have been handled by collective action of the stakeholders including the SROs.

Although the microfinance portfolio now seems to be well diversified across all the four regions of the country, it still is desirable to have more geographical spread out within the regions. Recent data has shown a gradual shift to urban areas in the microfinance operations. One reason for this could be the higher cost involved in serving the far-flung rural areas with low population density and at the same time ease of operations in urban areas.

Dr Alok Misra: As you do not entirely agree with the feeling that growth rates are too high and leading to heat in the market, do you think higher stake of domestic patient equity can be done to bring the sector a reasonable growth path? Both bankers and equity investors seem to be too happy pumping money.

Dr K Shivaji: As mentioned in my earlier response, while there appear to be no major concerns at this stage, I think the long-term strategy for balanced growth lies with all the stakeholders, be it MFIs, banks or equity investors. The industry needs to continue to follow a balanced growth coupled with client-centric approaches. Proper identification of clients, addressing HR issues at strategic level, and moving to deeper, interior geographies are certain areas MFIs/lenders and donors/investors must look at. Further, enhanced engagement with current and future borrowers on financial literacy could also address the demand side issues, if any. Patient capital can help, but we need to see that commercial considerations do not wither away. After all, the business has to be profitable for it to cover the vast excluded segments.

Dr Alok Misra: Microfinance emerged from the failure of formal sector banks to offer customized products to poor clients, but over the years it is seen that MFIs have not been able to diversify much beyond plain JLG loans. Recent changes have focused on increasing loan size and repayment frequency. Other loan products such as for education, solar lights, and so on are also more of a name change rather than feature change. What are your views on this?

Dr K Shivaji: We must appreciate the MFIs for having developed a sustainable model to reach out to the poorest and extend credit services, which the banking system could not address for multiple reasons. Their unique "feet on street model and doorstep credit delivery" has helped millions to access credit, which otherwise would not have been possible through the traditional banking model. However, this low-cost model has limited scope for product innovation and handling complexities related to multiple products. Many of the MFIs who have experimented with individual lending models, which relies on cash flow assessments, have realized that it requires improved skill sets. Given the skill sets of the ground level functionaries, this becomes a constraining factor for increased individual lending in many circumstances.

We also need to understand that the segment under question does not have very divergent needs. Most of their needs are around consumption and income generation activities only. So, most of them are either entrepreneurs who earn their livelihood through some income generating activity or they use part of these loans for consumption purposes, with some deployment towards an income generating activity.

Dr Alok Misra: The sector had requested RBI to include NBFC-MFIs as eligible BCs to offer savings services to its customers but after RBIs acceptance of the suggestion, NBFC-MFIs have majorly stayed away from being a BC. How do you see this?

Dr K Shivaji: Ideally, partnering as BCs with banks on the liability side to offer savings and other related services to their customers provides a good opportunity to the MFIs to complete their basket of offerings which otherwise they are constrained as MFI/NBFCs. Since for the MFIs the investment required would be incremental, better RoIs could also be expected vis-à-vis a stand-alone corporate BC arrangements. However, few critical challenges that are faced are in the area of conflict of interest and a new set of processes/compliances, and so on. There are multiple technology platforms interacting, reporting systems, multiplicity of audits, and so on. Moreover, MFIs are also grappling with the risk associated with cash collections and handling at the grassroots level. A few MFIs have tried undertaking this role, but the results have been mixed so far, thereby not inspiring an increased level of confidence in the business proposition. The business case for BC operations also has to become stronger to generate more interest. Overall, I feel that this is a worthy idea that should be pursued by all the banks.

Dr Alok Misra: The other players catering to microfinance segment such as banks, BCs, and NBFCs are not obligated to give data to microfinance CBs and are also not subject to interest rate caps leading to a discriminatory regulation. What steps is SIDBI taking to address this issue?

Dr K Shivaji: At present, there is some regulatory arbitrage available wherein the set of guidelines applicable for MFIs are not applicable for other financial players who are lending to the same segment of borrowers. As a result, we can find some variations in practices of different agencies. We are hopeful that the regulators would address some of these issues and gradually the regulation would move on the basis of product/client segment rather than the lending entity.

Dr Alok Misra: On interest rates, while NBFC-MFIs have been consistently bringing down rates, the rates charged by BCs, banks, and NBFCs continue to be around 26%. How do you view this rate differential in lending to similar segment?

Dr K Shivaji: There would exist some disparity in the interest rate, since different players in the industry have different cost structures and different service qualities. The interest rates under the SHG-BLP are even lower than the NBFC-MFIs. The insistence on "transparency" and "client education" by the regulator largely addresses this issue. To specify, borrowers are usually aware of the difference in the interest rates and are mostly in a position to make informed choice. They choose the channel that suits them the most, after considering both cost and convenience. In the long run, because of competition and advancement in technology, NBFCs and banks (under BC arrangement) would also have to reduce their interest rates.

Dr Alok Misra: SIDBI has been an active promoter of responsible business practices in MFIs. What are the significant initiatives taken by SIDBI during last year to improve client centricity of MFI operations?

Dr K Shivaji: SIDBI is one of the key stakeholders in the MF sector and, as mentioned earlier, has been an active promoter of the responsible finance agenda. Various initiatives undertaken by SIDBI are:

a. SIDBI has already made the Independent CoCA Assessments and a minimum benchmark score mandatory for availing loans by the MFIs.

b. A standard set of covenants called "Responsible Finance Conditions" are stipulated in all the loan agreements. Compliance with these conditions as well as the steps taken by the MFIs to address the weaknesses observed in the CoCA assessments are periodically tracked under the monitoring framework of the loans.

c. Through its presence on the boards of several MFIs, SIDBI also influences the improvement of the RF practices at the board level of the MFIs.

d. Through the lender forum, the responsible finance agenda, is jointly pursued with other lenders.

e. SIDBI has been extending capacity-building support to the MFIs to strengthen their RF practices as well as partly defraying the cost of external assessments.

f. In partnership with DFIDUK under the Poorest States Inclusive Growth Programme, SIDBI has supported large-scale financial literacy programs for MFI clients.

Though not directly related to microfinance activities, SIDBI has already had two group-level interactions with the proposed SFBs to better understand their needs so as to enable fruitful interactions in future.

The point I wish to make is that the process adopted by SIDBI is dynamic so as to enable it to facilitate continuous improvements in the sector.

Dr Alok Misra: While observers feel that the sector is getting overheated and generating client stress, as seen through higher loan sizes and instances of hotspots, the CoC reports funded by SIDBI show good performance of MFIs. Do you think the CoC assessment agencies are following the rigor?

Dr K Shivaji: As mentioned earlier, higher loan sizes have been mostly a result of the higher demand backed by the customers' needs. Also, MFIs graduate clients to a higher loan once their existing loan is successfully repaid. So I don't see a reason for client distress due to this as long as the regulatory guidelines with regard to income limits, overindebtedness, and fair recovery practices are being followed. Notwithstanding that, there could be some stray instances of hotspots, however, the regulatory regime is well entrenched to address these. CoCA assessments have been carried out over the years and may not necessarily capture the current ground realities. However, a defined periodicity of the CoCA assessments is now being considered by the lenders to make it more reflective of the current practices.

Dr Alok Misra: Post-2010, the role of MFIN as quasi regulator has become critical and it has also expanded its scope of work. Do you think the SRO model wherein members fund the SRO can be effective in monitoring and ensuring compliance?

Dr K Shivaji: Yes, SADHAN and MFIN both have been conferred the SRO status and their role would be critical in the times to come. SRO is a supervisory body that works under the direct purview of the RBI. SROs have been formed with the prime motive of putting in place an "intermediary system" so that all the issues are not escalated to the RBI level and also key threats to the sector can be mapped and addressed in a time-bound manner before they become too severe. Given the current challenges and the need for a closer supervision, this seems to be the best possible model in the given circumstances. The funding issues and more independent structures would evolve as more experience is gained. SIDBI is in constant dialogue with the SROs and extends continuous support towards strengthening their capacities.

Dr Alok Misra: SIDBI has been promoting NGO-MFIs since long, however, post-2010, bankers are not funding them enough leading to their gradual contraction. How do you view this? Will they survive or will the sector see transformation as NBFCs or mergers?

Dr K Shivaji: Traditionally, the NGO-MFIs have played an in important role in the evolution of the micro-finance sector in the country. Many of the NBFC-MFIs of today's time started off with their MF operations as societies/trusts/Section 25 cos and later transformed into NBFCs. SIDBI, in fact, supported many of them in the transformation process through its transformation loan scheme.

Understanding the need and importance of small structures of NGO-MFIs/societies etc. that have the wherewithal to reach out to the interiors of rural India, GOI, through SIDBI, operates the India Micro-finance Equity Fund (IMEF) where the mandate is to address the equity/quasi equity needs of the small and mid-sized MFIs.

However, post the AP crises, the regulatory environment has not been very favorable for NGO-MFIs. The regulatory stand seems to be converging towards the view that that significant microfinance player need to convert themselves into the regulated NBFC structure, which fosters a greater lender confidence and helps to attract the necessary equity for growth.

Dr Alok Misra: Lenders forum is a critical initiative of SIDBI to instill orderly growth of the sector. What are the new initiatives taken during last year by the forum?

Dr K Shivaji: The lender's forum is a voluntary platform of lenders, initiated by SIDBI even prior to the detailed regulatory guidelines for the sector being issued by the RBI. The objective of the forum is to work towards enforcing responsible finance practices in the MFIs through a set of common loan covenants. One of the important decisions taken in the last lender's forum meeting held in February 2016 was to harmonize the CoCA assessments and make it a periodic exercise. SIDBI has since organized a meeting of all its empaneled agencies, which conduct the CoCA exercise, in July 2016 where a draft of the harmonized indicators were presented and discussed. In order to foster greater transparency, some of the ideas that were discussed were increased sharing of information among the lenders through a common portal, institutionalizing loan portfolio audit, conducting joint field visits, having common lenders forum nominee/observers on the board of the MFIs, incentivizing MFIs to reach out to un/under penetrated pockets for credit delivery, and so one. Needless to say, SIDBI is committed to the issue and will constantly strive to make the lenders forum relevant to the emerging needs of the sector.

Dr Alok Misra: Currently, the sector has multiplicity of assessments/certifications/ratings, and I had alluded to this in the last year's report indicating an MFI needs to undergo nearly 7–8 such assessments and SIDBI can take a role in harmonizing and limiting these as there is significant overlap. What are your views on this?

Dr K Shivaji: Considering the nature of the microfinance business, being unsecured, vulnerable of the client segment and the attendant need to pursue a responsible finance agenda, independent assessments undertaken by the MFIs helps them to showcase their performance and fosters lender/investor confidence. Lenders generally insist on two types of grading, namely, capacity assessment rating (CAR) and CoCA, both of which, incidentally, have been pioneered by SIDBI. These assessments help the lenders get an independent view on MFIs financial and social performance respectively. As per regulatory requirements, for larger exposure, the banks are now also insisting on a bank loan ratings. A few of the MFI's additionally undergo social performance ratings, client protection assessments/certifications, governance ratings, and so on on their own volition, to showcase their specific strengths to investors and other stakeholder, which although is not mandatory. With a view to reduce the burden of multiple assessments, SIDBI has recently initiated discussions to explore the consolidation of CAR and CoCA into one single assessment.

Dr Alok Misra: There has been a lot of talk about PBs viability, but I also feel that PBs can be used by MFIs to strengthen their product diversity. What are your views on PBs and MFIs synergy?

Dr K Shivaji: There is scope for great synergies between the PBs and MFIs as the target segment that the former would be catering to is largely expected to overlap with MFI client segment, namely, bottom of the pyramid. Currently, the MFIs are not able to make cashless disbursements and collections, resulting in the huge cash carry cost as well as the associated risks. With a tie-up with PB, MFIs can devise newer efficient methods of transaction with the customers. MFIs can also devise methodologies for cash flow assessment based on the transactions in the PB account, which would help them manage the credit risk in a more efficient manner. For the PBs, this would also help in greater transactions in the customer accounts which would help in the improvement of their viability. Thus, the situation would be a win-win for both. Devising an appropriate cost-sharing mechanism between the two would be the key to realizing this synergy on the ground.

NOTES AND REFERENCES

1. Concerns/risks are covered in Chapter 5.
2. https://rbi.org.in/Scripts/BS_NBFCNotification-View.aspx?Id=9651, accessed on September 23, 2016.
3. https://rbi.org.in/Scripts/BS_NBFCNotificationView.aspx?Id=10144, accessed on September 23, 2016.
4. Report of the Committee to Recommend Data Format for Furnishing of Credit Information to Credit Information Companies, RBI.
5. https://rbi.org.in/Scripts/NotificationUser.aspx?Id=10227&Mode=0, accessed on September 23, 2016.
6. http://mfinindia.org/wp-content/uploads/2015/12/2nd-Edition-of-the-MFIN-CoC.pdf, accessed on November 2, 2016
7. http://www.smartcampaign.org/certification/certified-organizations, accessed on September 23, 2016.
8. PSIG. 2015, June. *Governance Practices among Microfinance Institutions.* Lucknow: MicroSave.
9. Vikas, Dia. 2015. *Transforming Lives.* Gurgaon: Dia Vikas Social Performance Report.
10. Ministry of Statistics and Programme Implementation, Government of India. 2014. *Key Indicators of Debt and Investment In India.* Ministry of Statistics and Programme Implementation, Government of India. Available at: http://mospi.nic.in/mospi_new/upload/KI_70_18.2_19dec14.pdf, accessed on September 23, 2016.
11. Porter, Michael E. and Mark R. Kramer. 2011, January–February. *Creating Shared Value, How to Reinvent Capitalism and Unleash a Wave of Innovation and Growth. Harvard Business Review.*
12. https://rbi.org.in/Scripts/BS_NBFCNotification-View.aspx?Id=9651, accessed on September 23, 2016.
13. MicroSave. 2014, November. *Code of Conduct Assessments for the Microfinance Sector: A Macro and Micro View of MFI's Compliance to the Code of Conduct.* Lucknow: MicroSave.
14. http://www.thehindubusinessline.com/money-and-banking/atal-pension-yojana-finmin-may-allow-mfis-to-play-a-role/article8327975.ece, accessed on September 23, 2016.
15. Inputs from Jenny Morgan, SEEP from SEEP's case study on disaster risk framework.
16. For detailed analysis, read Misra, Alok. 2014. *The Microfinance Bill: Need for a Fresh Outlook.* New Delhi: UNDP and Access.
17. http://www.prsindia.org/uploads/media/Micro%20Finance%20Institutions/SCR-%20Micro%20finance%20bill.pdf, accessed on September 23, 2016.
18. https://www.rbi.org.in/scripts/PublicationReportDetails.aspx?ID=608, accessed on September 23, 2016.
19. USSPM has six dimensions broken down into standards and essential practices.
20. http://www.bfil.co.in/media-details/, accessed on September 23, 2016.

21. Micrometer, issue 17, data as of March 31, 2016, Microfinance Institutions Network (MFIN).

22. These six MFIs account for 58.45% of microfinance portfolio reported by MFIN.

23. Customer-change and Transformation study, 2015, conducted by Shaishavi Project Consultants.

24. CGAP. 2014. *The Journey to Customer-centricity, How Janalakshmi a Financial Inclusion Service Provider in India is Transforming Through Customer-centricity.* Available at: https://www.cgap.org/sites/default/files/Other-Kaleido-Brochure-March-2014.pdf, accessed on September 23, 2016.

Role of MFIN as Self-regulatory Organization (SRO) in Promoting Responsible Finance

3

Chapter

3.1 BACKGROUND: INDUSTRY ASSOCIATION TO SRO

The microfinance industry started in India in the early 1990s, and its advent can be attributed to multiple factors: the realization of the inability of the formal banking system to reach the poor sustainably, the beginning of financial sector reforms in the early 1990s, and successful microfinance interventions across the world, especially in Asia and India by NGOs. The microfinance since the start was divided into two strands: one, the SHG model of microfinance and the other, in the form of existing NGOs, working in a range of developmental areas, including the microfinance component as an add-on to the existing work. The sector till the early 2000s was dominated by NGOs working as societies and trusts, and also as cooperatives in some cases. Community development was the theme on account of their close grassroots links with the people, field-based development orientation, and commitment. In this context, a high-level policy forum on 'Building India's Leadership in Microfinance' was organized by Friends of Women's World Banking (FWWB) in 1998.

The policy forum had two crucial outcomes. A paper[1] presented at a preparatory workshop suggested a three-track strategy to accelerate the spread of microfinance by "re-orienting existing financial institutions in favour of microfinance, encouraging new specialised MFIs who see this as their business, and establishing a network of community-based financial institutions (CDFIs)". The last part of the three-track strategy saw immediate action, with the leading microfinance stakeholders getting together to establish a network called Sa-Dhan, which came into being in July 1999. The other outcome was constitution of a task force by National Bank for Agriculture and Rural Development (NABARD) to arrive at a conceptual framework for sustained growth of microfinance. Besides other things, policy and regulation were the key terms of reference for the task force constituted by the RBI in 1998. In the year 1998, the sector was dominated by NGO-MFIs (registered as societies or trusts) and only a handful of NBFCs with the task force put their numbers at 500 and 5 respectively. On the aspect of regulation, the task force preferred self-regulation, arguing that regulation could stifle growth and rob the sector of its informality and flexibility. It recommended that all MFIs (registered as societies or trusts) register themselves with the SRO. Recognizing the unsuitability of the legal form of society or trust to undertake financial intermediation, it recommended that societies and trusts would have to transform themselves into cooperatives or companies once the sum of their deposits and loans exceed a certain level, tentatively proposed at ₹25 lakhs. This was in line with the view expressed in the paper cited above, which also said, "NGOs invented micro-finance but NGOs are not the best type of agencies to carry out micro-finance on a long-term sustainable basis."

3.1.1 Transformation of the Sector: Formation of a New Network—MFIN

The recommendations of the task force on SRO were not implemented, and the sector continued under dispersed regulation. Meanwhile, the sector started changing in the decade of the 2000s, as the limited nature of donor funds and the desirability of moving the sector toward sustainable operations was realized early. The profitability of microfinance was demonstrated, operational model was validated by external assessments, leading to flow of funds from banks, and the constraint of equity mobilization was met through transformation of the larger and medium MFIs into NBFCs, enabling the MFIs to attract shareholder equity. The transformation gave a big fillip to microfinance in India, with the sector touching an outreach of 26.7 million clients by March 2010. The growth of NBFCs also brought about a separate industry association, 'Microfinance Institutions Network (MFIN)', in 2009. While the MFIN website attributes the formation to the following: "As the NBFC-MFI industry grew, so did its need for transparency and better governance. It was against this backdrop that the industry felt the need for an organization that would establish a framework for fair practices and client protection for NBFC-MFIs and promote the development of a robust Microfinance industry in India"[2], industry observers opine that the varied membership base of Sa-Dhan was proving to be a constraint in adequately addressing concerns of NBFCs through Sa-Dhan.

Other than ushering in a new network, the growth and transformation of the industry also brought risks in the form of focus on increasing outreach at the cost of quality of lending, which led to various flashpoints like the Krishna crisis in 2007, Kolar in 2009, and finally culminated with the AP crisis of 2010.

3.1.2 Crisis of 2010 Wakes Up the Sector, and Regulation Ensues

The crisis brought RBI to the forefront and made it realize that the microfinance-focused NBFCs cannot be left to passive regulation in so far as they deal with vulnerable sections of the society. The RBI appointed a committee[3] to examine the regulatory issues arising from the AP Government's law to take control over lending activities of institutions that were under its jurisdiction. The Malegam Committee's recommendations[4] had a lot of new suggestions such as creating a new set of NBFC-MFIs, and most importantly it recognized the role of industry associations, especially in compliance, by saying:

> Industry associations must ensure compliance through the implementation of the Code of Conduct, with penalties for non-compliance.

> The Reserve Bank should have the responsibility for off-site and on-site supervision of MFIs, but the onsite supervision may be confined to the larger

MFIs, and be restricted to the functioning of the organizational arrangements…. It should also include supervision of the industry associations, in so far as their compliance mechanism is concerned.

MFIN formed in 2009 is an industry association, which claims it has 44 members (with another 5 in pipeline) who collectively constitute 80% of the MFI business. Similarly, Sa-Dhan is an association of community development finance institutions, which also includes MFIs. Both institutions have a Code of Conduct for their members.

By referring to the role of industry associations in monitoring compliance with a CoC, the committee hinted at the efficacy of the concept of self-regulation but did not say anything about the formal role of industry associations as SRO. The RBI issued detailed guidelines on creation of a separate category of NBFC-MFIs and other business rules relating to loan size, interest rates, collection practices, and permissible indebtedness levels in 2011, but it took more years to come up with guidelines on recognizing the role of industry organizations as SRO.

Before 2010, the industry had Sa-Dhan's Mutual Code of Conduct formulated in 2007, and compliance with it was voluntary. MFIN was beginning to take shape after its formation in 2009. The crisis brought MFIN and Sa-Dhan together in adopting an industry-level Unified Code of Conduct (UCoC) in December 2011, which postulated the acceptable practices related to "integrity and ethical behavior, transparency, client protection, avoiding overindebtedness, appropriate interaction and collection practices, privacy of client information, governance, recruitment, client education, data sharing, and feedback and grievance redressal"[5] that all member organizations would need to comply with. Their quasi-regulatory role began with this initiative.

3.1.3 RBI Gives Shape to Industry Associations as SRO

In November 2013[6], RBI issued guidelines on SRO for NBFC-MFIs, based on the recommendations of the Malegam Committee. Building on these recommendations of the Malegam Committee, emphasizing the role of industry associations, and assuming greater responsibility in ensuring compliance with the FPC, the guidelines detailed the process of recognition of industry associations as an SRO. The key reasons for according the role of an SRO hinged on effective monitoring of NBFC-MFIs' compliance with CoC, RBI regulations, and working in the best interest of the customer. While the membership of the industry association as per regulations still remains voluntary, the guidelines encouraged NBFC-MFIs to voluntarily become members of at least one industry organization/SRO, as the membership will be "seen by the trade, borrowers and lenders as a mark of confidence, and removal from membership will be seen as having an adverse impact on the reputation of such removed NBFC-MFI". These words emphasize the serious intent of RBI in according a high priority to the role of the SRO in ensuring customer protection. The shift to SRO to aid the direct regulation by the RBI is perhaps also an admission of the regulatory limitations of constantly monitoring an ever-growing sector dealing with a vulnerable section. The key functions attributed to the SRO in the policy guidelines of RBI are given in Box 3.1.

Box 3.1 Role of SRO as per RBI Guidelines

- Formulating and administering a CoC recognized by the RBI.
- Having a grievance and dispute redressal mechanism for the clients of NBFC-MFIs.
- Responsibility of ensuring borrower protection and education.
- Monitoring compliance by NBFC-MFIs, with the regulatory framework put in place by the RBI.
- Surveillance of the microfinance sector.

Source: RBI guidelines on SRO.

The guidelines, along with placing strong emphasis on borrower protection, by giving compliance and surveillance, bestow quasi-regulatory status to the SRO. The seriousness of the role is further evident in RBI prescribing a governance structure comprising of directors meeting the 'fit and proper' criteria of RBI and one-third of the independent members on the board.

Thus, what was prescribed by the task force in 1999 to bring common standards across diverse legal entities and pave the way for their eventual transformation to companies took shape in 2013 in the form of SRO guidelines by the RBI.

Considering that the SRO guidelines were applicable to NBFC-MFIs (entities regulated by the RBI), the guidelines stipulated that to be recognized as an SRO, the association must have at least one-third

of NBFC-MFIs as its members. Not surprisingly, MFIN whose membership exclusively included NBFC-MFIs was accorded recognition as SRO in June 2014. At present, its membership base comprises 56 NBFC-MFIs—almost the entire sector of NBFC-MFIs—while the total number of NBFC-MFIs listed on RBI website is 69[7]. Almost all NBFC-MFIs, which are not members of MFIN, have small operations. The total gross loan portfolio of MFIN members stands at ₹50,306 crore as on June 30, 2016, accounting for nearly 90% of the microfinance sector. Sa-Dhan was also recognized as an SRO later in March 2015. Although it is an association of community organizations, it also has NBFC-MFIs as members as part of the legacy—most NBFC-MFIs transformed from NGOs and have retained their affiliation, considering also the fact that Sa-Dhan was the only industry organization till 2009.

Since its formation, and more so in recent years, MFIN has played a vital role in shaping the responsible finance agenda of NBFC-MFIs. The focus on responsible finance flows from its role as SRO and more importantly from its mission statement:

"MFIN's primary objective is to work towards the robust development of the microfinance sector, by promoting:

- *Responsible lending*
- *Client protection*
- *Good governance and*
- *A supportive regulatory environment"*

The chapter focuses on MFIN, as its membership base is exclusively NBFC-MFIs, which dominate the microfinance market, as also the fact that SRO guidelines of RBI are directed at NBFC-MFIs. The other SRO, Sa-Dhan, is not being covered this year, as it works mainly with NGO-MFIs (though it also has membership of NBFC-MFIs) and on account of information availability.

SRO—A Unique Concept

The according of SRO status to an industry association by the regulator is unique to India, as the world over, although there have been community-based SROs, they have failed due to weak governance structures and are largely self-ordained, without the relevant backing of regulation. Typically, industry associations of microfinance institutions do not undertake work relating to monitoring compliance with standards as well as surveillance. The typical role of a network is to advance the sector through policy advocacy, sharing of best practices, fostering peer learning, and training and capacity-building of members.

Sanabel[8] (The Microfinance Network of Arab Countries) was set up in 2002 as a regional association of seven Arab countries. Over the years, it has become a prominent network and has 90 members from 13 Arab countries. Its listing of membership benefits are typical of the work of a network described above, namely

- Annual conference: scholarships and discounted registration.
- Trainings courses. These courses are updated, contextualized to local realities, and delivered in Arabic, English, or French.
- Training of Trainers (TOT) workshops.
- Sanabel's newsletters and website.
- Promoting peer learning activities and exchanges.
- Data dissemination from the region and globally on Sanabel's website.
- Regional benchmarking reports featured in the Microbanking Bulletin (MBB) and the annual Arab Benchmarking Report.
- Providing access to new projects and activities brought to the region for the first time such as social performance management.

Similarly, if another example of a national network is seen, that is, Credit & Development Forum (CDF)[9] in Bangladesh, typical network-related activities dominate its work area. CDF's membership includes prominent MFIs like Grameen Bank, BRAC, and ASA. The activity profile of CDF includes capacity-building support through trainings, networking, and advocacy to advance the interests of MFIs and building a conducive policy atmosphere, collecting industry data, and disseminating it, facilitating exposure visits and special projects. Under special projects, at present CDF is implementing a social performance project, which includes raising awareness to its members on social performance. Compliance and regulation remain under the state body 'Microfinance Regulatory Authority'.

Thus, India is the only example of industry associations adding on the SRO role to their typical network role. Regulation being a public good is typically funded by policy funds, but the industry associations in India do not receive any such funding and depend on subscriptions from members

to undertake their roles. In such a scenario, what has been done till now, especially by MFIN, needs special mention as its members are all NBFC-MFIs for whom the regulation applies, as also the fact that they account for the lion's share of the microfinance market.

3.2 ROLE OF MFIN IN PROMOTING RESPONSIBLE FINANCE

The significant work undertaken by MFIN in areas of responsible finance can be seen across five pillars, namely (a) monitoring compliance with code of conduct, (b) grievance redressal of clients, (c) data collection and dissemination, (d) CB ecosystem monitoring, and (e) client education. The other areas of its work include advocacy for sustainable growth of the sector, networking and information dissemination to stakeholders, resolution of field issues like client distress, and misinformed action on MFIs by local authorities, as well as regular reporting to the RBI. These multifarious and sometimes seemingly contrary activities of advocacy and monitoring compliance require a strong governance system.

As MFIN combines the dual role of advocacy and acting as an SRO, it is necessary to have a robust governance structure. The SRO guidelines of the RBI do not go beyond stipulating that the board should have one-third of the independent directors. The current governance structure of MFIN has evolved over the years, and in addition to the mandatory board subcommittees on human resources, finance, audit, and nominations, it has two more committees for the SRO function, that is, the enforcement committee (EC) and the SRO committee (Figure 3.1). The EC consists of three independent members and two industry members, with the SRO head acting as the ex officio member. The main function of the EC is properly enforcing the industry CoC and monitoring adherence to regulatory norms of the RBI/government. The EC also handles issues arising out of disputes between members and issues pertaining to client grievance redressal (CGR). The EC reports to the board and has been empowered to (a) issue warnings, (b) censure, (c) levy fines for violation of regulations/extant guidelines, and (d) recommend suspension/termination of any member. Consisting of majority external members backed up by wide array of powers and reporting to the board through SRO committee,

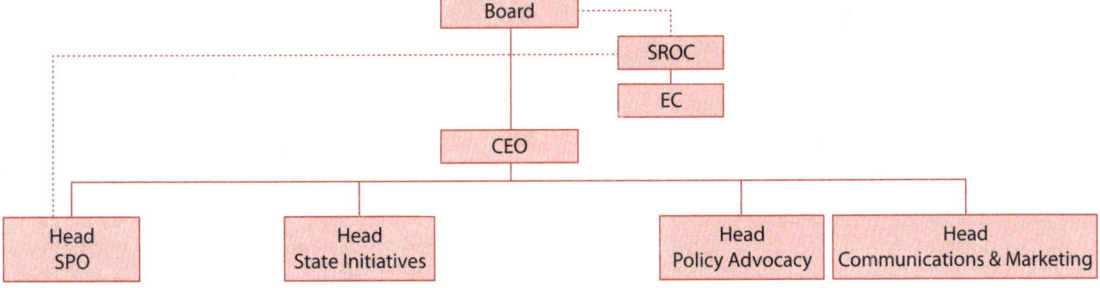

Figure 3.1 MFIN Governance Structure

it is an effective body. The SRO committee acts as an appellate authority for the EC, and it also looks after policy issues. It consists of two independent members of the board, two other board members, and one eminent person from outside. The SRO head (staff of MFIN) has a team and reports to the CEO as well as to the SRO committee. As per MFIN CEO, the dual reporting is due to the fact that the CEO is the nodal person communicating with the regulator (RBI), as well as appraising SRO team's performance in conjunction with the committee.

The effectiveness of the SRO committee lies to a large extent in its ability to influence the sector toward responsible finance by way of advisories. During the last year, the SRO committee issued the following advisories:

1. *Advisory on Third-party Products (TPP)*: Members to disclose full information on cross sell of TPP, including any product associated with any of the subsidiaries of the company.
2. *Advisory on Pending Insurance Claims*: Data on pending insurance claims should be submitted by members quarterly to the SRO; the key highlights are published within closed user group for members.
3. *Advisory on MFIN Toll-free Number*: Members to display MFIN toll-free number on loan cards, in branch, and in vernacular language, and the number to be made a part of client education and staff trainings.

These advisories are directly related to customer protection, reflecting the concerns emerging in the field related to product offerings, and are highlighted in Chapter 2. It is satisfying that the governance structure evolved by MFIN over the years gives due importance to its role as an SRO, ensuring independence and balancing the performance versus conformance roles of the board.

Apart from the above committees, MFIN has set up task forces of members to have focused attention on topical issues. Presently, there are four such task forces, of which one is on CB. In line with the theme of the report, the role of MFIN in strengthening responsible finance agenda is described in detail in the following section. The description follows key themes of responsible finance and not the MFIN nomenclature. For example, MFIN as an SRO has surveillance as a major function, and under it are subsumed activities such as compliance with industry CoC, grievance redressal, and SRO reports to the RBI: These aspects have been narrated separately in the report based on their relevance to promoting a client-centric industry. Similarly, its advocacy and communication roles have not been included.

3.2.1 Industry Code of Conduct and Compliance

The UCoC was adopted in December 2011. The UCoC comprises (a) core values of microfinance, (b) CoC, (c) guidelines on client protection, and (d) guidelines for institutional conduct. It is termed unified as the UCoC combines elements from the earlier voluntary CoC, client protection principles developed by the Smart Campaign, RBI regulatory guidelines for NBFC-MFIs, as well as the FPC of RBI applicable to NBFC-MFIs. The UCoC also has additional aspects like hiring and deployment of staff, which are not covered by other initiatives.

Being mandatory, MFIN, the industry association of NBFC-MFIs, monitors compliance with it through self-reported data from member MFIs on a quarterly basis. MFIN has developed a quantitative index, called Industry Compliance Index (IC Index), comprising 94 indicators from the UCoC, and organized it under four broad heads (Disclosure, Customer Engagement, Institutional Process and Transparency—Annexure 3.1). Based on the

---

Box 3.2 Promoting Responsible Finance—Second Edition of Code of Conduct

Keeping in view the tremendous changes brought about in the industry landscape, MFIN took the initiative of facilitating and coordinating a multistakeholder working group, consisting of representatives from SIDBI, IFC, Sa-Dhan, and MFIN, to pull together the second edition of the Industry Code of Conduct. The second edition of CoC was released on December 8, 2015 at the Access Assist Conference in New Delhi.

The salient features of the revised code emphasize more robust standards on corporate governance, measures to reduce client overindebtedness, mandating use of Aadhaar over a period of two years, strengthening grievance redressal management, and enforcement of the CoC through the SROs. The revised code also includes a supplementary document 'MFIs Commitment to Customers', recommended by the working group, which is to be used as a separate one pager pull out, to be given to the customers at the time of loan disbursement.

Source: Author.

---

self-reported data, member MFIs are scored on their compliance level, and this scoring is overseen by the EC of MFIN. While the UCoC was revised in 2015 through a working group constituted by MFIN, which included Sa-Dhan (Box 3.2) and other stakeholders, the key changes relating to responsible finance have been outlined in Chapter 2. The IC Index's self-reported score of members during 2015–16 shows a very healthy compliance level across the four broad heads (Figure 3.2)

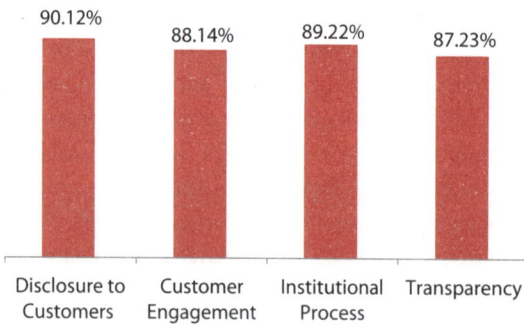

90.12%   88.14%   89.22%   87.23%

Disclosure to Customers | Customer Engagement | Institutional Process | Transparency

Figure 3.2 Scores on IC Index of MFIN Members (Self-reported Data)

Source: MFIN Annual report, 2015–16.

While requiring NBFC-MFIs to report compliance on nearly 100 parameters on a quarterly basis was a creditable task in itself, as it involved moving the sector from voluntary compliance mode, MFIN realized the limitation of this approach in it being based on self-reported data. To remove this deficiency, during the last year, MFIN has moved toward a system of independent verification of self-reported data. For this, MFIN has empaneled external agencies to conduct annual verification of each member's compliance.

During late 2015 and early 2016, MFIN started the pilot of external validation and termed it as third-party evaluation (TPE) and did 12 such TPEs. Learning from the pilot exercises, and to ensure reporting consistency, a reporting template has been developed by MFIN for the TPE exercises. The reporting template shared with the author shows that the scope of evaluation is very detailed and goes beyond CoC compliance. The following broad areas are covered in the TPE:

- Key operational and financial information.
- Governance structure—details of board composition.
- Products offered by the MFI.
- Validation of CoC compliance across all parameters and comparison with self-reported score.
- Evaluation of credit bureau and KYC compliance.
- Reporting of any other significant issue—TPP and field issues.
- Reporting on any good practice seen in institution's operations.

This is a very exhaustive coverage of issues, and in view of that it is prudent that reporting standardization has been attempted by MFIN. The other good thing relates to the fact that compliance with the CoC is to be seen in both 'policy' and 'practice'. Based on noncompliances reported in TPE reports, MFIN informs the MFI concerned, seeking it to comply on the deficiencies. In all cases, where MFIs fail to respond, such issues and critical concerns are reported to the EC. For the next phase (July 2016–March 2017), MFIN has made a plan to conduct 20 TPEs, which will take the total number of TPEs to 29, covering more than half of its members.

The introduction of external validation by MFIN is a very welcome step in the objective assessment of NBFC-MFIs compliance with the CoC. According to informal information, in most cases the score obtained by member MFIs is lower than what was reported in self-compliance mode, and this reflects the credibility of the exercise. However, at present the reports are not made public, remaining private with MFIN and members, and only summary findings are reported to the RBI. It would be useful and more credible to place these compliance reports in public domain, so that the same can also be used by other stakeholders like lenders, rating agencies, and researchers, but probably the imperatives of being a member-funded organization constrains public disclosure. RBI, which is the ultimate regulator, can take the initiative of making it public, for the sake of transparency. Barring this solitary factor, it is a very healthy practice and enables its member MFIs to systematically measure, manage, and integrate responsible business practices through gap analysis, benchmarking, and tracking progress.

3.2.2 Grievance Redressal and Dispute Resolution

Addressing the grievances of microfinance clients in a time-bound manner is a major client-centric practice and one which restores confidence in the system. MFIN has assiduously worked at both levels, that is, standardizing grievance redressal systems at member MFI level, by putting in place a three-tier grievance redressal mechanism (GRM), and running a quarterly grievance redressal tracker at the MFIN level. The dispute resolution covered here does not pertain to the disputes between member MFIs, which are handled by the EC of the board. The disputes here relate to the problems faced by MFIs in field due to unjust actions by local leaders or state apparatus, and it merits inclusion here—as suspension or disruption of MFI activity ultimately leads to adverse impact for the clients. Grievance redressal systems act as early warning systems for problems in the field, and if such a system is effective, then it can lead to course correction.

Moving the Sector Toward Best Practices in Grievance Redressal

In order to keep an eye on timely disposal of complaints by member NBFC-MFIs, member MFIs are required to submit their CGR data in a standard template quarterly (Annexure 3.2) with the SRO wing of MFIN. The MFIs are given a time of 15 days to resolve the complaints, and if the complaints remain unresolved within the stipulated time, then the matter is referred to the EC. Due action is taken against

erring institutions according to the standard operating procedure (SOP) and internal rules of procedure (IRP) of the EC. The EC is empowered to issue show cause notices, censures, warning, and penalty orders in cases of noncompliances on a range of issues looked into by it, like CoC/FPC compliance, grievance redressal, and submission of data to the CB.

The illustrative list of some of the penalties defined by MFIN is as follows:

* The penalty applicable for each client where an MFI has violated the two lender limit is ₹5,000 per transgression.
* A penalty of ₹1 lakh per month for nonadherence to weekly submission of data to credit information companies (CICs) for three months.

Additionally, outbound calls are made by the manager, grievance redressal at head office, and MFIN's state teams on a sample basis to these clients, based on the information available in the grievance tracker. As a norm, 20 such calls are made every month by the state teams. The proactive work on this front is reflected in the GRM at MFI level as indicated in Chapter 2. All the institutions have established multiple channels for grievance registering and time-bound systems for resolution or escalation of the complaints received. The efficacy of the process was checked by seeking the details of grievances from MFIN for the quarter ending June 30, 2016, and the data provided are as follows:

* Number of complaints pending at the beginning of the quarter—1315.
* Number of complaints received during the quarter—7181.
* Number of complaints redressed during the quarter—7058.
* Number of complaints pending at the end of the quarter—1438.

While monitoring the grievance handling process is one aspect, MFIN has taken steps to tone up the GRM among its members so as to match global best practices. To strengthen GRM in the microfinance industry, MFIN took 40 existing GRMs and commissioned the Smart Campaign to study and cull out good practices from these GRMs. The other task was to work on a three-level GRM framework, which could cover the capacity of all sizes of MFIs. Based on these principles, Smart Campaign was asked to develop a comprehensive architecture of

Grievance Redressal Mechanism			
Standards	Level I: Basic GRM Framework	Level II: Intermediate GRM Framework	Level III: Adequate GRM Framework
Explanation of different Levels	This level constitutes the minimum standard for GRM practices. It is based on the mapping research exercise and includes all directives from RBI FCP + COCA + selected standards of CPP #7 (Mechanism for Complaints Resolution).	This level constitutes a transitory stage and ensures that MFIs are making efforts to transition to Level I. It is based on the mapping research exercise and includes all directives from RBI FCP + COCA + selected standards of CPP #7 (Mechanism for Complaints Resolution).	This level constitutes the adequate standard for GRM practices. It is based on the mapping research exercise and includes all directives from RBI FCP + COCA + all standards of CPP #7 (Mechanism for Complaints Resolution).

Figure 3.3 GRM Framework

Source: MFIN.

GRM for the microfinance industry. The study had the following objectives:

- Analysis of MFIs' GRMs.
- Three different levels of GRM framework that could be adopted by NBFC-MFIs.
- Identify best practices.

Based on the study which covered 45 MFIs, a 'Three Level Progressive Framework' was jointly developed by MFIN and Smart Campaign (Figure 3.3).

Within the framework, Level III demonstrates 'adequate indicators for GRM framework', while Level II shows that the institution is making progress and is categorized as the 'intermediate level'. Level I, the basic level, demonstrates the minimum level that all institutions irrespective of size need to be at. Across the three levels, there are 9 broad parameters (commitment, communication, visibility and access, active and effective, continual improvement, resources, personnel and training, remedies, and external review) and 17 indicators across the three levels (detailed framework in Annexure 3.3). The GRM framework was rolled out in 2015, with the intended aim to move from Level I to II and II to III in an incremental fashion to bring all organizations to a uniform level. In order to make it easy for member MFIs to track progress, as well as to empower staff handling it to make changes, MFIN has designed a GRM accelerator tool (see Box 3.3). The tool enables MFIs to have a graphic visualization of their current stage through a dashboard.

The rolling out of the framework was backed up with a capacity-building work. Realizing the differences in institutional capacity and resources, the 'MFIN Three Level Progressive Framework' is developed in such a way that it factors in the capacity of different MFIs and provides guidance to the MFIs to reach to the next level in a span of a year or so. In order to share the framework with MFIN members and strengthen GRM practices in the

---

Box 3.3 GRM Accelerator

MFIN has internally devised and developed a new self-evaluation tool called GRM Accelerator. The tool is based on the three-tier GRM framework, also developed by MFIN. To ensure that the staff handling GRM is empowered to scale up and strengthen the systems and processes for GRM, 'GRM Accelerator' helps to monitor GRM framework progression. The tool has a dashboard and gives a graphical overview of organizational performance. It has been shared with the members for internal tracking of progress and GRM strengthening.

Source: MFIN.

industry, three workshops were conducted by MFIN and Smart Campaign during the period August–December 2015. The objectives of these one-day GRM workshops were to disseminate the framework and support peer learning amongst members. The workshops were conducted for senior management of MFIs, SRO coordinators at MFIs, and GRM heads of the member MFIs.

As mentioned above, while toning up of GRM at the level of member MFIs is one aspect of work, MFIN has gone a step further and set up an MFIN toll-free number '18002700317' in July 2015. This toll-free number gives direct access to microfinance clients to reach out to the SRO with their grievances and is based on cloud telephony, allowing for recording of each call. The SRO GRM is an appellate-level mechanism. Once the complaint is forwarded to the MFI by the SRO, an initial resolution time of 15 days is given to the MFI concerned to resolve the issue and close the case. Thereafter, the case is reported to the EC. To popularize the number

---

In last one year (July 2015–June 2016), the MFIN toll-free number received 7,446 calls.

among microfinance clients, stickers of MFIN toll-free number were printed by MFIN and sent to the member MFIs, and it has resulted in good number of complaints being registered at the toll-free number. Such comprehensive work in ensuring a robust grievance redressal system for the clients at own cost is heartening and can serve as a model for other national and regional networks.

Work on Resolution of Disputes Affecting Clients

In order to deal with field situations, MFIN, in its role as an industry organization, has a separate vertical called the 'state initiative' team. The state initiative team covers all the states where MFIN members are operating either directly or through affiliated state associations (Figure 3.4). Although it has its

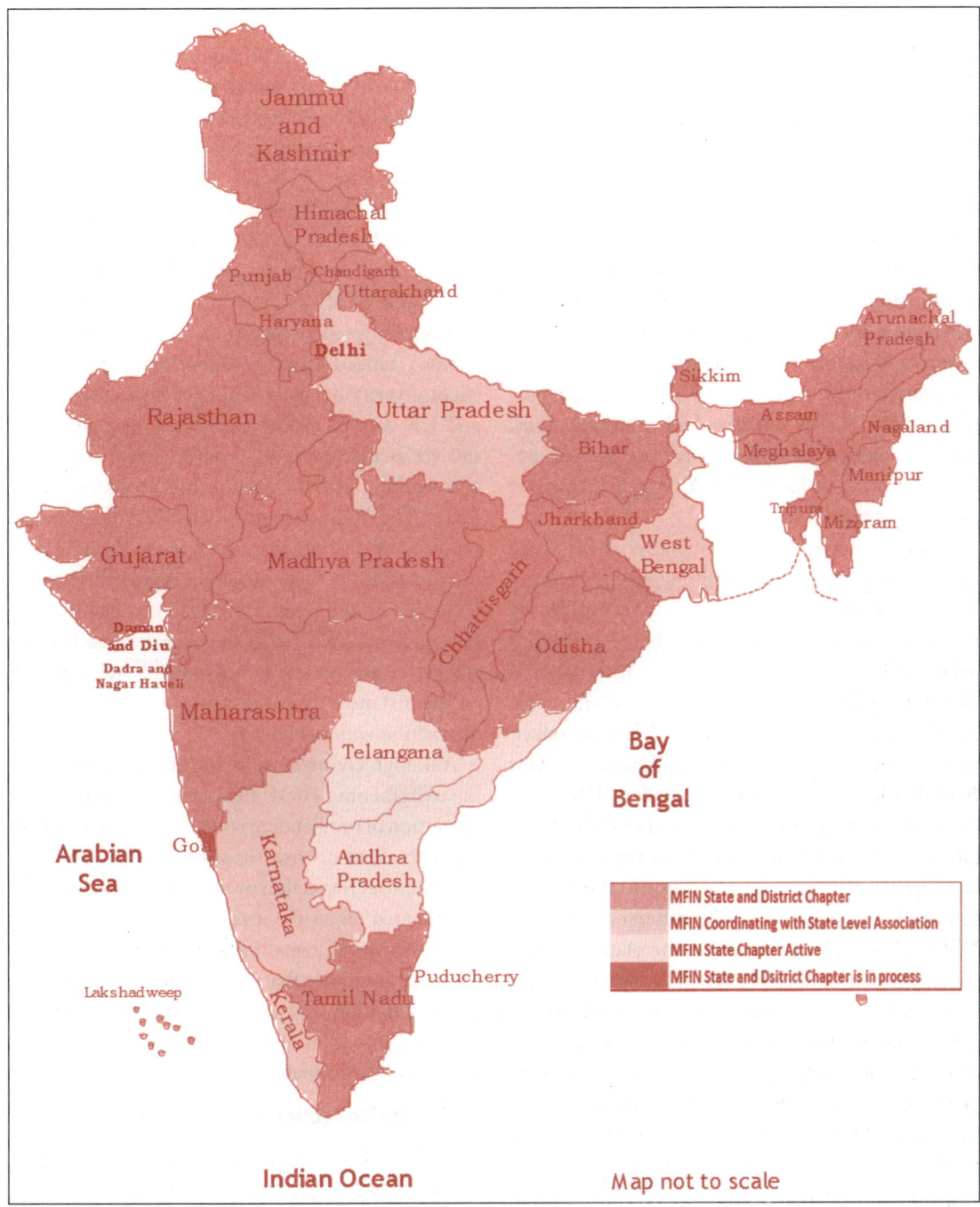

Figure 3.4 Coverage of MFIN State Initiative

Source: MFIN.

Note: This figure is not to scale and does not depict authentic boundaries.

staff (one each) in five regions, the MFIN state initiative work covers 25 states through 13 state chapters and 411 district forums. It has created state-level and district-level chapters for extending its reach. The MFIN state initiative team also engages with three state-level associations, namely UPMA—Uttar Pradesh Microfinance Association, AKMI—Association of Karnataka Microfinance Institutions, and KAMFI—Kerala Association of Microfinance Institutions. MFIN's state- and district-level engagement has created collective platforms at the state and district levels by setting up and operationalizing state chapters and district forums. These platforms have played a significant role in strengthening understanding of stakeholders of national initiatives and in promoting universal financial inclusion and the role played by NBFC-MFIs in that context. This initiative has brought greater coordination among members in their field operations and helped in creating a more receptive environment to enable member institutions to operate. Compared to the staff strength, the work and outreach of MFIN state initiative look a bit ambitious, but MFIs opined that it is effective and the district-level platforms of local MFIs activated through it have played a good role.

During the last year, the member MFIs faced several instances of disruption by state authorities under the Protection of Depositors' Act (PIDA) by many state governments. Although the PIDA has been in existence for quite some time, the active use of it in the past years is the fall out of recent scams associated with chit funds, with the most talked about being the Saradha chit fund scam in West Bengal, wherein depositors were duped through Ponzi schemes. Although none of the NBFC-MFIs fall under the purview of PIDA, as they are regulated by the RBI and are nondeposit-taking institutions, low awareness on the difference between NBFC-MFIs and chit funds at the state and district administration levels have led to problems for NBFC-MFIs in southern, eastern, northeastern, central, and northern regions. There were instances of branch offices being sealed and staff members arrested, leading to stoppage of operations, affecting clients. MFIN, through its state initiative team worked on this, through a process of constant engagement with state authorities, to educate them about the difference. MFIN also engaged with the offices of the chief secretaries of various states,

state finance departments, and state law and order machinery of Bihar, Jharkhand, Chhattisgarh, Assam, Kerala, Madhya Pradesh (MP), Orissa, Maharashtra, Uttarakhand, Tripura, and Tamil Nadu to bridge the gap between understandings on the implementation of PIDA in the respective states. This was supplemented by state-level interfaces with the police department and NBFC-MFIs in various states, to generate awareness among the police officials on the role of NBFC-MFIs and their difference with chit funds. The RBI has been supportive of MFIN's work and has played its role by writing to the state governments about the regulatory status governing NBFC-MFIs.

The other set of issues which the state initiative team of MFIN had to handle were cases of client suicides, wilful default, and client stress due to pipelining of loans by ring leaders. Around 20 such cases came to MFIN's attention, and all such cases were investigated by the MFIN state initiative team. Actions ranged from field-level interaction with clients, verifying facts through field interactions and CB data of clients concerned, engaging with the vernacular press to ensure correct reporting, and working with local authorities to address these issues. The findings of such field-level instances are reported by the state initiative team to the MFIN SR for inclusion in their quarterly report to the RBI. However, as the reports of field investigations are not made public (though shared with members for corrective actions), it is not possible to comment on the instances except by way of press reports and interaction with MFIs.

Although credible work has been done by MFIN in strengthening GRM, field-level monitoring, and resolution of problematic issues, the efficacy of dealing with client distress situations and the ability to induce corrective action by member MFIs cannot be commented on, as the investigation reports are not public. However, reporting of such instances to the RBI is an assurance that the regulator is kept abreast of the situation and can take remedial actions if need be. This in itself is a significant improvement to the pre-2010 situation.

3.2.3 Data Collection and Dissemination

Data is an integral part of the microfinance sector's ecosystem for benchmarking, analysis, and informing policy. Although the work of data collection and dissemination is not directly related to responsible finance, it provides analytical insights to policymakers, practitioners, and researchers to see the progress of the sector toward responsible finance. Before MFIN, the sector suffered from acute lack of data on both operational and financial parameters, with MIX and the annual Bharat Microfinance Report of Sa-Dhan being the only data source. While the Bharat Microfinance Report was an annual publication and contained only limited data points, MIX data update had a time gap, it shared the limitations of data coverage with Bharat Microfinance Report, and often the financial and operational ratios were not accurate. Over time, MIX has also restricted much of the data available without any payment.

MFIN has more than adequately filled this void by providing wide-ranging data and analytics on its member NBFC-MFIs. As MFIN members account for an overwhelming share of the microfinance market, the MFIN data publications have become synonymous with the status of microfinance industry. It first started publishing the quarterly MicroMeter[10] in June 2012 and has continued since then as a quarterly publication. The MicroMeter provides a snapshot of a wide range of operational data such as MFI-wise loan portfolio, branches, average loan sizes, portfolio at risk, overall all-India figures, and other useful information such as funds flow to the sector. This provides the industry with a feel of sector's growth as well as allows for benchmarking for MFIs. From March 2016 issue of the MicroMeter, MFIN has added more areas such as pricing, ratings grade, and cost of funds. The utility of data lies in its timeliness, and the MicroMeter meets this yardstick with its publication timeline of 45 days after the end of the quarter. In addition to the MicroMeter, MFIN has an annual publication called 'MicroScape', which gives detailed financial information based on audited financial statements. Last year, it added another publication. MFIN published its inaugural edition of MicroSpread, which provides district-level data of member MFIs on key operational indicators such as number of MFIs operating, branches, loan accounts, loan amount outstanding, and disbursements. However, this publication is currently only available to MFIN members and associates.

The utility of the data being published by MFIN can be seen in the fact that reports on the microfinance sector such as this report or the state of the sector report make generous use of it, and investors, bankers, analysts, and policymakers eagerly wait for it. While these are the reports in public domain, MFIN, through its role as an SRO, reports to the RBI and provides the regulator with critical information necessary for policymaking. As gathered from MFIN CEO, as part of the SRO mandate from the RBI, MFIN is required to submit quarterly reports to the RBI. The reports cover the activities and developments of the SRO and typically cover compliance issues, dispute resolution among member MFIs, CGR issues, actions taken by the EC, and appeals escalated to the SRO. In addition, in case of field level 'hot spots', the findings of the investigation conducted and action taken are also conveyed to the RBI. As part of its work with the CB, MFIN does regular data monitoring and shares critical data points emerging from it, such as the heat map showing the extent of microfinance penetration and instances of multiple lending with the RBI.

This role feeds into the responsible finance agenda, as it enables policymakers to take suitable action, points analysts and researchers in the direction of key issues facing the sector (most news articles are based on MFIN data, and so are analyst reports), and more importantly enables the member MFIs to benchmark and improve their performance.

3.2.4 Credit Bureau Ecosystem—Avoiding Overindebtedness

It is fair to say that a major cause of the AP crisis in 2010 related to the absence of a system to assess indebtedness level of prospective microfinance clients. In the absence of any robust evidence, the loan appraisal process depended to a large extent on the subjective assessment of client's income and liabilities by the loan officer. Furthermore, the focus on growth often resulted in short-circuiting of this already weak process, leading to cases of client distress. Recognizing this critical gap in the ecosystem, it is to the credit of MFIN and its members that they started investing in setting up the country's first CB High Mark (now CRIF High Mark) way back in 2010. Today, there are four CBs, two of which—CRIF High Mark and Equifax—have mature microfinance bureaus to whom MFIs regularly upload data on a weekly basis. With the RBI's mandate that data should be uploaded to all CBs, the other two bureaus, namely Credit Information Bureau (India) Limited (CIBIL) and Experian, are also setting up MFI bureaus. CRIF High Mark was the first CB focused on microfinance operations due to this initiative and has been followed by Equifax. It is this ecosystem-building work which has now improved the credit appraisal process as well as enforceability of RBI regulations on loan size-based tenure, maximum indebtedness level, and limit on number of lenders lending to the same client. The leapfrogging of Indian financial sector ecosystem through biometric-based Aadhaar has further strengthened the CB processes.

Monitoring and development of credit information system is one of the core areas of MFIN's work. MFIN's credit bureau standards issued in 2012 stipulate that all MFIN members should submit full credit data to all credit bureaus on a weekly frequency. A monitoring report is shared by the bureaus with MFIN every month. The bureau data are analyzed by MFIN to ensure (a) timely submissions, (b) comprehensiveness of data submitted, (c) rejection rate, (d) frequency of data submission, and (e) report (credit information report—CIR) usage. The analysis and the points emanating from it are brought to the notice of the EC for review. Due to active monitoring, the weekly submission of data to all the functional CBs has become the norm, with very few cases of noncompliance, and those also usually relate to technical issues. Active monitoring of compliance, issue of notices, levy of penalties, and reporting of noncompliance to the RBI have led to a paradigm shift in data submission.

One of the most important initiatives taken by MFIN in recent times has been strengthening the quality of KYC documents, so as to uniquely identify each borrower. As the CIRs were capturing only a limited credit profile, leading to cases of multiple lending and overlending, MFIN decided to promote Aadhaar ID usage amongst clients, so as to plug gaps because of multiple KYCs. MFIN issued a directive on KYC standards in August 2015, which has been gradually refined based on field situation, and the current instructions require MFIs to achieve state-wise Aadhaar seeding, with ≥ +5% on state-level coverage. The directive had a gradual, incremental plan for Aadhaar seeding. According to the MFIN CEO, currently the Aadhaar coverage of MFIN member clients captured in the bureaus is around 70%, and it is hoped that by the next year it

> Every week 40 million loan accounts are updated by NBFC-MFIs on CBs and 6 million credit enquiries are made with the CBs.

will be 100%. The enormity of the changes is evident—from a zero capture of credit history in 2010, in six years the sector has moved to 100% coverage under CB, and 70% of client databases have a unique national ID—Aadhaar. The internal task force on CB is responsible for strengthening the CB ecosystem, and during the last year it took steps such as improving the data quality submitted to the bureau, standardizing field for data query, and supporting the board to come up with new guidelines on KYC. The new KYC guidelines envisage member MFIs to capture minimum two KYC documents.

Apart from the CB, the other key initiative taken by MFIN to check indebtedness of clients relates to capping of maximum indebtedness at client level. While the RBI regulations allow for a maximum credit exposure of ₹1 lakh to each client, MFIN has voluntarily agreed to keep it at ₹60,000. Considering that the earlier regulatory limit was ₹50,000, MFIN felt that doubling it at one go may not be prudent, and an incremental approach is to be adopted. Probably, this can be taken as a good example of balancing the advocacy and SRO role and is illustrative of the fact that a member-based and -funded organization can take prudential measures to guard the clients as well as institutions. These measures have led to the industry-watchers saying that now there is little room for institutions' inability to assess credit risk.

3.2.5 Client Education

Educating clients is mentioned as one of the objectives of SRO functioning in the RBI guidelines, and the same is clubbed with 'responsibility of ensuring borrower protection and education'. The earlier sections show the work done by MFIN in ensuring borrower protection, compliance with extant regulations, and orderly growth of the sector, and these seem to have taken much of the bandwidth of MFIN in past six years. MFIN CEO Ratna Viswanathan[11] acknowledges this and was of the view that "Phase 1 was focused on effective surveillance, grievance redressal and dispute resolution. The data part has been an activity since start, and at present we are only strengthening it. Client literacy is the next phase, which starts in 2016." She implied that having stabilized Phase I activities, client education is the next focus area. MFIN has plans for developing a short film in different languages around loans, repayment, tenure and interest rate, and a mobile phone app, with basic information and that uses symbols rather than letters or numbers, which clients can access on their phones.

While client education, which is an integral piece of responsible finance framework, is already being done by MFIs on their own as mentioned in Chapter 2, MFIN has already started doing some work in this area. During the last year, in an effort to raise awareness on CB and the merits of maintaining a good credit history, MFIN in partnership with IFC undertook a 'Credit Bureau Awareness Project'. Under this project, a suite of campaign modules like posters, picture cards, animation, banner pans, and comic book (Figure 3.5) have been designed to disseminate knowledge about CB awareness amongst clients. This was borne out of the practical insights from field, which showed that clients have little awareness about CB and more so about the personal information captured in it. In 2015–16, a pilot with a few MFIs has been initiated to test the suitability of the CB modules. It is a good initiative inasmuch as it will educate the clients about the merits of providing correct IDs to lenders as well as from over-borrowing by trying to conceal information. The work relating to publicizing the toll-free number

Figure 3.5 Cover Page of the Comic Book
Source: MFIN.

mentioned above can also be seen as MFIN's client education work. However, as the CEO opined, this area needs to be further strengthened in the near future and is the focus of MFIN this year.

3.3 SUMMING UP: WELL DONE BUT MORE TO DO

The role played by MFIN in ensuring that its members follow a sustainable path and comply with regulatory architecture, as well as in building a responsible ecosystem for microlending, is praiseworthy. It becomes more so if the angle of being funded solely through member contribution, sans any grant or policy funding, is factored in the analysis. In recent years, it has also been able to demonstrate its effectiveness as an SRO, mainly on account of putting in place a good governance system as well as having an efficient organizational leader. However, it will not be out of place to say that the concept of combining advocacy and SRO functions has a design contradiction from a theoretical standpoint. It has been able to balance these roles in recent times, mainly due to the current leadership, which believes that good governance and efficient discharge of SRO functions feed into building the credibility of the organization for advocacy work. However, as institutions are permanent and people are not, it will be wise to have a stricter firewall between SRO and advocacy work, and at the same time, reduce the dependence on member funds for SRO work. As an SRO, MFIN is engaged in market surveillance and monitoring compliance, which is the domain of regulation, and globally, regulatory or quasi-regulatory bodies are always public-funded to protect their neutrality. Further, the demands on manpower and resources for efficient functioning of the SRO will grow in future, as the sector is already touching a portfolio of ₹55,000 crore, and the resources required for it cannot be met solely through member funds. Funding of SRO through public funds will also ensure that the public disclosure will increase, as currently being a member based organization, critical aspects of its functioning such as field investigation reports, CB data, and so on are not disclosed, thus reducing transparency in its functioning. A good platform has been built, and public policy should ensure that the scope of the SRO is enhanced in future through public funds, which will also guard against the inherent issue of design.

While the following may or may not see the light of the day, the current good work being done by MFIN can be further strengthened through a few additional things. In the governance structure, while the regulations call for one-third of the independent members, it will be wise to better that with majority independent members on the lines of the SRO committee. Furthermore, the independence criteria should be clearly defined to exclude people providing direct services to the member MFIs, such as funding. The other aspect which needs to be worked on is sharing of information in public domain. Sharing of field investigation reports—in a generic form—without names to begin with, grievance redressal tracker, and credit penetration across states/districts should be a good first step. In an era of the Internet, and widespread information sharing, absence of authentic information in public domain only serves to distort facts, and several newspaper reports in recent times are testimony to it. Availability of authentic information will help address distorted news and foster a fact-based understanding of the issue. One of the primary reasons for the AP crisis in 2010 was inaccurate and distorted reporting of events by the vernacular press, and that shaped the public as well as policy perception of microfinance. The recent initiative of broadening the data availability in MicroMeter, which is available to all, by way of including loan pricing data, is a welcome step in this direction and will help inform the perception about microfinance rates of interest.

Another key aspect relates to the data on social performance/responsible finance. While making this suggestion, it is acknowledged that this is more of a wish list, considering the resource base and staff strength. The current data points mainly focus on operational and financial performance, and with respect to social performance, it is limited to number of women clients and average loan size. The theme of this report is based on the globally accepted premise that microfinance is a double bottom-line industry, and it needs to demonstrate both sides. MFIN, as an ecosystem builder, has to take a lead in this and build a reporting system which captures key dimensions of social performance, such as poverty outreach, social goals and objectives, progress in achievement of social goals, and compensation ratio between the top and bottom in an institution. Most of its members do capture this information, and the SPTF has developed best practices and critical indicators to be captured to demonstrate social performance. Like the data disclosure point, this will enable MFIN to demonstrate that its members have robust systems to demonstrate their social impact and not rely on anecdotal cases to prove that.

It is hoped that client education will receive the priority of MFIN in the current year. While the steps to be taken by MFIN to promote client education, such as a mobile phone-based app and a short film, are good steps, it will be prudent to conserve its resources for disseminating best practices in client education to its members and nudging them toward more credit plus activities. This seems very doable now by all institutions, as profitability has returned and institutions have resources to invest in credit plus activities. It is believed that implementation of these suggestions will further enhance the role of MFIN in promoting responsible finance.

ANNEXURE 3.1
Industry Compliance Index Parameters of MFIN

Section	S. No.	Parameter
1. Disclosures to Customers		
1.1 At Branch	1.1.1	Displays the basis and effective rate of interest charged for all loan products prominently in vernacular language.
	1.1.2	Displays the company GRM followed by the company in vernacular language.
	1.1.3	Displays contact details of company's grievance redressal officer in vernacular language.
	1.1.4	Displays MFIN toll-free number for registering client grievances/disputes.
	1.1.5	Displays contact details of regional RBI office in vernacular language.
	1.1.6	Displays client protection principle (as mentioned in Industry CoC) in vernacular language.
	1.1.7	Displays fair practices code in full spirits of RBI guidelines in vernacular language. The FPC to include the following:
	1.1.7. A	A statement articulating commitment to transparency and fair lending practices in vernacular language.
	1.1.7. B	A declaration that the MFI will be accountable for preventing inappropriate staff behavior and timely grievance redressal in vernacular language.
1.2 In Loan Card	1.2.1	Provides loan cards to customer for each loan product disbursed.
	1.2.2	Adequately reflects information which identifies the customer.
	1.2.3	Accurately displays the basis and effective rate of interest charged for the loan product given.
	1.2.4	States that no penalty is charged in delayed payment.
	1.2.5	States that no security deposit/margin is being collected from the customer.
	1.2.6	Fully displays all other terms and conditions attached to the loan.
	1.2.7	Clearly states that the grant of loan is not linked to any other product/services offered by the MFI or third party.
	1.2.8	Clearly shows acknowledgments by the MFI of all repayments including installments received and the final discharge.
	1.2.9	Clearly states commitment to transparency and fair lending practices as prescribed by RBI.
	1.2.10	Displays the contact details of grievance redressal officer of the company and MFIN toll-free number for registering client grievance/disputes.
	1.2.11	Displays all entries in vernacular language.
	1.2.12	Clearly gives fee structure of noncredit products (if any).
1.3 In Loan Agreement	1.3.1	Provides customers a copy of loan agreement for each loan disbursed.
	1.3.2	States all terms and conditions of the loan.
	1.3.3	States that pricing of loan involves only three components, namely interest charge, processing charge, and insurance premium (which includes administrative charges in respect thereof).
	1.3.4	States that no penalty is charged on delayed payment.
	1.3.5	States that no security deposit/margin is being collected from the borrower.
	1.3.6	States that the moratorium (between the grant of the loan and the due date of the repayment of the first installments) is not less than the frequency of repayment.
	1.3.7	Statement of an assurance that privacy of borrower data will be respected.
	1.3.8	Statement articulating commitment to transparency and fair lending practices in vernacular language.
	1.3.9	Has a declaration that the MFI will be accountable for preventing inappropriate staff behavior and timely grievance redressal.
	1.3.10	Has a declaration that the MFI will not lend to borrower with more than two NBFC-MFIs loans.
	1.3.11	Has a declaration that recovery of loan given in violation of the regulations should be deferred till all prior existing loans are fully repaid.

(Continued)

(Continued)

Section	S. No.	Parameter
1.4 In Loan Application Form	1.4.1	Includes product information details.
	1.4.2	Indicates list of documents to be submitted with the application form.
	1.4.3	Indicates the time frame within which loan applications will be disposed.
1.5 In Loan Sanction Letter	1.5.1	Reflects the amount of loan sanctioned along with the terms and conditions including annualized rate of interest.
	1.5.2	A borrower-signed copy of sanction letter with acceptance of terms and conditions is in company's record.
2. Customer Engagement		
2.1 Loan Processes (Sanction/ Disbursement/ Repayment)	2.1.1	KYC requirement of the MFI are fully aligned with MFIN KYC standards.
	2.1.2	Uses CIR for every loan granted.
	2.1.3	Staff conducts full due diligence. A copy of due diligence is available in the client's loan file.
	2.1.4	Loans are disbursed only at a central location (center meeting/branch office).
	2.1.5	More than one individual is available at loan sanctioning and disbursement.
	2.1.6	Loan is repaid only at a central designated place (center meeting).
	2.1.6	Validity of CIR.
	2.1.7	Field staff goes for collecting repayment at the place of residence or work place of the client only if the client fails to appear at central designated place on two or more successive occasions.
	2.1.8	Loan repayment is only collected by employees (MFI staffs). Outsourced recovery agents are not used for collection.
2.2 Customer Education/ Rights/Welfare	2.2.1	MFI has a well-structured financial education module to train customers.
	2.2.2	Customers are charged for undergoing the financial education module.
	2.2.3	Takes written customer consent for any third-party disclosure (privacy of client data).
	2.2.4	MFI has a policy to suspend recovery of loan from client/group in the event of unfortunate demise of insured client and/or her spouse.
	2.2.5	Average length of training program which is given to customers during a loan cycle.
	2.2.6	Coverage of customers through training under the financial education module
	2.2.7	Updates accurate information and loan data of customers to CBs as per prescribed cycle.
	2.2.8	Takes written customer consent for sale of noncredit financial products or other nonfinancial products.
	2.2.9	Coverage of clients through livelihood training or other development programs/inputs.
3. Institutional Processes		
3.1 HR	3.1.1	Recruitment policy of MFIs provides for necessary minimum qualification of field staff.
	3.1.2	Company has a comprehensive training manual for the field staff.
	3.1.3	Training module for the field staff includes Industry Code of Conduct.
	3.1.4	Training module for the field staff focuses on appropriate behavior toward customers.
	3.1.5	Training module for the field staff focuses on appropriate recovery practices.
	3.1.6	Training module for the field staff focuses on protection of customer's personal and financial information.
	3.1.7	Training module for the field staff focuses on assessment of client's income, cash flows, and indebtedness.
	3.1.8	Average length of training given to a staff in one calendar year.
	3.1.9	Percentage (%) of field staff covered under training programs every year
	3.1.10	Incentive structure of field staff provides for service quality.

Section	S. No.	Parameter
3.2 Customer Complaint Redressal System	3.2.1	Every complaint is recorded and a log is maintained at branch/region/head office.
	3.2.2	The redressal system has at least two levels of escalation protocol.
	3.2.3	MIS of redressal system at least captures client information, nature of complaints, action taken, and turnaround time on a monthly basis.
	3.2.4	MIS of redressal system generates periodic reports on complaints received and handled and shared with the board.
	3.2.5	Has a dedicated toll-free number to register complaints.
	3.2.6	Offers outbound calls to collect customers' feedback/complaints.
	3.2.7	Complaints are resolved and disposed within a turnaround time as per the company's policy.
3.3 Audit and Compliance	3.3.1	Has an IA team.
	3.3.2	Has a detailed audit manual.
	3.3.3	Has designated a compliance officer.
	3.3.4	Compliance officer's approval is necessary for all product launches/product and process changes.
	3.3.5	Periodicity of IAs.
	3.3.6	Rotates the statutory auditor (individual auditor after 5 years and audit firm after 10 years).
3.4 Board	3.4.1	Management submits a compliance (CoC/FPC/RBI directions) report to the board on a periodic basis.
	3.4.2	Management submits a customer redressal report to the board on a periodic basis.
	3.4.3	At least one-third of the board of directors are independent.
	3.4.4	Has audit committee of the board with an independent director as chairperson.
	3.4.5	Has at least one female director.
	3.4.6	Has a board-approved risk management framework.
	3.4.7	Board-approved internal exposure limits have been fixed to avoid any undesirable geographical concentration.
	3.4.8	Has written and board-approved curative debt restructuring policy to address the problems of genuine hardship of borrowers
4. Transparency		
4.1 Website	4.1.1	Displays on website complete details of all loan products offered, including interest rates.
	4.1.2	Displays on website noncredit financial products offered (if any) and applicable charges in detail, including insurance premium collected.
	4.1.3	Displays on website client grievance system.
4.2 CICs	4.2	Complete data are shared with all CICs having a functional MFI bureau on a weekly frequency.
4.3 Quarterly Data Reporting	4.3	Quarterly data reporting to MFIN Micrometer in last four quarters.
4.4 Annual Data Reporting	4.4	Annual data reporting to MFIN MicroScape for the financial year 2013–14.
4.5 Pricing Data	4.5	Reports pricing information for all loan products to MFIN.
4.6 Additional Information	4.6	Adverse observation in statutory auditors' report regarding prudential norms will be given as a narrative in RB Index reporting.

Summary

Section	No. of Parameters
Disclosure to Customers	**37**
At Branch	9
In Loan Card	12
In Loan Agreement	11
In Loan Application Form	3
In Loan Sanction Letter	2
Customer Engagement	**18**
Loan Process (Sanction/Disbursement/Repayment)	9
Customer Education/Rights/Welfare	9
Institutional Process	**31**
HR	10
Complaint Redressal System	7
Audit and Compliance	6
Board	8
Transparency	**7**
Total	**93**

ANNEXURE 3.2
Customer Grievance Redressal Tracker of MFIN

Complaint No.	Date of Complaint	Client Name	Client Relationship No.	Client Address	District	State	Client Contact No.	Complaint Related with	Details of Complaint	Action Taken
123456	February 1, 2016	Raya	AP-01-2001		Patna	Bihar	8506018101	Third-party Products and Services		
786900	March 2, 2016	Maya	1611661		Delhi	Delhi	187656789	Loan		

Status of Complaint	Is the Client Satisfied with the MFI Decision?	Date of Complaint Closed	Turnaround Time	Further Appeal by the Client (if any)
Closed	Yes	February 12, 2016	January 11, 2000	No
Open				

Summary of Customer Complaints

NBFC-MFI Name

#	Details	Count
1	No. of complaints pending at the beginning of the quarter	
2	No. of complaints received during the quarter	
3	No. of complaints redressed during the quarter	
4	No. of complaints pending at the end of the quarter	

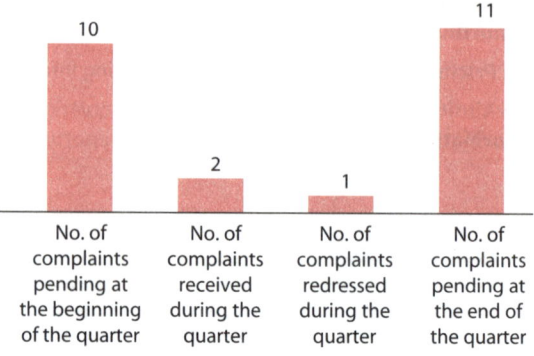

Source: MFIN.
Note: The above figure is illustrative.

Three Levels of Grievance Redressal Mechanism

	Standards	Level I: Basic GRM Framework	Level II: Intermediate GRM Framework	Level III: Adequate GRM Framework
	Explanation of different levels	This level constitutes the minimum standard for GRM practices. It is based on the mapping research exercise and includes all directives from RBI FCP + COCA + selected standards of CPP #7 (Mechanism for Complaints Resolution).	This level constitutes a transitionary stage and ensures that MFIs are making efforts to transition to Level I. It is based on the mapping research exercise and includes all directives from RBI FCP + COCA + selected standards of CPP #7 (Mechanism for Complaints Resolution).	This level constitutes the adequate standard for GRM practices. It is based on the mapping research exercise and includes all directives from RBI FCP + COCA + all standards of CPP #7 (Mechanism for Complaints Resolution).
1	**Commitment**			
1.1	GRM framework or policy has been approved at the board level and the board acts as an overseer of processes under GRM.	GRM framework or policy has been approved at the board level.	Level I + the complaint resolution reports are shared with the board.	Level II + grievance redress policy should be detailed including staff roles and responsibilities, escalation matrix, description of informing clients on options to register complaints, and the usage of feedback for improving product and process.
2	**Communication**			
2.1	Front-line staff informs clients on how and where to submit a complaint during the product application process (application interview, orientation sessions, disbursement speech, etc.).	Front-line staff informs clients about where to submit their complaints through at least two channels—one verbal and one written.	Level I + front-line staff reiterate this information to clients several times during the credit process (application interview, orientation sessions, disbursement speech, etc.).	Level II + clear printed information on promotional materials (brochure, group registers, etc.).
3	**Visibility and Access**			
3.1	Names and contact details (telephone/mobile numbers and email address) of the (a) nodal officer/grievance redressal officer (b) MFIN, and (c) RBI are displayed prominently, and clients are communicated about their rights to contact the nodal officer.	Names and contact details (telephone/mobile numbers and email address) of the (a) nodal officer/GRO, (b) MFIN, and (c) RBI are displayed in loan card and branch in vernacular language.	Level I + communication to clients about their right to contact the nodal officer.	Level II + clients are aware about their rights to contact the nodal officer.
4	**Active and Effective**			
4.1	MFIs have set procedures for responding and resolving complaints.	Has at least one client feedback channel which responds and resolves client complaints.	Level I + established multiple client feedback channels with procedures for responding and resolving complaints for at least two feedback channels.	Level II + all multiple client feedback channels have systems for responding and resolving client complaints received from all feedback channels.

(Continued)

(Continued)

	Standards	Level I: Basic GRM Framework	Level II: Intermediate GRM Framework	Level III: Adequate GRM Framework
4.2	Type of response (along with time frame for resolution, person in charge of solving the complaint, and potential compensation) is categorized under different heads and time taken to acknowledge and resolve a formal complaint (including complaints lodged through information technology) is reasonable.	Complaints are not categorized but are addressed on the basis of severity + all complaints are resolved within maximum 30 days.	Complaints are categorized and addressed on the basis of severity + all complaints need to be resolved earliest within seven days.	Level II + type of response is categorized on the basis of factors like severity, type, product, process, or person + all complaints are acknowledged and resolved within minimum three days.
4.3	Complaints are captured at field level (from branches, POS, and BCs), and clear, regular reports are sent to the head office (HO) or complaint handling staff without errors.	Complaints are captured and resolved at field level and are mandatorily documented.	Level I + complaints are documented and resolved + monthly closure reports are sent to GRO at HO.	Level II + at least weekly reports are sent to HO + reports are audited by IA.
4.4	Institution monitors the number of clients who used the mechanism over a period of time. Considering the size of the institution, the number of complaints received is sufficient.	Management is aware about the general trend of increase or decrease of complaints.	Level I + monitoring of active usage of GRM on quarterly basis for at least current year + the number of complaints is showing an increasing trend.	Level II + monitoring of active usage of GRM for at least two-year period + considering the size of the institution, complaints are sufficient (around 1% of the client base).
5	**Continual Improvement**			
5.1	GRM is reviewed every year and changes are made to the system.	NA	GRM is reviewed and management is aware of the changes.	Level II + management has reviewed and made tangible changes to the system, product, and process based on the GRM inputs.
6	**Resources**			
6.1	MFI has sufficient back-end technology to log, resolve, and forward incoming calls to the concerned person and department.	Institution uses simple MIS like excel sheet to record incoming calls but the excel tracker is not comprehensive at HO level. Also, at branch level, complaints are documented in simple register/excel but are not forwarded to the HO.	Level I + branches send closure reports to GRO at the HO.	Level II + branches have MIS software or comprehensive excel sheet tracker to record incoming calls/feedback + updated trackers from branches are sent to the HO daily.
6.2	MFI has budget for managing GRM activities	NA	There is an ad hoc budget for GRM activities.	There is a committed budget for the GRM activities.
6.3	MFI has an efficient outbound calling system.	NA	Client awareness on GRM is checked during loan utilization (LU) checks.	Level II + outbound calling system.

	Standards	Level I: Basic GRM Framework	Level II: Intermediate GRM Framework	Level III: Adequate GRM Framework
7	**Personnel and Training**			
7.1	Institution has designated an independent staff (from operations) for registering complaints and ensuring that they are resolved in time.	Institution has staff for registering complaints at HO but he/she may belong to operations department.	Institution has designated an independent team of staff at HO to register complaints.	Level II + designated staff ensures that all complaints are resolved on time, and the branch has staff designated to register complaints and escalate and report to the HO.
7.2	Institution's induction training includes a session on how the complaint mechanism works, the LOs role in the process, and how to appropriately manage complaints until they are fully resolved.	Basic level of training on GRM is provided as part of CoC training.	Level I + staff is trained on communicating with clients but branch- level staff is not trained to record or escalate complaints.	Level II + staff is trained to record and escalate the complaints and resolve within a stipulated time.
7.3	MFI has a clear escalation matrix and staff knows who to turn to within the institution in case of a complaint.	NA	Basic-level escalation matrix and some training is provided to staff on the escalation process.	Level II + MFI has a clear/ structured escalation matrix and staff knows who to turn to in case of a complaint.
8	**Remedies**			
8.1	MFI has made adjustments to operations, products, and communication materials in the last year based on complaints and suggestions. In response to customer complaints, MFI applies sanctions or penalties on staff.	NA	Some adjustments to process/products based on client complaints + few staff sanctions.	Level II + clear changes made to operations, products, and communication materials + list of applied sanctions.
9	**External Review**			
9.1	IA or another monitoring system conducts sample checks (10% of clients) to verify if complaints have been resolved to client satisfaction.	IA randomly checks with 1% of clients if complaints are resolved.	IA randomly (2–5%) checks if complaints have been resolved.	IA or another monitoring system conducts sample checks (10% of clients) to verify if complaints have been resolved to client satisfaction.
9.2	IA checks client's awareness about different mechanisms to submit a complaint.	NA	IA randomly checks client awareness on how to handle complaints.	Level II + IA regularly checks Client's awareness on how to handle complaints + reports are sent to the HO on the findings and action is taken.

Source: MFIN.

NOTES AND REFERENCES

1. Mahajan, Vijay, Bharti Gupta Ramola, and Mathew Titus. "Dhakka Starting Microfinance in India.".
2. http://mfinindia.org/history/, accessed on September 29, 2016.
3. The committee was chaired by Mr Malegam, a member of the Central Board of RBI.
4. https://www.rbi.org.in/scripts/PublicationReportDetails.aspx?ID=608, accessed on September 29, 2016.
5. http://www.microfinancefocus.com/sa-dhan-and-mfin-release-joint-code-of-conduct-for-mfis-in-india/
6. http://mfinindia.org/wp-content/uploads/2014/06/SRO_NBFC-MFI_27112013.pdf, accessed on September 29, 2016.
7. https://www.rbi.org.in/scripts/BS_NBFCList.aspx, accessed on September 29, 2016.
8. www.sanabelnetwork.org, accessed on September 29, 2016.
9. www.cdfbd.org, accessed on September 29, 2016.
10. http://mfinindia.org/mfin-publications/, accessed on September 29, 2016.
11. Conversation with the author spread over four meetings in July and August 2016.

Clients' Voices: Evidence from the Field*

4.1 INTRODUCTION

The microfinance sector in India has bounced back after the monumental crisis of 2010 and is now registering a growth, which has never been seen before. Chapters 2 and 3 detailed the possible drivers of growth or the factors which are giving comfort to the lenders and investors. Dominance of the sector by NBFC-MFIs which are regulated closely by the RBI, proactive role of MFIN in monitoring compliance of the sector with regulatory and voluntary norms, as well as positive assessments coming from external reviews such as ratings and CoC assessments have provided funders with a sense of comfort. The practices in the industry have also shown a great improvement, especially in transparency, mandatory CB checks for measuring indebtedness, grievance redressal systems, as well as passing on efficiency gains to clients in the form of reduction in interest rates. However, amidst these comforting factors, there are voices of concern on the scorching pace of growth. These voices have moved from murmur to a recurrent pitch in recent times, and the primary basis for these is based on meta data showing saturation in pockets as well as occurrences of client distress and mass defaults. Experts feel that this is symptomatic of high money supply in saturated areas and loosening of controls in rush for growth leading to client distress.

The next chapter analyzes the meta data reported by MFIN as well as sourced from CB to examine these claims. However, it needs to be emphasized that it is equally important to know about the feelings and perceptions of clients. Is the stress and excess money supply reflected in their responses?

And whether the improvement in practices of MFIs has reached the clients and is valued by them. For a client-centric industry, the ultimate cornerstone of success has to be the positive changes in lives of clients. For the purpose of this report, to ascertain the changes at client level, two studies were commissioned by ACCESS ASSIST under the Poorest State Inclusive Growth (PSIG) Programme of DFID, Government of UK, implemented by SIDBI.

One study was commissioned to examine the drivers of overindebtedness of microfinance borrowers in saturated areas. The primary objective of the study (referred to as OID study[1]) was to assess the level of overindebtedness of clients and reasons for it in high-MFI concentration areas. This was conducted by IFMR-LEAD in three states—Uttar Pradesh (UP), Karnataka, and MP. These are the three states where significant overindebtedness has been reported in recent times. Within these three states, three taluks were selected which reported highest proportion of borrowers servicing more than three loans according to the reports accessed from the CBs. A quantitative survey with 2,100 households was conducted in these three taluks, supplemented by focus group discussions (FGDs). The study looked in detail at repayment pressure and stress associated with it.

The other study 'Voices of MF Clients' (referred to as voices study) was conducted by M2i to identify sources of key concerns and worries of clients and to obtain their feedback on MFIs' processes and products. This study involved two phases. In the first phase, 10 FGDs and 20 in-depth interviews were conducted with clients of 5 MFIs in 3 states. In the second phase, a quantitative survey was conducted where 1,080 clients of 14 MFIs in

* The chapter is benefitted from significant contribution by M2I.

5 states were interviewed. The FGDs and surveys were conducted in the districts known to have high concentration of MFIs.

The voices study is inspired by a similar study titled, My Turn to Speak: Voices of Microfinance Clients, carried out by Accion's Smart Campaign and Bankable Frontier Associates in four countries[2]—Benin, Pakistan, Peru, and Georgia. The Accion study was also conducted in two phases—the first phase involved qualitative techniques such as FGDs, ranking exercises, skits, and photographs by clients; the second phase involved quantitative surveys with about 1,000 clients in each country. The issues and concerns highlighted in the Accion study were considered while designing tools for the voices study in India. Qualitative tools used in the Accion study such as FGDs, in-depth interviews, and photographs by the clients were also used with required contextual modifications.

Although both these studies are in the finalization stage, it was considered important to include key aspects from their draft findings. The draft reports have many unanswered questions, and as such only major themes have been taken for this report. In this chapter, the key findings of the OID study and the voices study are presented on the lines of the Smart Campaign's CPP.

4.2. APPROPRIATE PRODUCT DESIGN AND DELIVERY

Much of the microfinance practiced in India is inspired by the model pioneered by the Grameen Bank of Bangladesh. Organization of clients in groups and centers, predisbursement trainings, standardized loan products, and joint liability are essential components of this model.

Variations in products and processes of MFIs are influenced by the demand of clients, offerings of the competitors, and efficiency considerations. The voices study obtained feedback of clients about the products, processes, and methodologies followed by the MFIs. Total 77% of the respondents found the processes followed by the MFIs to be simple and convenient. Only 5% of them found them to be difficult or very difficult. Among the specific subprocesses of the MFIs, clients find compulsory group trainings (CGTs—16%) to be the most difficult process followed by KYC and documentation (10%). It is important to note here that 49% of the respondents could not point to any specific subprocess to

be most difficult. The fact that training and KYC emerge as difficult areas is comforting on the flip side as it shows that MFIs are adhering to processes with rigor.

Client satisfaction is important for client retention and for reducing risks. The voices study found the MFI clients to be generally satisfied with the loan products offered by the MFIs. Total 77% of the respondents expressed satisfaction with the loan amount, 93% with the loan tenure, and 96% with the loan frequency.

When posed with the question that whether they faced any problem with the loan products, 59% of the respondents reported facing no problem. Total 13% of the respondents felt that the loan size was inadequate, while 10% felt that the interest rate and fees were higher. Only 6% of them felt that the loan given only for income generation purposes was a constraint. These findings sit uneasily with the fact that over the last six years, MFIs guided by productivity concerns have moved toward fortnightly/monthly repayments. Furthermore, there is not much differentiation between products and the sector continues to have same loan features—basically institutions are competing without any significant comparative advantage in products. The question that whether the high satisfaction level is 'real' or is a reflection of limited choice has not been explored by the study.

Joint liability is an essential element of the microfinance methodology practiced by the MFIs. However, this is also a source of stress for many clients, particularly when the loan sizes are going up. The voices study explored the areas of concerns experienced by clients in dealing with the MFIs (Figure 4.1), and joint liability along with the fear of nonrepayment of loans emerges as a major source of worry and concern for the clients.

Not surprisingly, 23% of the clients in the voices study said that they would prefer individual lending methodology for loans of large sizes. When it comes to the factors which drive choice between two MFIs for the clients, loan size emerges as the clear preference (28%) followed by interest rate (27%). This

> **Clients' Voices**
>
> *When one member of the group does not repay we have to pay on behalf of her. This is the thing which I hate the most about the MFIs.* —An MFI client in MP

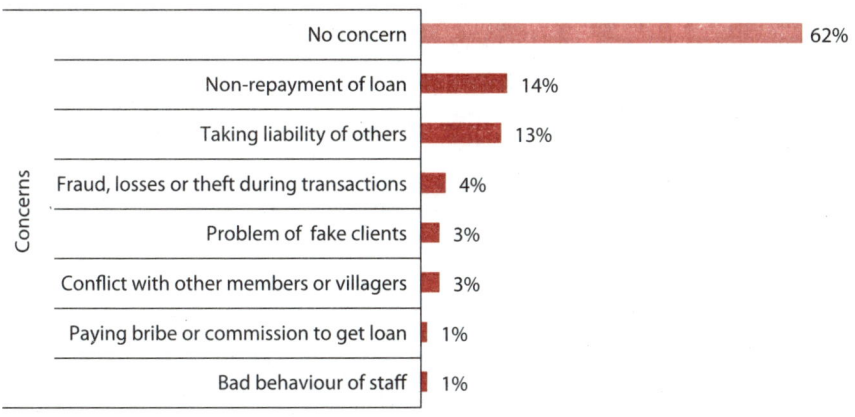

Figure 4.1 Client Concerns in Engaging with MFIs (n = 1,080)

Source: Voices Study, 2016.

is natural in a situation of perennial cash shortage experienced by microfinance borrowers, which tests the MFIs' ability to stick to repayment capacity analysis and avoids pushing excess money. The study found the evidence that MFIs are pushing credit over rigorous assessment of repayment capacity.

Most of the MFIs face the issue of high client drop out and surprisingly MFIs trying to give loans higher than what is required by the clients has emerged as the most important reason for the dropouts (20%) followed by delay in sanctioning loans (19%). Insufficient loan amount was cited as the reason by 14% of the respondents who had for some reason dropped out of the MFIs in the past.

At present, MFIs are not able to offer savings products unless they act as BC of a bank. However, on being asked whether clients would prefer MFIs over banks if they are able to offer savings products, 80% of the clients expressed their preference for saving with MFIs over banks. This indicates a general level of trust of clients with the MFIs. This also shows the comparative advantage of MFIs over other channels in last mile financial inclusion. With the entry of banks in microfinance and transformation of nine MFIs as SFBs, the competition is set to intensify and MFIs will do well to build on this strength by offering savings as BC. At present, this has not seen much traction and the focus has been on retailing credit as a BC (Box 4.1).

Overall, it appears from the study that in a situation of limited options, MFI clients are generally satisfied with the product design and delivery. On their part, the MFIs can further improve the product design and delivery by allowing more flexibility in loan sizes and adopting processes to make

---

Box 4.1 Joint Liability as a Source of Stress for the Clients

Under joint liability mechanism, clients need to not only repay their own installments but also contribute in case one or more clients do not bring their installments in the group meetings. Need for such a contribution is also often not known until the last moment, creating stress and uncertainties for the clients on an ongoing basis.

In each meeting, clients generally bring additional amounts to contribute in case someone in the group does not repay. Joint liability or bearing the cost for other group member's inability to pay due to any reason can be either of a temporary nature or of a permanent nature. Liabilities where certain group members fail to arrange money due to sudden crisis or emergencies are temporary in nature. The group members recover the money from the delinquent members afterwards. In the sample of the voices study, about 33% of the respondents reported fulfilling their obligation for joint liability on one or more occasions and getting their money back from the delinquent clients.

In certain situations when the delinquent client is not able to repay the installments at all, she either migrates or refuses to repay installments. In such situations, joint liability becomes of a permanent nature where other members of the group have to bear losses.

It is interesting to note that when clients contribute for joint liability, some of them do not tell their husbands or other members in the family. They feel that in case they tell their husbands, they will become angry and will ask them to withdraw from the group.

The process of enforcement of joint liability by the MFIs is also stressful for the clients. Most MFIs adopt strict policies for enforcement of joint liability. MFI loan officers do not leave the place of meetings until the entire amount due for the meeting is collected. If delay persists, other staff members of the organization also come to the village to persuade group members to repay. Resulting commotion, arguments, and counterarguments often become embarrassing for the group members, particularly for the delinquent members. The process of the enforcement of joint liability is often known to extend till late in the evening, resulting in an unpleasant experience for the clients.

Unpleasantness related to the enforcement of joint liability often extends even after the MFI staff members leave the place of meeting after recovering their amounts. After contributing for joint liability, the group members continue their recovery efforts by following up the delinquent members. Intensity of this follow-up depends on perceived likelihood of them not being able to recover the money from the delinquent client at all.

Source: Voices Study.

enforcement of joint liability to be a less stressful experience for the clients.

4.3 PREVENTION OF OVERINDEBTEDNESS

Prevention of overindebtedness has been one of the key focus areas of the framework of regulation and self-regulation in the regulatory regime specified by the RBI. Regulatory limits have been specified for the number of NBFC-MFIs who can lend to a client and their overall indebtedness. Reporting to CBs has been made mandatory, and the MFIs also need to use information from the CBs in their credit appraisal. Quality of information received from the MFIs has also improved over the years on account of increased usage of Aadhaar as the primary document for identification of clients.

The OID study asked clients to report the number of loans they had taken. According to this study, more than 27% of the respondents had two or more loans: 22% of them had two loans, 4% of them had

Table 4.1 Average Current Outstanding Loan among Clients

State	Average Loan Amount for Current Outstanding Loans (in Rupees)
Karnataka	29,134
MP	37,218
UP	30,326

Source: OID Study.

three loans, 1% of them had four or more number of loans, and the balance had only one loan. The average loan amount outstanding per client in three states was quite high (Table 4.1).

The study also looked at the source of repayment, and more than half of our sample borrowers sourced their loan repayment installments either through their savings or from income generated from nonagricultural or business-related occupations, which for a majority of them was represented by money generated through working as an unskilled laborer. Across the three states, only 8% of the clients in UP and less than 1% of the clients in Karnataka use another loan or borrow money from friends/relatives to make repayment.

The OID study defined overindebtedness in terms of proportion of net income which goes in servicing household and business debts of clients or if there is delay in repayment obligation of clients three times in a row. Clients who spend more than 40% of monthly net incomes, or profit after taxes in the case of enterprises, on the payment of monthly credit installments are considered overindebted. On the basis of these criteria, the OID study found that 10% of the sample population was overindebtedness. The study also found a correlation between number of loans and overindebtedness (Figure 4.2) using

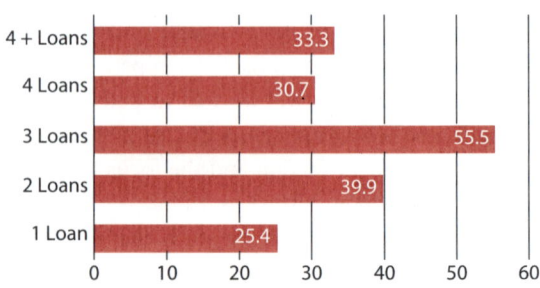

Figure 4.2 Correlation between Number of Loans and Overindebtedness

Source: OID Study, 2016.

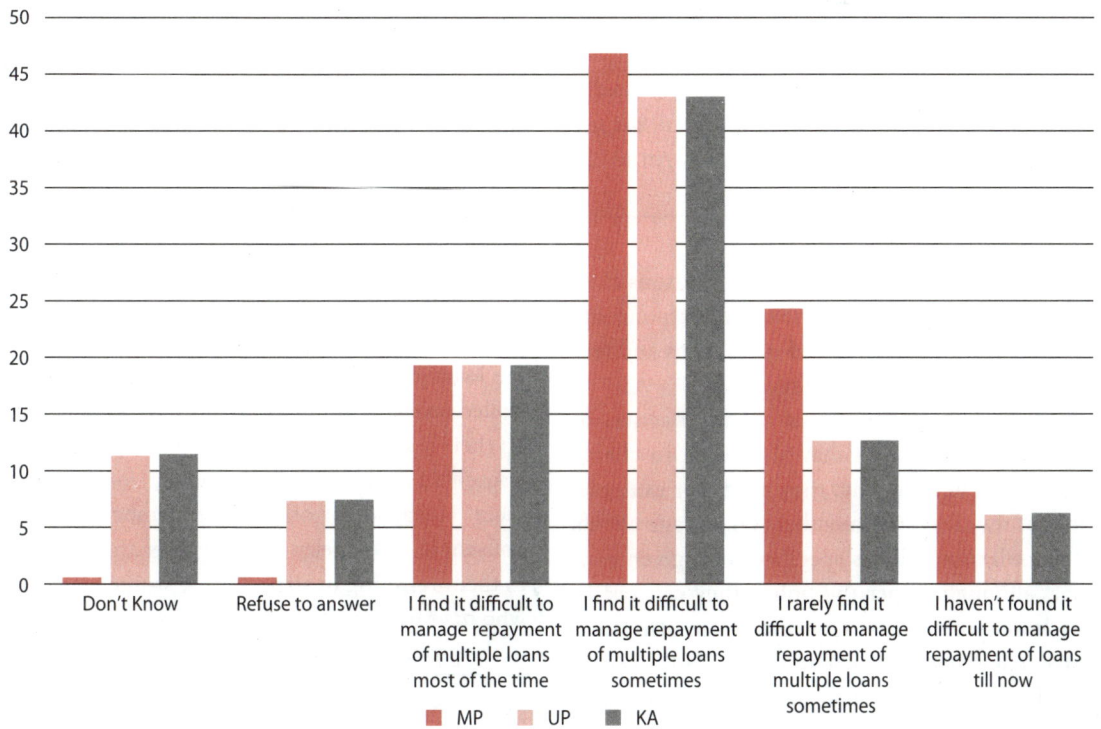

Figure 4.3 Repayment Stress (Clients in %)

Source: OID Study, 2016.

multivariate regressions tests. Borrowers with three loans were the most OID at 56%.

The higher loan sizes coupled with multiple loans also adds to the repayment stress with nearly 45% of clients in all three states reporting feeling anxious on the higher end of a scale, when it came to making loan repayments (see Figure 4.3). However, notwithstanding the difficulties that some borrowers have faced in making loan payments, especially multiple loan payments, most of the respondents felt that the loan uptake had ultimately been more beneficial than not having a loan at all (more than 85%). Borrowers who struggled to repay the loans, as well as those who never struggled, believed that their incomes improved because of taking loans.

The voices study inquired the clients about their understanding of the MFIs' policies regarding indebtedness (Figure 4.4). During the past few years, results from the CBs have emerged as the most important criteria in the loan appraisal process of the MFIs. MFI staff members during the training and appraisal process inform clients about the RBI's policies on overindebtedness. Total 88% of the clients were found to be aware of CBs and their functioning. They know that the details of the loans

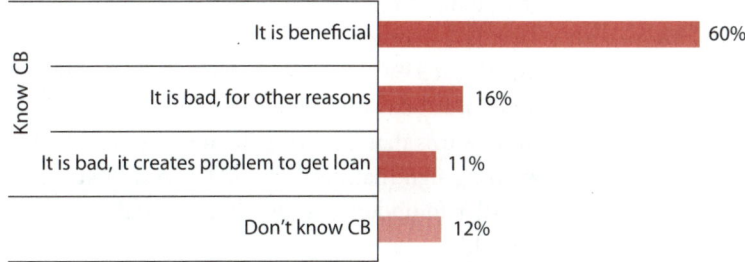

Figure 4.4 Client Perception about Credit Bureau (n = 1,080)

Source: Voices Study, 2016.

taken by them from any MFI are available to all MFIs through the CBs. They are also broadly aware of the RBI's directions regarding indebtedness from the MFIs. Clients said that the MFI field staff members also emphasize the need to take loans responsibly and not beyond their repayment capacity. Most of the clients the voices study team interacted with were found to be aware of the need to take loans which they could comfortably repay.

As part of their appraisal process, the load officers of the MFIs ask clients about their household indebtedness. More than 75% of the respondents in the OID study reported informing about all their existing loans to loan officers while attempting to

> **Clients' Voices**
>
> *A woman takes loan and if the man (husband) does not repay, it is the woman who then has to bear all the difficulties and problems.* —An MFI client in UP

acquire new loans. The most common reasons cited for not disclosing all current loans the respondents had were fear of being refused more loans and fear of their existing loans getting recalled.

The voices study found that certain practices of the field staff members may also result in clients taking loans beyond what they need. For example, some of the field staff members encourage clients to take maximum loans specified for a given loan cycle, although as per the policy they can opt to take lower sized loans. The study team also came across a few instances where clients had dropped out of an MFI and joined another MFI to again become eligible to be the first-cycle client for lower sized loans.

The OID study also found that more than a quarter of the borrowers admitted to having struggled to make repayments over the past 12 months. This is corroborated by the voices study which found that 33% of the respondents had contributed for joint liability during the past one year. The OID study warns that this struggle to repay is an early-warning sign that needs to be taken into account in order to understand possible overindebtedness (Box 4.2).

> **Box 4.2 Repayment of Installments as a Major Source of Stress**
>
> Arranging money for repayment of installments has emerged as a major source of stress for the MFI clients. The problem is accentuated on account of ever-increasing loan sizes and clients obtaining loans from multiple sources. As the loan installments become due within 15–30 days of loan disbursements, there is stress on the cash flows of the households in the entire duration of the continuance of loans. With increasing loan sizes, clients prefer fortnightly and monthly installments as it provides them some time to arrange for the cash.

Not repaying loan installments has adverse social consequences for the clients and their households. In the case of nonrepayment, other clients put pressure on the delinquent clients to repay. They often go to the delinquent clients' household to force repayments. Clients therefore try their best to avoid situations of nonrepayment.

An additional source of stress is created by the fact that the women clients are often not in control of household cash flows. Only 13% of the loans have been utilized by an activity controlled solely by women. Clients have to depend on their husbands or other male members of the household who hand over money for installment. Husbands or other male members of the household often delay handing over the money to them resulting in stress for the women clients who have to face consequences of nonrepayment in the group meetings.

Source: Voices Study.

According to the OID study, the most common coping strategy adopted by the respondents to meet their loan repayment obligations on time, and to meet household expenses, was to cut back on spending (more than 35%) followed by taking money out of savings, borrowing food or money from relatives, and working extra to earn more money. Other sacrifices, made by fewer borrowers, included postponing paying of bills or taking loans from informal money lenders.

4.4 TRANSPARENCY

Transparency in interest rates charged by the MFIs is one of the most important aspects of the regulatory framework specified by the RBI and the CoC prescribed by the industry associations. MFIs are required to disclose declining balance interest rates, fees, and other terms and conditions to their clients. They are also required to provide receipts to the clients for all the amounts they receive.

The voices study inquired the clients whether the MFI staff members told them the interest, charges, and other terms and conditions of loan and whether they understood them. Almost all clients reported MFI staff members informing them about interest rates and other charges during the group trainings or during group meetings. Loan cards with interest

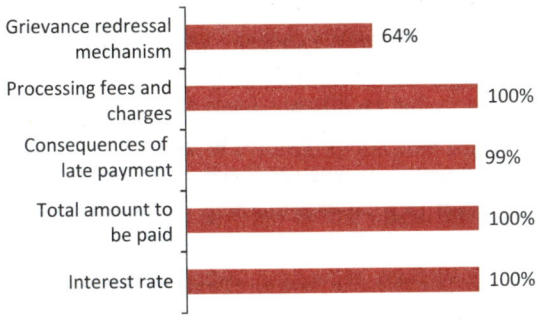

Figure 4.5 Clients' Awareness (n = 1,080)

Source: Voices Study, 2016.

rates and other terms and conditions of the loans were also found with the clients. Clients were also found to be aware of interest rates, processing fees, and installment amounts.

The voices study also found that the clients were generally aware of the interest rates which the MFIs charge, although they were not able to appreciate meaning and significance of reducing balance interest rate (Figure 4.5). As part of their training process, MFIs simply tell the declining balance interest rate to the clients who are not used to such rates in their day-to-day usage. While clients were able to distinguish large interest rate differences between different service providers, they could not identify minor differences in the rates of interest. For example, clients were aware that MFIs' interest rates are lower than those of money lenders; it was difficult for them to compare interest rates of different MFIs. MFI clients typically tend to compare absolute amounts of interest which they pay in different MFIs; these are not always comparable given difference in loan tenures and loan amounts.

It appears that the MFIs have made sincere efforts to communicate interest rate and other terms and conditions to the clients. In order to further improve clients' understanding, they should make additional efforts (through financial awareness trainings or otherwise) to ensure that the clients understand the nuances of interest rates and they are able to compare interest rates across institutions.

4.5 FAIR AND RESPECTFUL TREATMENT OF CLIENTS

The FPC of the RBI for the NBFCs and the CoC of industry associations require MFIs to deal with their clients in a polite manner. MFIs are specifically prohibited from using abusive language during their interaction with the clients or using coercive practices for recovery of their loans.

The voices study explored whether clients were satisfied with their staff members and whether there had been instances of misbehavior or other malpractices by the MFI staff members. The study found that the MFI clients were generally satisfied with their staff members and did not report any instances of significant misbehavior or other malpractices. It emerged during the FGDs that some of the clients, however, had issues with the way the loan officers sometimes speak to them. The clients reported that the loan officers shout at the clients if they are late or delay contributions in the case of enforcement of joint liability. The study indicates that most of the clients have accepted this as normal and do not report this as a case of misbehavior or unfair treatment. "If we make mistakes, we will naturally get scolded", was the typical response of the clients. Only a few clients were vocal about the fact that the loan officers should not shout under any circumstances. Some of the clients, in fact, empathized with the loan officers that as they had pressure to maintain timeliness and targets, they were bound to be frustrated in case their schedules are disturbed because of delays caused by the clients.

The study also notes that the clients found the branch managers and supervisors more polite in their dealings rather than the field staff members who interact with them on a regular basis. It is apparent that with experience and repeated trainings, the MFI staff members understood the importance of being polite.

Figure 4.6 shows clients' desire for overall better MFI experience. Reduction in interest rate

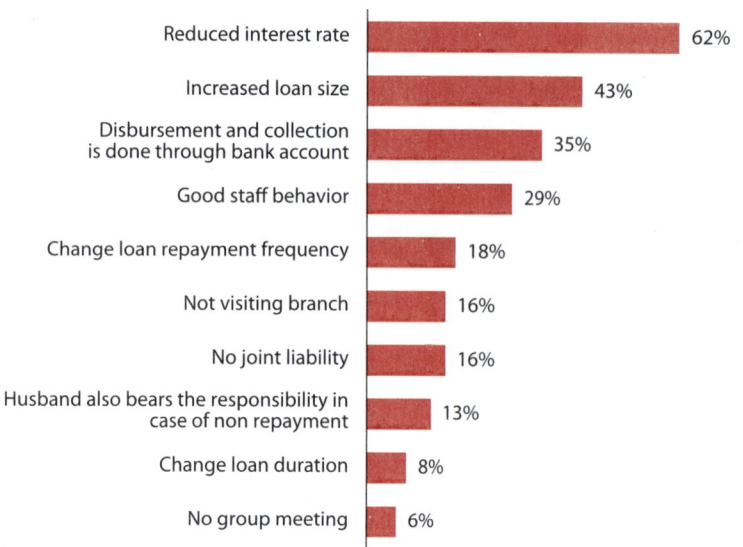

Figure 4.6 Clients' Desire for Better MFI Experience (n = 1,080)

Source: Voices Study, 2016.

and increase in loan sizes emerge as the two most important desires of the MFI clients to improve their overall experience with the MFIs.

While the MFIs have been taking steps to ensure that clients do not experience unfair treatment on account of their practices, association with MFIs have also exposed them to frauds and losses which are not directly or intentionally caused by the MFIs (See Box 4.3). The MFIs need to be aware of the potential of losses caused to the clients due to such cases. The MFIs will need to improve their internal controls and undertake client awareness programs to further improve experience of clients with the MFIs.

Box 4.3 Potential of Frauds and Losses as a Source of Client Stress

Association with the MFIs has resulted in costs beyond the interest amounts for many clients. Following are some such examples:

- Influential center leaders or unauthorized agents in certain cases obtain bribes from the clients for facilitating loans from the MFIs. They are sometimes encouraged by the MFI staff members who can reach their client origination targets with the help of these leaders and agents.
- Clients have recounted instances where they were approached by some people for forming groups for giving them loans. After collecting the 'processing fees', these people never returned.
- There have also been instances where an unauthorized person collected loan installments prior to the scheduled day of the meeting. On the scheduled day of the meeting when the regular loan officer came for collecting installments, clients had to pay again.
- Clients get fake notes during loan disbursements or collections.
- Clients have also reported losing money on account of counting errors or theft during group meetings.
- Some of the MFIs have a practice where one person from the group collects loan installments from all the members in the group and has to deposit this in the branch offices of the MFIs. Sometimes this amount is lost during transit.

Source: Voices Study.

4.6 PRIVACY OF CLIENT DATA

MFIs collect KYC documents, photographs, and household information as part of their appraisal process. The Voices Study tried to explore concerns of clients regarding privacy of information and documents which they provide to the clients (Figure 4.7). Discussions with clients revealed that

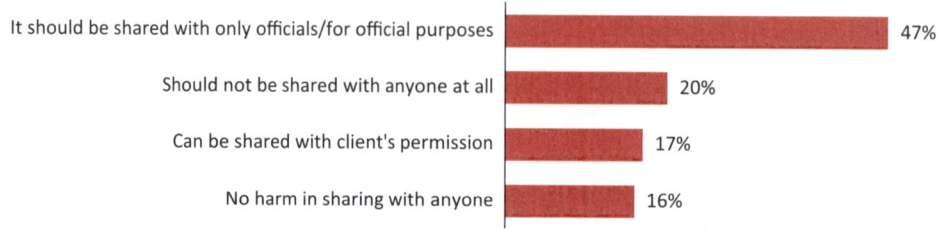

Figure 4.7 Clients' Opinion on Maintaining Privacy of Their Personal Data and Documents (n = 1,080)

Source: Voices Study, 2016.

they believed that their documents were kept in safe custody and would not be misused. The study notes that in this context, one of the issues to be considered is that the clients are not aware of the manner in which the information could be misused.

It was also observed that most of the MFIs do not return the KYC documents and photographs obtained from the clients in case their loan applications are refused. Most clients strongly feel that in case their loan applications are refused, the KYC documents and photographs should be returned to them.

Box 4.4 Objects MFI Clients Relate To

One of the questions which were asked in the voices study during the FGDs was about the objects in the real world which the clients associate with when they think about MFIs or processes related to microfinance. These associations reveal a lot about clients' perception of the MFIs. Schools, temples, computers, and wall clocks are the four items which clients relate MFIs to.

Clients associate MFIs with schools on account of the focus of MFIs on discipline and timeliness, fixed schedule and agenda, and opportunity to learn.

Like schools, MFI group meetings have fixed schedules—groups meet at fixed days of the month/week/fortnight at the specified time and at the specified venue. There is a pledge at the beginning of the meeting, attendance of clients is marked, and there is a fixed agenda for transactions. At the end of the meetings, there is again a prayer and then a formal dismissal.

During the group or center meetings, clients are expected to maintain discipline—they are required to come on time, sit in the specified order, undertake transactions in the specified manner, and maintain decorum. In many groups,

clients are expected to pay a fine in case they are late for the meeting. There may be penalty in the form of denial of loans in case a client is absent for several meetings.

Clients' participation in MFIs is also associated with learnings. At the most basic level, MFIs teach clients how to put their signatures. Additionally, clients learn about financial products and institutions during the course of their interaction with the MFIs. Many MFIs also educate clients about the need to save and borrow responsibly.

Association with schools is so strong that many clients when they want to say that it is the time to go to center meetings say that it now the time to go to school.

Clients' association of MFIs and their processes with temples (or other places of worship) is related to the stress clients face relating to repayments and other uncertainties relating to transacting with the MFIs on a periodic basis. People typically go to temples or other places of worship and pray when faced with situations bearing stress and uncertainty. Before every meeting, clients face stress related to whether they will be able to get adequate amounts for repaying the installments, whether all clients of the group will pay their installments on time, and whether there will be any disagreements within the groups during the meetings. Clients also fear about loss of money on account of frauds, theft, fake notes, and counting errors. Under such stress, clients silently pray that nothing untoward happens in the group meetings and it passes off without any incident.

Source: Voices Study.

4.7 GRIEVANCE REDRESSAL MECHANISM

A responsive and reliable GRM can ensure protection of clients' interest in the event of any issues. Regulations for the MFIs require them to set up effective mechanisms to ensure redressal of grievances. Senior management and boards of the MFIs are required to review the functioning of the GRMs on a periodic basis.

In voices study, it was found that all the participating MFIs had set up formal GRMs where a toll-free number was specified on which clients can call to register their complaints. It was also found that

---

Clients' Voices

Why to use the telephone number and complain, why to risk someone's job? You never know what will happen if we make the phone call. —An MFI client in UP

---

the loan officers inform clients about the GRM during the group trainings. The numbers are also mentioned on the loan passbooks provided to the clients and displayed on the office premises of the MFIs. Total 64% of the interviewed clients were found to be aware of the toll-free numbers and the process to register complaints. Only 6% clients, however, used this mechanism to complain or to ask the questions.

The study reports that the clients were more comfortable talking to a person who they know rather than to some unknown person. Most of the clients had access to respective branch managers' numbers. Clients called the branch managers in cases of queries or complaints. Clients also put their questions to the supervisors in case they visited their centers. Branches are also accessible to the clients; they visit the branches to resolve their queries.

Only 13% clients said that they would prefer using toll-free number to seek any information from the MFI. Remaining 85% said that they would either approach the branch managers, supervisors, or the group leaders to seek any information (Figure 4.8).

The study also reports that the clients empathize with the loan officers and they are often reluctant to

complain about them to their supervisors. The clients feel that negative feedback about the MFI field staff members may jeopardize their career.

SUMMING UP

Both studies even though at their draft stage throw up findings which support the positive story of microfinance as narrated in earlier two chapters as well as issues mentioned in the following chapter. It is amply demonstrated that MFIs have made significant progress in transparency and grievance redressal but a lot needs to be done in preventing overindebtedness and proper behavior in client interaction. Field staff members continue to push for higher sized loans and despite CB checks, there is substantial multiple lending. Field practices show that almost full reliance on CB check is not advisable as there are critical gaps in CB reports (details in Chapter 5). Higher sized loans and multiple loans to a client are causing repayment stress and this is supplemented by cases of pipelining—where somebody else uses the loan but the client has to repay. Repayment problems coupled with continuance of strict enforcement of zero delinquency lead to inappropriate behavior and collection practices.

MFIs need to urgently address these gaps which are being repeatedly flagged in various studies and reports. These can be addressed by improving credit appraisal and not relying solely on CB reports, delinking incentives from portfolio growth as under current practices field staff members have incentives to give higher sized loans and training of field staff on behavioral aspects. These have to be supplemented with moving away from zero-delinquency culture as 100% recovery from a client segment with fluctuating income is at odds with client centricity and it forces field staff members to indulge in strong arm tactics to recover loans.

NOTES AND REFERENCES

1. IFMR-LEAD. 2016. *Study on the Drivers of Over-indebtedness of Microfinance Borrowers in India: An In-depth Investigation of Saturated Areas.*
2. http://smartcampaign.org/tools-a-resources/1075, accessed on September 30, 2016.

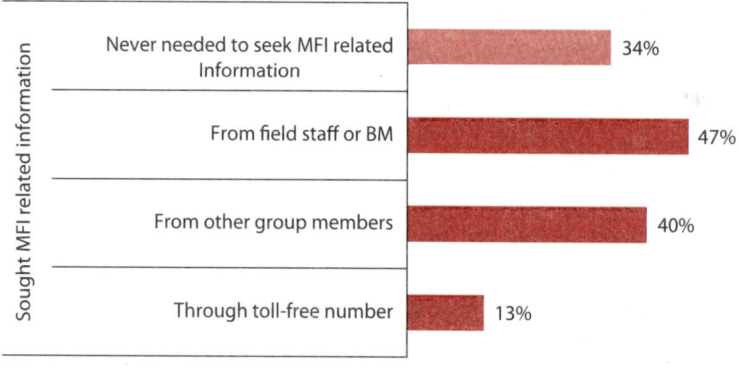

Figure 4.8 Preferred Means to Seek Information (n = 1,080)
Source: Voices Study, 2016.

The Lingering Shadows of Risks on Microfinance: A Macro and Micro View

5.1 HAVE RISKS DECREASED OR INCREASED? COMFORT AND CONCERNS COEXIST

The last six years have been watershed years for the microfinance industry in India. During this period, the industry not only weathered the crippling blow of AP crisis but has also flourished as demonstrated by a two-fold increase in its gross loan portfolio, and that too after excluding the largest player, Bandhan (as it transformed as a bank last year). It has been followed by a greater recognition of MFIs, especially NBFC-MFIs, with nine of them being awarded SFB license. This has been possible through the elaborate regulatory structure and business rules, put in place by the RBI, as well as industry initiatives, to nudge the industry toward a sustainable path. The growth of microfinance industry has been backed by increasing equity investments, higher debt lending by banks, and entry of international investment funds through the nonconvertible debenture (NCD) route. Banks have also started using NBFC-MFIs as BCs in lending, in addition to the securitization route. The return of heady buoyancy in the sector rides on the comfort of regulation and other external checks, such as ratings, IC Index monitoring by MFIN, CoC assessments, loan portfolio audits, and CPP certifications.

It was mentioned in Chapter 3 that the score of NBFC-MFIs on the IC Index during 2015–16 was 89%, demonstrating a high degree of adherence to the Industry Code of Conduct. Eleven NBFC-MFIs being CPP-certified so far show that these institutions meet the global standards in client protection. The ratings data[1] show that out of 44 NBFC-MFIs with current rating, 9 fall under 'adequate safety'

and 21 under 'moderate safety', and these institutions make up for the dominant share. CoC assessments also show a high score. All these measures are backed by the comfort of the RBI's regulatory oversight through onsite and offsite monitoring. Thus, the external checks provide comfort especially on the responsible finance side of it, pertaining to appropriate behavior with clients, pricing transparency, checking over indebtedness, grievance redressal, and diversification of product offerings, as these aspects form the core of CPP, IC Index, and CoC assessments. Investors and lenders have taken this comfort in their decision matrix, and they feel that the sector is de-risked and is following responsible business practices.

However, as the sector is involved with the poor and the vulnerable, it will always be subject to intense external scrutiny. During the last year, there have been murmurs as well as published articles, reflecting concerns over the high growth being shown by the industry. These concerns come from two aspects—high growth and instances of client distress, suicides, or mass defaults, linked to oversupply of credit. The Wire published an article in January 2016 with the headline 'Why Microfinance is Becoming a Bad word All Over Again'[2]. The article is based on several instances of suicides and running away from home by microfinance clients in eastern UP due to overindebtedness and inability to repay loans. The article cites individual cases to show that CBs are not foolproof, with clients having as many as seven loans against the prescribed ceiling of two lenders, extensive prevalence of pipelining of loans (loan taken by the client but passed on to another person for a small monetary gain), and presence of ring leaders. It goes on to say that these instances are a direct result of pressure to expand business at all cost, in order to keep the private equity investors happy. In another article in January 2016[3], Professor Sriram took a contrarian view stating that the regulations ensure that macro-level data analysis will not show worrying signs and that incidents like the one quoted by 'The Wire' have to be seen in the perspective of large microfinance client base of over 33 million. Despite taking a different perspective, he admits that such instances have lessons to be learned that the sector will do well to thoroughly analyze these sporadic events, and if needed, implement corrective measures.

In a more recent article published in 'The Mint' in July 2016, 'Signs of Froth in Microfinance'[4], the writer argues that the sector is growing too fast, and she gives three primary reasons for it. First, she says that the microfinance market potential is not that huge, as the low-risk market segment catered by MFIs is not that large. Second, the CB report reliance is not foolproof, as KYC documents can be manipulated. Finally, a critical point on contextual variation is made. It is pointed out that the current growth states of Bihar and UP differ enormously in women empowerment, as compared to earlier growth states of south.

These news items, coupled with vernacular press reporting and opinions of many sector experts, have changed from a murmur to a louder noise, that another crisis is around the corner, and so people have started talking of AP crisis V.2. Many view that the drivers or indicators of the crisis pointers remain the same, and thus if something happens in future, the only difference will be that this time it will be with its foreknowledge.

This view sits contrary to the picture emerging out of institutional assessments as described above and leads to the question as to where does the reality lie? Considering the importance of this topic, a separate chapter was devoted to the analysis of risks in the last year's report. The analysis[5] showed concerns on pockets of saturation, cases of client distress, higher loan sizes, higher staff productivity, and changes in loan features to boost productivity, rather than keeping needs of the clients as the guiding principle. The analysis was based on macro as well as institutional data and was supplemented with data from a CB. A similar analysis with more data points has been done this year to provide insights into the situation. As against a nuanced and data-based analysis, much news which shapes public and policy perception is based either on a very generalized macro data or overplaying isolated cases.

Unfortunately, history shows that the financial sector is dependent to a large extent on perception, and MFIs face the double challenge in dealing with a sensitive client segment, as well as belonging to the financial sector. In this context, it is imperative that they remain aligned to client-centric practices and keep the welfare of clients at the core of operations. This is the only panacea to mitigating another risk event, and MFIs need to ensure that the exuberance of growth does not dilute focus on client-centric practices as well as investments in human resources and control systems. The enormity of the responsibility on the microfinance sector is much higher than ever. While the earlier crises can be explained by the absence of suitable regulatory framework, or tools for measuring of double bottom line performance, there is no such alibi available anymore. Any major crisis now will show that the practice differed widely from policy and put to naught the validity of various external assessments which pointed toward a responsible sector. It is also likely to lead to severe regulatory measures.

Moreover, more than the institutional effect, the effect on 33 million clients will be enormous. Even after six years, microfinance operations have not started in AP and Telangana. This close link between responsible finance and institutional risks is often subsumed by including risks under financial analysis. History shows that institutional viability and sustainability is inextricably linked to client welfare, and thus the sector has to ensure that it proactively mitigates the emerging risks or possible risks.

5.2 GROWTH AND ITS GEOSPATIAL DIMENSIONS

As much of the concerns stem from the enormous portfolio growth, it is imperative to analyze the growth magnitude and its spatial distribution. High growth gives rise to concerns, as it is the phase of growth in the past that brought the 2010 crisis. However, it must be reiterated that growth per se is welcome, as financial inclusion for all will be the bedrock for building an inclusive India. Also, the challenge of financial exclusion, especially asset-side inclusion, remains high as brought out by FinScope consumer survey, 2016. The return to the high-growth path achieved by NBFC-MFIs[6] during

2014–15 accelerated further in 2015–16, with the sector recording an annual increase of 91%—almost doubling the portfolio. The growth is even more remarkable, as it excludes the portfolio of Bandhan Bank, which accounted for 23.75% share in NBFC-MFIs loan portfolio last year. According to the recent data, the growth engine marches on, with the NBFC-MFIs recording a growth of 89% in the first quarter of 2016–17 over the first quarter of 2015–16. This level of annual growth makes the annual growth of 46% achieved by the sector in 2010 look insignificant. This growth rate becomes even more of a puzzle if seen with the two successive droughts in the country, which have caused rural distress in nearly half of districts. Naturally, questions are being raised on the growth quality, saturation in pockets, and emergence of a situation where money is chasing clients, rather than it being the other way. The first point of analysis relates to examining the growth regions, its concentration, if any, and comparison with the past.

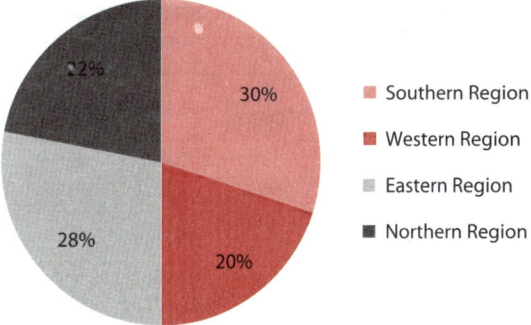

Figure 5.1 Regionwise Share in NBFC-MFI Portfolio, March 2015

Source: MFIN Micrometer, Issue 13.

Even without Bandhan Bank, which accounted for 24% market share in 2014–15, the annual growth in portfolio was 91% in 2015–16.

5.2.1 Portfolio Distribution across Regions has Improved

This dimension of growth is closely associated with risk, as concentration in a few markets could lead to saturation of those markets. In the years after 2010, the microfinance market in India has moved distinctly away from a southern states domination (South Indian region accounted for 55% market share in 2010). By 2015, the sector had an even regional distribution with the region accounting for highest share having 30% share and the region with lowest share having 20% share—not much difference (Figure 5.1). The figures for March 2016 were expected to aggravate the skewness, as Bandhan Bank, a major Pan-India MFI with dominant presence in eastern India, is no longer a part of the microfinance numbers. Figure 5.2 shows that the impact has been there but still the regional pie is balanced.

The share of the southern region has increased, as Bandhan's exit has led to a drop in the share of the eastern region coupled with the fact that five out of six largest NBFC-MFIs are headquartered in the southern region (Janalakshmi, BFIL, Ujjivan, Equitas, and GFSPL). However, what stands out is

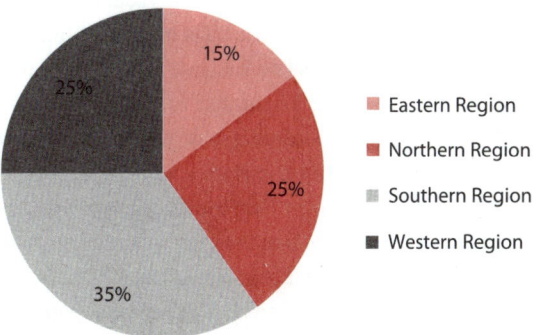

Figure 5.2 Regionwise Share in NBFC-MFI Loan Portfolio, March 2016

Source: MFIN Micrometer, Issue 17.

the fact that the eastern region's share is still at 15% despite the exclusion of the biggest player from the numbers. Furthermore, it is good to see that the northern and western regions have 25% share each in the total portfolio, while in earlier years (prior to 2014), these regions accounted for much lower share.

5.2.2 State-level Statistics Remain Skewed: Similar to Past but Growth Happening across All States

The regional spread has balanced out, but as indicated in the last year's report, regional share does not provide many insights into saturation. There is a need to look at state-, district-, and may be pin code-based market penetration. An analysis of state-level data shows that other than the obvious displacement of West Bengal from the list of top five states, nothing has changed much since 2015. The top five states in terms of loan portfolio account for 55% of the total sector outstanding as against 58% share in total loan portfolio in 2015 (Table 5.1).

Table 5.1 Loan Portfolio Share of Top Five States in 2010, 2015, and 2016

| | 2010 | | | 2015 | | | 2016 | |
State	Portfolio (₹ Crore)	% Share in Total	State	Portfolio (₹ Crore)	% Share in Total	State	Portfolio (₹ Crore)	% Share in Total
Andhra Pradesh	52.1071	29.53	West Bengal	60.19	14.99	Tamil Nadu	82.5521	14.93
Tamil Nadu	23.8709	13.52	Tamil Nadu	57.00	14.20	Karnataka	66.3068	12
West Bengal	21.0628	11.93	Karnataka	43.70	10.88	Maharashtra	58.5361	10.59
Karnataka	18.9769	10.75	Maharashtra	38.72	9.65	Uttar Pradesh	57.4821	10.40
Odisha	12.0041	6.80	Uttar Pradesh	33.91	8.45	Madhya Pradesh	41.0544	7.43

Source: State of Sector Report, 2010, MFIN MicroMeter Issues 13 and 17.
Note: This excludes NPA portfolio in AP for 2015 and 2016.

The balanced spread seen in regional analysis gets a bit skewed at this level, as five states accounting for nearly 60% of the loan portfolio is not a very healthy indicator. State-level skew has not improved much since 2010, when AP accounted for 70% share. On the positive side, poorer states of UP and MP now figure in the list of top five states.

It is interesting to see that the annual growth figures across states show that the highest annual growth during 2015–16 took place in five states which do not figure in the list in Table 5.1. These states with the highest growth rates are Jharkhand, Kerala, Chhattisgarh, Assam, and Bihar, and Jharkhand tops the list with 108% annual growth. The annual growth analysis across states shows that portfolio build-up is happening across all states with MFI presence and is not restricted to top five states. The difference between highest growth rate state (Jharkhand with 108% annual growth) and lowest growth rate state (West Bengal with 53.71%) is almost half, but most of the states have shown an annual growth rate of 75%[7] (state-wise portfolio and clients in Annexure 5.1). The impact of high growth across states has resulted in continued skew, as those with existing high base are also growing at a near similar speed.

The growth observed across states has implied that NBFC-MFIs now cover almost 85% of districts in India, which is a creditable achievement (Table 5.2). It is important to note that 23 districts of AP and Telangana have been taken as districts with no MFI presence, as at present operations have not resumed there. As these were traditionally high-microfinance penetration states in the past, their inclusion takes

the outreach to 90% of districts. Of the 569 districts covered by NBFC-MFIs, 448 have more than 5 MFIs, with numbers reaching as high as 25 and 28 in some districts.

> NBFC-MFI operations cover 85% of the districts in India.

The growth dimensions at state level do not match the comfort provided by a balanced regional spread. However, the fact that NBFC-MFIs now cover 85% of districts and the spread of growth across all states is encouraging, it is hoped that state-level figures will show improvement in coming years, as the market gets saturated in states with higher share in loan portfolio—even though the figures from last year (2015–16) do not indicate this.

5.2.3 District Level: The Skew Gets Alarming[8]

With 448 districts having presence of five or more MFIs, one expects that the legacy of state-level skew would get corrected in future, as the outreach has been established and growth is happening across states. However, the analysis of district-level data shows that even within states, growth is happening in only selected districts.

Top 80 districts in terms of loan portfolio account for 60% of NBFC-MFI portfolio, and top 50 account for 45% of the portfolio. This shows that the growth story is highly uneven, with mere 7.5% of districts in India accounting for nearly 50% of the portfolio, and the remaining 50% portfolio is spread across other 519 districts with the presence of NBFC-MFIs. What is more worrying is the fact that out of top 80 districts, 59 belong to top 5 states of Tamil Nadu, Karnataka, Maharashtra, UP and MP, and these 59 districts make up for 46% of the all-India gross loan portfolio of NBFC-MFIs. The break-up

Table 5.2 Presence of NBFC-MFIs across Districts

No. of Institutions	0	<2	3–5	>5
Districts	107	24	97	448

Source: CRIF High Mark.

of these 59 districts according to states, and their share in the all-India portfolio given in Table 5.2, shows a highly lopsided growth of the industry, and the intense portfolio built in these districts has the distinct possibility of leading to market saturation and multiple lending (see the portfolio and number of MFIs in top 80 districts in Annexure 5.2).

> Total 59 districts in 5 states account for 46% of the all-India portfolio of NBFC-MFIs and remaining 54% is spread across 510 districts.

Merely 33 districts of Tamil Nadu and Karnataka (which make up 5% of total districts in India) account for nearly 30% of NBFC-MFIs all-India portfolio. This is an alarming level of concentration, and it calls for correction. Industry experts feel that even within these districts, there are pockets of high saturation and pockets of low credit penetration—that is why it seems that a pin code-based analysis is needed to fully explore the dynamics of skewed growth. Responsible finance at the sector level implies going to less penetrated areas, and that was also the reason for the emergence of microfinance. Sadly, the growth considerations have led to overlooking this aspect.

The other aspect which has changed over the years in microfinance is that the credit exposure has largely become urban. The list of districts mentioned in Table 5.3 proves that. The five districts in MP figuring in the list are Indore, Bhopal, Jabalpur, Ujjain, and Sagar—all prominent cities. Similarly, in UP, the list of eight includes all major cities and urban centers—Varanasi, Allahabad, Ghaziabad, Agra, Meerut, Gorakhpur, and Saharanpur. MFIN data[9] also reflect that, showing that 60% of all-India portfolio of its members is urban. These areas are those with higher level of existing banking penetration.

The pattern of loan use also shows urban concentration, with 64% of loans going for nonagricultural use. Probably, high urban orientation and low share of agriculture in loan use also explains the high portfolio growth, despite widespread rural distress in the country. As NBFC-MFIs rely on priority sector funding from banks to grow, the regulator and MFIN as industry bodies need to pay immediate attention to this and insist on mandating wider spread of growth.

The district-level concentration has led to a situation, where even leaving the outlier Bangalore, the minimum level of credit in each district has touched ₹200 crore, with a maximum of ₹6.24 crore. Bangalore is an exception because the outstanding credit level as on March 31, 2016 was at ₹1,453 crore.

In addition to NBFC-MFIs, there are other institutions involved in a similar type of microlending, using the group methodology, and they also cater to the same segment. These institutions are banks and NGO-MFIs, through the BC route. If the lending from them is included in the analysis—which should be—the credit saturation in these 59 districts becomes even worse. The analysis presented in Figure 5.3 is based on the CRIF High Mark CB data and, therefore, only includes those institutions which provide data to the CB.

As shown in Figure 5.3, leaving the outlier case of Bangalore, seven districts have microlending portfolio in the range of ₹700 to ₹999 crore, and 18 in the range of ₹400 to ₹699 crore. Overall, 50 districts have micro loan portfolio in excess of ₹3 billion. The levels will be much higher, if figures of lending by other players who do not report data to the CB, including SBLP, are included.

This is a clear indication of credit saturation from meta data analysis, though for a more granular understanding, the per capita exposure, population, and level of economic development need to be seen.

Table 5.3 **Share of Top Five States—District-wise Analysis**

State	No. of Districts in Top 80 Districts by Loan Portfolio Size	Percentage Share in All-India Portfolio (%)
Tamil Nadu	22	17.70
Karnataka	11	10.34
Maharashtra	13	9.78
Uttar Pradesh	8	5.12
Madhya Pradesh	5	3.40

Source: CRIF High Mark Credit Bureau.

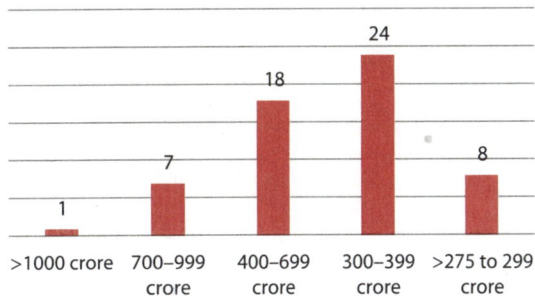

Figure 5.3 Microlending Portfolio Range in Top 58 Districts as in March 2016

Source: CRIF High Mark.

However, the meta data at district level show sure signs of market saturation and are analyzed further in later sections through the examination of multiple borrowing and presence of multiple lenders in these districts.

It is no surprise that the heat map generated by CRIF High Mark shows these dark patches of saturation in India map. In order to show the contrast, the position in respect of 2015 and 2016 is shown in Table 5.4 and the heat map in Figures 5.4, 5.5, and 5.6. As other microlenders are an important part of the analysis, it is imperative to include them in the analysis along with NBFC-MFIs.

Table 5.4 Frequency Distribution of Districts by Credit Portfolio in 2015 and 2016

Loan Portfolio (₹ Crore)	Number of Districts— NBFC-MFIs		Number of Districts— All Microlenders Including NBFC-MFIs	
	2015	2016	2015	2016
< 0.25	436	317	321	272
0.25–0.50	74	91	79	78
0.50–1	76	100	103	82
1–2	61	78	90	110
>2	29	80	83	134

Source: CRIF High Mark.

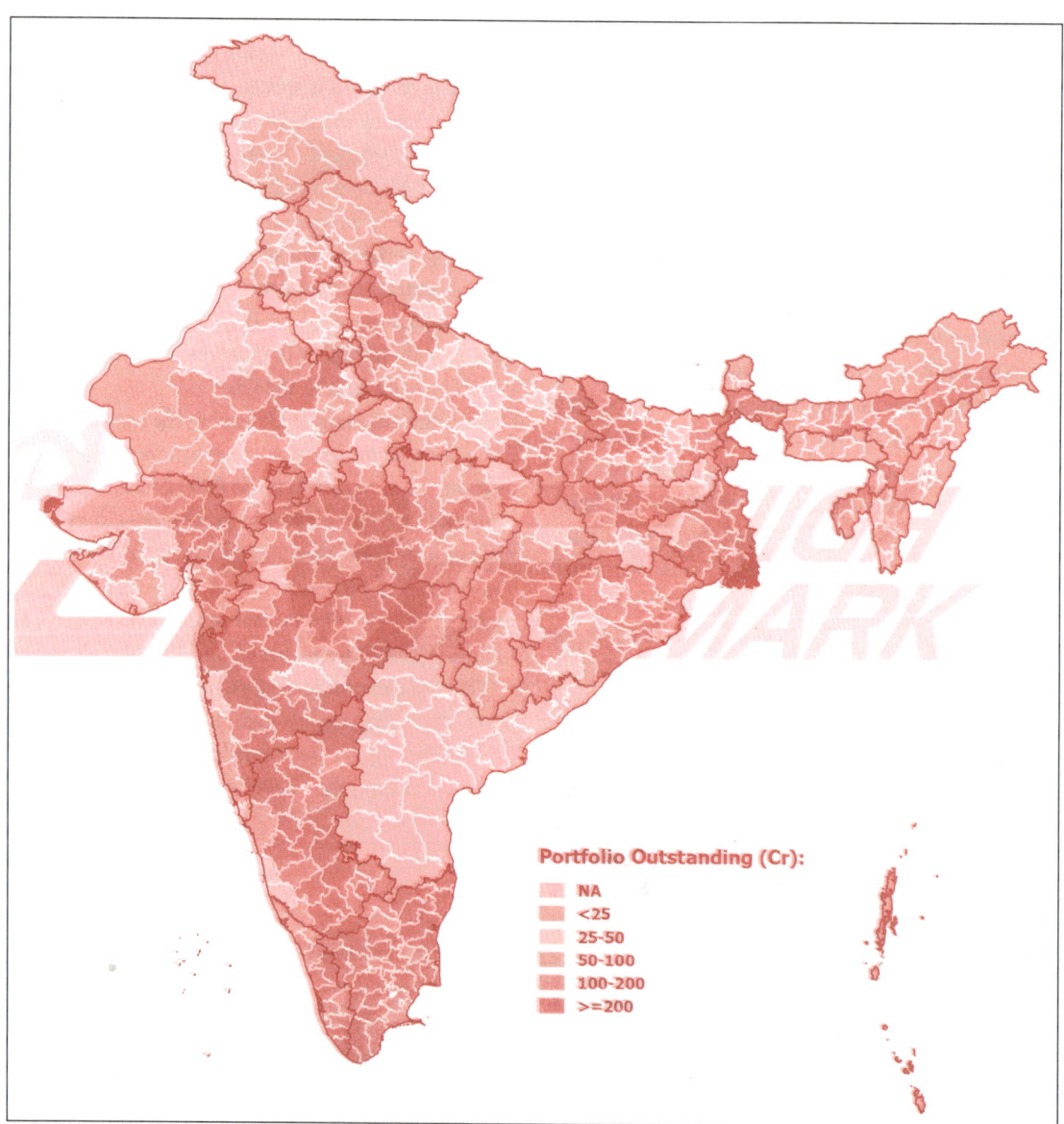

Portfolio Outstanding (Cr):
- NA
- <25
- 25–50
- 50–100
- 100–200
- >=200

Figure 5.4 NBFC-MFIs District Penetration in 2015

Source: CRIF High Mark.

Note: This figure is not to scale and does not depict authentic boundaries.

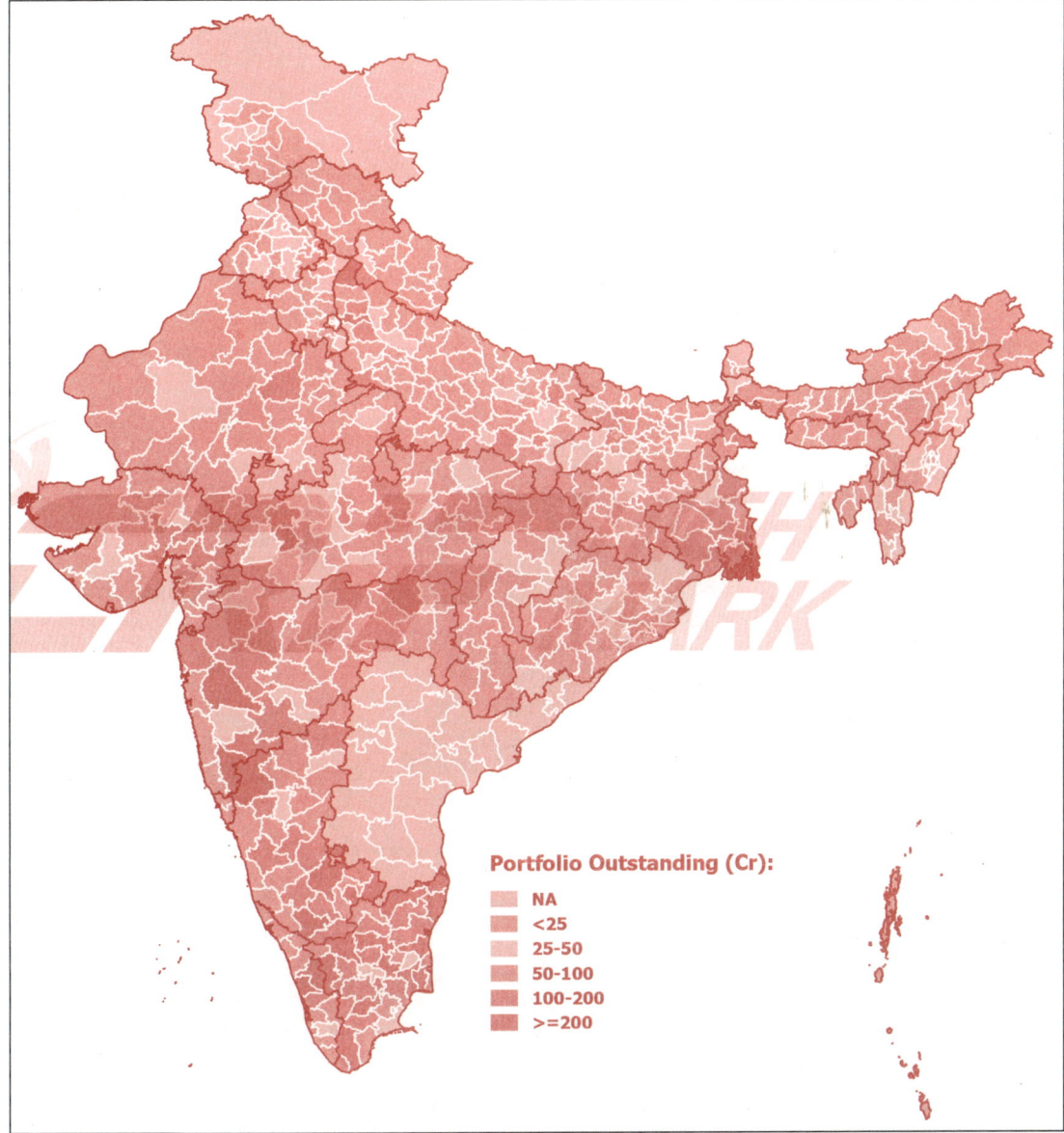

Figure 5.5   NBFC-MFIs District Penetration in 2016

Source: CRIF High Mark.
Note: This figure is not to scale and does not depict authentic boundaries.

The jump in the number of districts with more than ₹2 billion of loan portfolio in the case of NBFC-MFIs is 175%, and as stated above all top 80 districts now have more than ₹2 billion of loan portfolio. If all microlenders are considered, 134 districts in India now have more than ₹2 billion of microcredit. This does not include the SBLP, as well as banks lending small amount loans in individual mode. The heat maps show that more vividly—with darkest shade showing districts with more than ₹2 billion portfolio.

Figure 5.6 clearly shows that except for the desert area in Rajasthan, the ravines near UP and MP border, the mountains and northeast, and all other areas have good level of credit penetration. Having seen the highly skewed situation from geospatial angle, the following section analyzes the institutional story of NBFC-MFIs.

5.3 WHAT IS HAPPENING AT INSTITUTIONAL LEVEL?

The analysis of institutions is necessary to know if the growth is happening all across the spectrum or in the case of select institutions. The data available

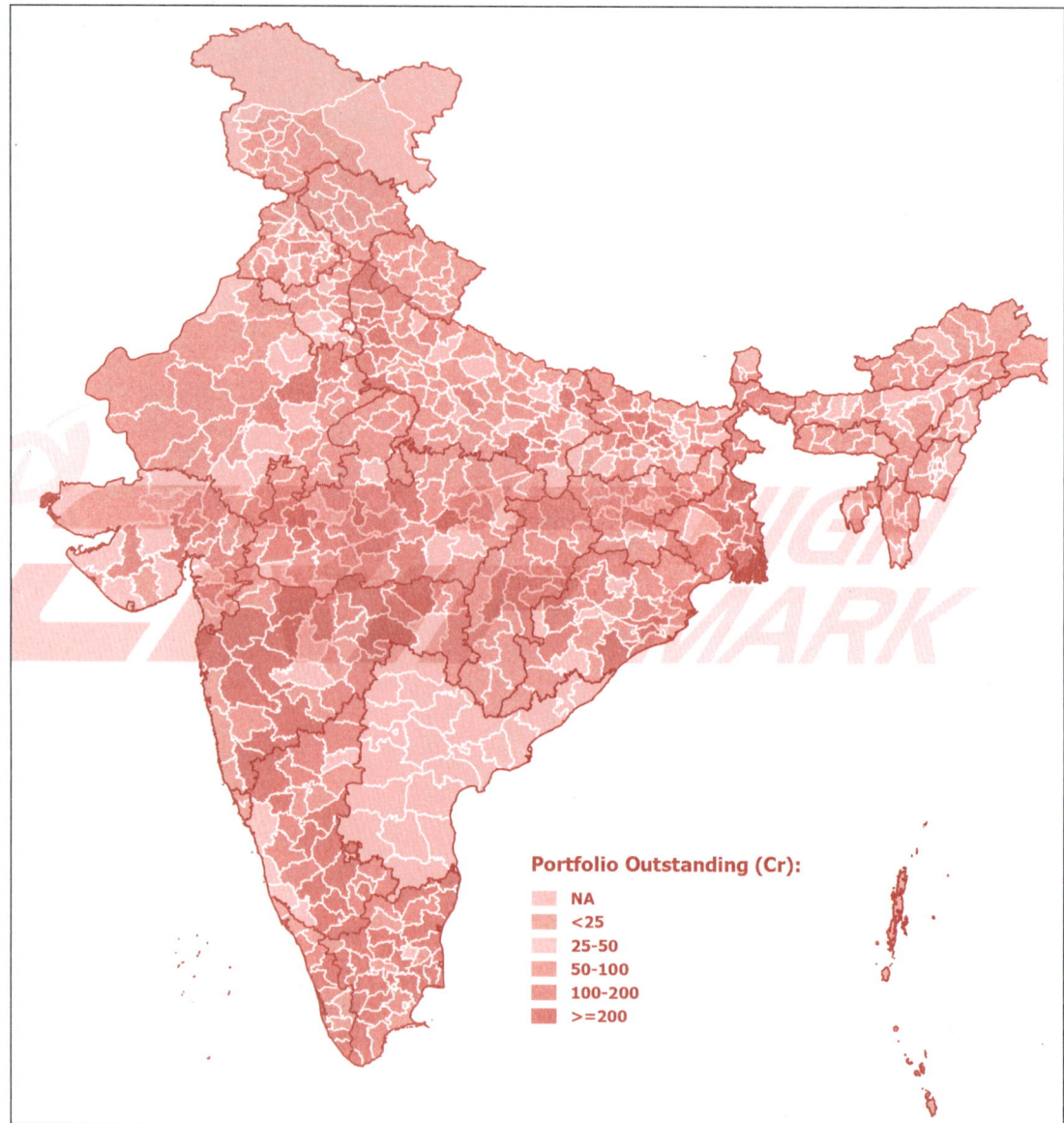

Figure 5.6 Microlenders District Penetration in 2016
Source: CRIF High Mark.
Note: This figure is not to scale and does not depict authentic boundaries.

from MFIN also allow for a micro analysis of the factors of growth, that is, how the growth is being achieved.

5.3.1 Growth at a Scorching Pace: Mid- and Small-sized Institutions also Join the Bandwagon

The narrative is focused on top 20 institutions among MFIN members like the last year, as these institutions account for 89% of portfolio share, while the balance 11% share is accounted by 36 other institutions with loan portfolio ranging

from ₹571 crore to ₹16 crore. The exit of Bandhan Bank from this year's list was expected to lower the share of top 20 institutions, but the high growth of Janalakshmi has ensured a portfolio share similar to the previous year, for the top 20. Last year, Bandhan constituted 23.75% of total NBFC-MFI portfolio, while this year, Janalakshmi accounts for 20% share.

The annual growth rate achieved during 2014–15 by top 20 NBFC-MFIs[10] by portfolio size (Figure 5.7) shows that seven of them had annual growth rate in excess of the national growth rate of 91%. During 2014–15, the growth rate was 61%. It is

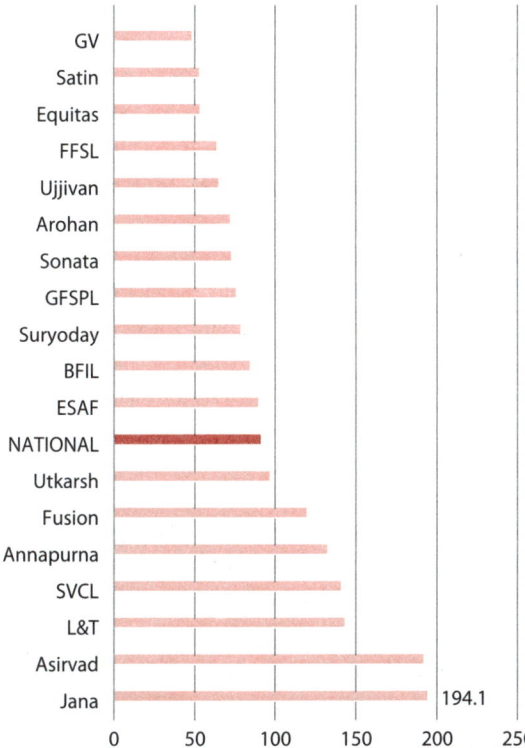

Figure 5.7 Annual Growth Rate of Top 18 NBFC-MFIs in 2015–16

Source: MFIN MicroMeter, Issue 17.

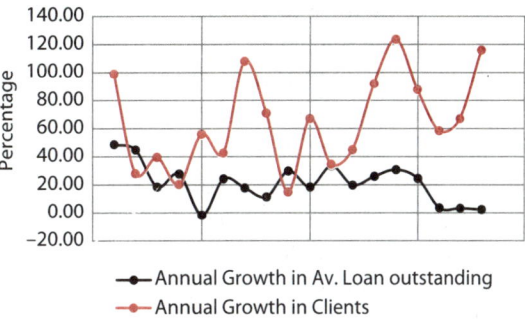

Figure 5.8 Annual % Growth in Average Loan Outstanding per Client and Number of Clients of Top 18 NBFC-MFIs in 2015–16

Source: MFIN MicroMeter, Issue 17.

5.3.2 Breadth or Depth? Data Show Breadth but…

Growth can be achieved either by adding more clients in same location, spreading the operations to new areas, or increasing the loan size for the existing customers. The analysis shows that during 2015–16, NBFC-MFIs did well by placing more emphasis on client accretion than increasing loan size as measured by average loan outstanding data (Figure 5.8).

The data in respect of top 18 NBFC-MFIs show that except in the case of 4 institutions, all other 14 institutions had much higher growth in the number of clients, rather than growth in average loan outstanding amount per client. In the case of Janalakshmi, the market leader, the number of clients grew by 98%, as against 48% increase in average loan outstanding per client. What is more noteworthy is the fact that in the case of Satin, the average loan outstanding fell by 1.57%, and four other institutions show growth of less than 5% in average loan outstanding amount. Overall, as against an average 20% increase in loan outstanding, the client growth rate was around 50%. This is heartening, as it implies that the focus is on increasing outreach as against pushing more credit to the same client. The pattern follows through the spectrum of 56 NBFC-MFIs, with the group recording an annual increase of 46% in clients during 2015–16—the combined client base as on March 2016 stands at 33 million clients. It is another matter that district-level concentration shows that client growth is happening in areas of existing operations, rather than going in new geographies.

However, field investigations show that the loan size is also increasing at ~40%, and its impact on average loan outstanding figure will show up with

disconcerting that six MFIs in top 20 had growth rates in excess of 100%, with Janalakshmi growing at 194%, almost tripling its portfolio in one year. The lowest growth rate amongst top 20 is 48%.

Thus, while the annual growth rate of bigger institutions keeps surging at an alarming pace, the other key feature of 2015–16 has been the growth observed in other 36 NBFC-MFIs[11]. Out of these 36 MFIs, 16 recorded a growth in excess of the national growth rate of 91% and notably 14 grew in excess of 100%. So, in the overall universe of 56 NBFC-MFIs, 20 institutions grew by more than 100%. Even though the small size inflates the growth percentage, there is something beyond growth when institutions grow by 400% and 900%.

Thus, overall, the growth story is not limited to specific institutions; the sector as a whole is growing at a scorching pace—as a responsible industry, the fact that 56% yearly growth in 2010 led to loosening of controls needs to be kept in mind. As in the case of geographical analysis of growth, in the case of institutional analysis, it is critical to have a look at the growth drivers (institution-wise details in Annexure 5.3).

a lag, as the increase in number of clients lowers the average amount. The analysis suffers from this limitation, as MFIN does not provide data on loan size ranges. The other available data point, on average loan amount disbursed per account, also suffers from a similar limitation. Furthermore, interaction with other industry experts brings forth another limitation of this analysis. This relates to the uniqueness of client numbers. It is not clear whether the data captures the uniqueness of a client, that is, if one client has three loans from the same institution, whether it is counted as one client or three clients. In field, in many instances, clients have more than one loan from the same institution, and the way it is counted determines the validity of this analysis. It seems that the truth lies in between, with some institutions reporting unique clients and some equating loan accounts with clients. Thus, while the analysis of the available data shows positive trend, more data points are needed to refine both measures.

5.3.3 Productivity: Signs of Correction or Build-up for Growth?

In this growth phase, it is critical to analyze as to what is happening with the case load and portfolio being handled by field officers. The sector has seen a surge in staff productivity, especially field officer/loan officer productivity. This surge has been flagged as a serious quality issue, as higher case load leads to weakening of relationship with the client and reduces it to a transactional mode. Microfinance is built on the edifice of personal understanding of client needs, and dumbing this vital block can lead to a disconnect among clients.

The figures for growth in clients handled per loan officer and credit portfolio for top 18 MFIs show a mixed picture and some good signals (Figure 5.9).

The ratio of clients managed by loan officers has shown a very high increase (>50%) in the case of one institution, high (25–50%) increase in the case of three institutions, moderate (0–25%) increase in the case of three institutions, and most critically, it fell in the case of 11 NBFC-MFIs. This is a significant data point from 2015–16, as it shows that institutions have realized the excess case load issues and are taking corrective actions. Similarly, credit portfolio managed by loan officers fell in the case of six institutions. Overall, it shows that while a large part is correcting the high load on loan officers, a few are still increasing the productivity. A word of caution needs to be made, as even at reduced levels the productivity remains high (Table 5.5; details in Annexure 5.2).

The productivity even at reduced levels is also high, averaging around 500–600. In recent years, a few other tasks have got added to loan officers' work, apart from credit, and that needs to be factored in. Many institutions now require their loan officers to sell consumer durables, such as solar lamps, and almost all work on other financial services, such as insurance and remittances. The same work force, with only credit portfolio to look after five years back, had productivity of around 250 clients, which has now more than doubled. This is creating stress at field officer level, and if the decreasing trend seen in 2015–16 is an acknowledgement of this, it is a welcome step.

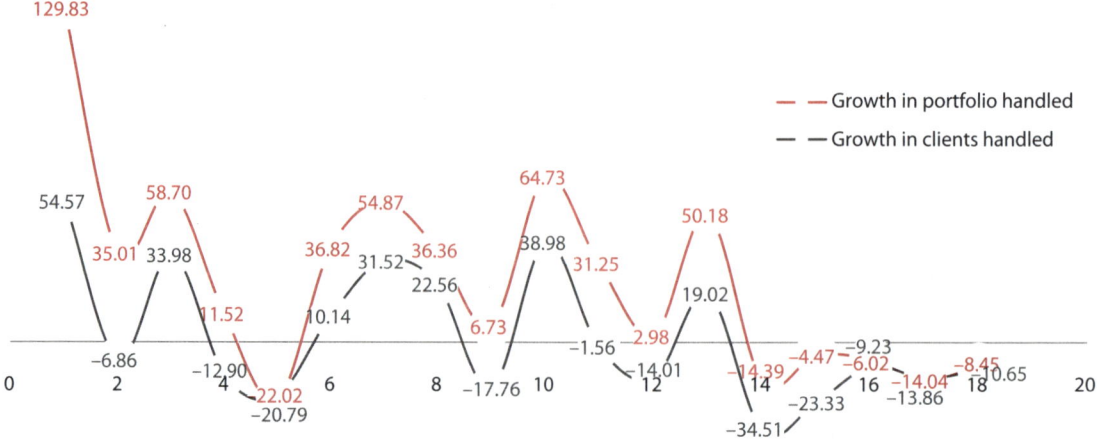

Figure 5.9 Annual Growth in Portfolio and Clients Handled by Loan Officers—Top 18 NBFC-MFIs

Source: MFIN MicroMeter, Issue 17.

Table 5.5 **Frequency Distribution of LO Productivity among Top 18 NBFC-MFIs**

No. of Clients Handled by Loan Officers	No. of MFIs
800–900	3
700–799	3
600–699	4
500–599	4
400–499	5

Source: MFIN Micrometer, Issue No 17.

Why Does Correction Seem Like Build-up for Growth?

A deeper dive into numbers, as well as interaction with industry watchers, reveals that buoyed by growth, MFIs are ramping up staff capacity. Equity investments and debt have started flowing and the build-up of off-balance sheet portfolio is also taking place at a healthy pace. The MFIs know that funds utilization depends solely on the availability of field-level manpower, and that has led to high-paced hiring. During 2015–16, top 18 NBFCs increased their field staff strength by 42%. If this is seen along with data from the past few years, 2015–16 stands out as an exceptional year. It is seen that some MFIs more than doubled their field staff strength during the year (Figure 5.10).

Except Ujjivan which had a negligible growth in staff strength of 3.6%, all others recorded healthy growth. Five out of eighteen doubled or more their loan officers' staff strength. As new recruits take time to build case load, it seems that this high level of hiring is a key factor in the reduction of productivity across many MFIs. This aspect reduces the positive side of self-induced correction in the industry.

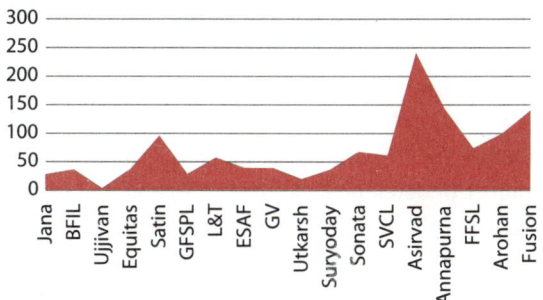

Figure 5.10 Annual Growth (%) of Loan Officers during 2015–16—Top 18 MFIs

Source: MFIN MicroMeter, Issue 17.

Such large-scale recruitment needs to be backed by equally large investment in training and capacity-building. Going back to 2010, one of the important lessons of the crisis related to this aspect. As more and more hiring took place, training was overlooked, and in many cases branches were being handled by all new staff[12]. From a responsible finance view point as well as for sustainability, MFIs must accord priority to training. It is almost impossible to build staff quality with such massive recruitment, and it also serves as a reason for continuing with limited product choices. It is easy to scale up with a relatively untrained workforce, offering the same product across the operational areas. New products based on context and needs of clients require more resources, staff training, as well as time for scaling up. Chapter 2 detailed the new credit products being introduced, but all such initiatives suffer from low outreach. It seems that in an era of high growth, the race is more for outreach, rather than for being client-centric. The analysis that MFIs are building up staff strength to support their growth plans is corroborated by a growth rate of 89% in the first quarter of 2016–17. (Institution-wise clients and loan portfolio handled per loan officer in Annexure 5.3.)

5.3.4 How is Such High Productivity Being Sustained?

The high levels of staff productivity seem to be riding on two factors. One relates to technological advances at the field level. Many MFIs have moved toward cashless disbursement, providing tabs to field officers to optimize group lending process, and this has resulted in loan officers spending lesser time in group meetings than ever before. MFIs proffer this as the primary reason for increase in productivity. Although this is one of the factors, the more important factor relates to shift of the industry to monthly or fortnightly repayment tenure. The weekly repayment mode, which was the main operational paradigm of microfinance, requires frequent interactions by way of weekly group meetings and collection of repayments. This, along with maintaining cohesion in the group, requires time and has been historically cited as the main reason for higher transaction costs in loan delivery. In recent years, realizing this limitation, the sector has increasingly moved away from weekly repayments to fortnightly or monthly repayments. With this change, the same loan officer can handle more clients, as the frequency of group meetings decreases from weekly to fortnightly or monthly. Technological processes such as entry of records in tabs in place of earlier manual records add to efficiency gains.

This shift was flagged in the last year's report, and the data for 2015–16 show that the trend has accelerated. If the data for top 80 districts in the country in terms of microfinance portfolio are examined, the number of districts having more than 50% weekly repayment loans is mere 9, while in remaining 71 districts the share of weekly loans has fallen to less than 50% (Figure 5.11). This trend compared with the data for 2015, when 22 districts had more than 50% weekly portfolio. Field observations suggest that in the next one–two years, nearly all loans will be of fortnightly or monthly repayment cycle. Even fortnightly and monthly data for 2015–16 show that the monthly repayment share is increasing at the expense of fortnightly repayment. The shift would have been even more pronounced but for two major lenders, that is, BFIL and GFSPL sticking to weekly repayments. While MFIs opine that clients are now demanding fortnightly and monthly repayments, this assertion sits oddly with the fact that loan sizes have gone up, and longer repayment frequency increases the repayment installment for the client. M.R. Rao, CEO of BFIL, pointed out that weekly repayment is the preferred option for its clients, a fact that has come across strongly in market surveys and in its regular VoC channel, wherein customer feedback is regularly taken. Udaya Kumar, CEO of GFSPL, concurs with this view. This is very paradoxical, as MFIs operating in same areas and with similar clients have different customer feedback. However, as the trend and industry talk suggest, the shift is more due to productivity concerns.

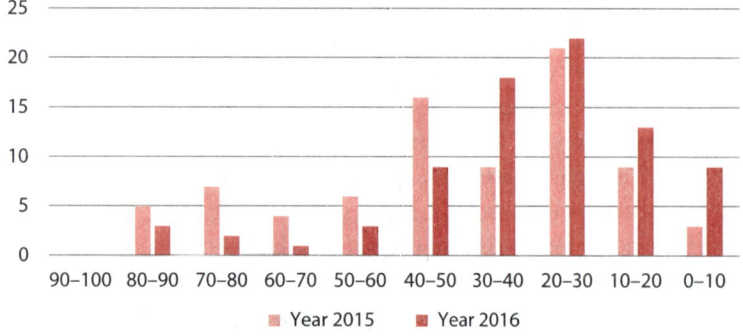

Figure 5.11 Frequency Distribution of Weekly Repayment Portfolio in Top 80 Districts

Source: CRIF High Mark.

5.4 FUNDERS AND ASSESSORS: FUELING GROWTH BUT ARE THEY FACTORING IN RISKS?

The above geographical and institutional analysis brings out several areas of concern. These are high geographical saturation, growth in high credit penetration market, increasing loan sizes with shift toward fortnightly and monthly repayments, and high loan officer case load. Frequent instances of client distress add to this list and point to the fact that on several counts, there is room for caution and corrective action. However, the engine fueling growth—investors and lenders—seems to be comfortable with the market situation. It is evident from the growth in debt funding from Indian banks, which grew from ₹21,737 crore in 2014–15 to ₹33,706 crore in 2015–16. Annual growth of 55% in debt funding underlies the fact that banks continue to believe in the growth story. Foreign investment funds have also joined the bandwagon and are increasingly using the NCD route for funding. The growing interest of institutional investors is evident from the fact that their share along with other than banks in debt funding of MFIs has gone up to 40%. In 2012–13, bank funding of MFIs constituted 75% of total debt funding, but it has gone down progressively over the years, reaching 60% in 2015–16.

What is providing this level of comfort to investors and lenders? responsAbility, a major global microfinance investment fund, feels that the public policy push and supportive regulation have brought the financial inclusion to the forefront in India. It also says that the policy has accepted that one-size-fits-all does not work, and there has to be a differentiated architecture of financial institutions. It sees a strong momentum for the MFIs and goes on to say "The long awaited political and regulatory backing has handed the sector a high-quality pen to write its next chapter"[13]. ICRA Limited, a leading credit rating agency, in its report[14] on the sector, also places high importance on the supporting policy framework, pointing out that the RBI and the Government of India have announced a number of developments supporting financial inclusion and MFIs during the last 18 months. The aspect of regulation that is most comforting to the analysts, besides regulatory clarity on NBFC-MFIs, is the safeguard of credit bureaus. ICRA's report says:

The good credit quality has been supported by several safeguards put in place by the regulators, such as data sharing through credit bureaus, restrictions on overall leveraging of ₹100,000 per borrower and stipulation that not more than two MFIs can lend to the same borrower.

Market size is another argument that is frequently heard to justify high growth. ICRA's report places the market size as ₹2.8–3.4 trillion as against the current outreach of ₹1.1 trillion, including SBLP and Bandhan Bank, and cites this as the reason for seeing continued growth of the sector. The report does cite instances of community, political, and ring leader issues in some pockets, exclusion of SBLP data from CB, and greater focus on collection of dues over group dynamics as some of the issues to be corrected, but for its future outlook on the sector predicts growth and good profitability. Riding on the positive assessment, ICRA upgraded ratings of 12 MFIs during 2015–16 as against nil downgrade and attributes the upgrades to "increased scale of operations on the back of better liquidity and improved capital structure".

Thus, while rating agencies and investors riding on regulatory comfort retain their positive outlook despite highlighting a few concerns, the other sources of institutional assessments also point to a comfortable scenario. CPP certifications of the Smart Campaign, which is a global benchmark, have also given their affirmation to 11 leading NBFC-MFIs in India. The CPP certification indicators have a strong emphasis on balanced growth, with one standard 'prevention of overindebtedness' focusing exclusively on saturated markets, assessing multiple borrowings through multiple checks and client-level assessments. Top MFIs meeting these standards imply that risks associated with growth impacting clients adversely are not seen through these certifications. In this holy grail of affirmation from all around—rating agencies, investors, other external assessments, and backed by the comfort of regulation—critical issues outlined in the above section are being ignored. Reliance on CB and regulatory limits on indebtedness level act as important building blocks of this comfort, and hence it is imperative to examine what does CB data tell us and what it does not.

5.5 INSIGHTS FROM CREDIT BUREAU DATA ON MULTIPLE LENDING AND INFORMATION GAPS

Establishment of microfinance-focused CBs in 2011 has been one of the pillars of regulatory framework, as it allowed MFIs to have a check on indebtedness

level of the client. As of now, there are four functional CBs in India, with two of them focusing mainly on microfinance. Up to last year, every credit institution was required to be a member of at least one CB. In 2015, the RBI revised the guidelines[15], realizing that as CB records provide information of a borrower in respect of its member institutions only, it mandated that credit institutions should become member of all CBs. The MFIN CoC for its members also says that MFIs will agree to share complete client data with all the RBI-approved CBs, as per the frequency of data submission prescribed by the CBs. Thus, as of now, at least in the case of NBFC-MFIs, the dataset with CBs is uniformly shared, and progressively all other RBI-regulated CBs such as banks and NBFCs have also started sharing data with all CBs. This has plugged the gap which institutions could exploit earlier, that is, the gap between the two CBs' records and use of the bureau report which enables them to disburse loans—as there were cases where one CB showed more than two loans against a client, while the other showed less than two loans.

As the issue of market saturation is hotly contested, data points other than total credit size at district/state level also need to be analyzed. Growth advocates opine that while the volume of credit has increased, the CB checks ensure that indebtedness is kept in check and there are negligible cases of multiple lending to the same client. The analysis of the extent of multiple lending presented here includes all microlenders, including NBFC-MFIs lending through the group mode. Thus, it includes data reported by banks, NBFCs, and NGO-MFIs for their group lending. From a responsible finance angle as well as risk perspective, enlargement of analysis, rather than focusing only on NBFC-MFIs clients, is necessary, as the client segment remains the same.

Data obtained from CRIF High Mark in respect of 80 districts with highest credit penetration show an alarming trend (Table 5.6) and provide additional support to the saturation logic seen through spatial and institutional analysis (district-wise details in Annexure 5.4).

Eleven districts have more than 6% clients having >2 micro loans. The figures will come down if only NBFC-MFIs are taken into account, but that will not reflect the true picture. All of these 11 districts are spread across West Bengal, Maharashtra, and Tamil Nadu. While, Maharashtra and Tamil Nadu

Table 5.6 Clients with More Than Two Loans in Top 80 Districts

Percentage of Clients with More Than Two Loans	Number of Districts
More than 8%	4
6–8%	7
4–6%	14
2–4%	21
0.1–2%	34

Source: CRIF High Mark.

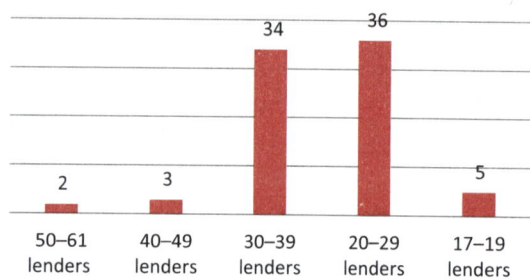

Figure 5.12 Number of Microlenders in Top 80 Districts
Source: CRIF High Mark.

are in the top five states, with highest loan portfolio of NBFC-MFIs, West Bengal does not figure, as Bandhan is now a bank. The level of multiple lending has shown significant increase in one year. As on March 31, 2015, the highest percentage of clients with more than two loans was 3.61%, and it was in only one district. The number of districts with less than 1% clients having more than two loans has come down from 36 to 22. The extent of multiple lending across these 80 districts is logically related to the size of microlenders present in the district. The data on active microlenders present in these 80 districts show that the range is from 17 to 61 lenders in a district, with an average of around 30 lenders per district (Figure 5.12).

5.5.1 Gaps in Credit Bureau Reporting

The CB data suffer from two limitations: institutional and lending methodology limitation and technical limitation. On the first aspect, the data analyzed above need to be supplemented by the fact that it does not include individual lending by NBFC-MFIs, banks under small borrowal accounts, nonreporting institutions like cooperative banks, and NGO-MFIs, as well as the SBLP. If all this is factored into the analysis, the multiple lending per client

is likely to go up significantly in these districts. In such a scenario, it is naïve to deny the increase in multiple lending breaching the regulatory norm and increasing the risk profile of the sector.

The other aspect pertains to the technical aspect of client identification. The KYC documents taken by different institutions differ, thereby increasing the chances of a client taking multiple loans from different institutions, based on different KYC documents. The client can offer a voter card to one, a ration card to another, and an Aadhaar card to the third. Such a client will not figure in the above list, as the system will show him/her as three different clients. MFIN, as the industry body, has tried to address the situation by requiring its members to take at least two KYC documents, including Aadhaar, as well as to focus on matching the Aadhaar penetration levels in the state. CB experts feel that the capture of Aadhaar can substantially check multiple identities of the same client, as it is unique and based on biometric authentication. CGAP and IFC, in their publication on credit reporting in the case of microfinance clients, stress the point of unique identity saying that

> [T]he challenge of uniquely identifying base-of-the-pyramid customers for credit reporting purposes is significant in many countries. Yet, without a reliable means of uniquely identifying borrowers, credit reporting mechanisms are more costly to implement, and the quality of data is reduced—in some cases to the point of rendering the data of little or no value[16].

Even though the universal acceptance of Aadhaar will eventually eliminate the problem of duplicating identity, two more factors need to be addressed to make the system foolproof. First, the acceptance of Aadhaar as the mandatory KYC document has to be extended to all credit institutions and not be restricted to NBFC-MFIs. Second, Aadhaar as a KYC document is not enough, and to reap its full potential, it has to be backed by e-verification of identity through Aadhaar's cloud-based system. During field visits by the author, it was observed that Aadhaar number as KYC is not enough as deliberate wrong input is also being resorted, resulting in nonmatching of records. Institutions feel that graduating to Aadhaar-based e-KYC is costly, but leading institutions like BFIL are already moving toward that. It is being realized that the cost of investment in technology is small, compared to the risks to the institution in the absence of it.

In addition to these technical issues in CB reporting, the exact authenticity of data being reported to the CBs is also not so clear. As an example, the case of the gross loan portfolio of NBFC-MFIs was analyzed. The CoC specifies that NBFC-MFIs have to submit data to all functioning CBs, and as such that the gross loan portfolio on a particular date reported by any of the CB should match the data reported by MFIN. However, it does not. MFIN reported the gross loan portfolio (reduced by the off-balance sheet portfolio) of its members as on March 31, 2016 at ₹43,666 crore, while CRIF High Mark reported ₹51,800 for its members' gross loan portfolio—a difference of ₹8134 crore.

> Gross loan portfolio of NBFC-MFIs reported by MFIN and CB differs by ₹81.34 billion—raising questions on the data validity.

Regular Occurrence of Hot Spots Adds to the Evidence—the Case of Kala Kahar

In the last year's Responsible Finance report, it was observed that

> What is worrying is that similar local incidents have started happening again with great regularity in the past one year or so, and this time the geographical location is vastly different. Late last year, there were two reported incidents in Erode (Tamil Nadu) and Nanded (Maharashtra) of client unrest, due to problems in repayment. Since the middle of 2015, there have been several such incidents like Amroha and Azamgarh (both UP), Narsinghpur and Burhanpur (both MP), and as this report goes to press in September, another incident is being reported from Sagar in Madhya Pradesh. Discussions with MFIs involved in these areas disturbingly show that there is a striking similarity between these events, and the events of pre 2010 years[17].

These incidents continued to occur during 2015–16 in different areas—be it Sitarganj, Vidisha, or Varanasi. These incidents, starting from Krishna crisis of 2007, Kolar in 2009, and AP in 2010 till date have a striking commonality of reported client distress or suicide due to multiple loans, pipelining of loans, community incitement, and local political interference—the only difference being scale and place. Industry sources say that the last year has seen around a dozen cases of suicides and half

a dozen cases of localized nonpayment by clients. It is well acknowledged that these cases have to be seen against the 31 million outreach of MFIs. However, they have two important lessons—the first one relates to the existence of pockets of saturation and the second one relates to gaps in CB reporting.

As this section is about CBs, the case reported from Narsinghpur in MP acts as a pointer to the gaps. MFIN did not share the field investigation report, citing confidentiality, so the findings reported are from the interaction of the author with the staff of MFIs. Kala Kahar, a women microfinance client, committed suicide in May 2015, and it was reported that she was under stress because of the excessive debt from MFIs. The reasons are avoided here, as there are differing versions, but the fact that she had multiple loans from NBFC-MFIs, despite the regulatory limitation on two lenders, is more critical. The informal accounts from MFI staff indicate that she had outstanding loans from six NBFC-MFIs at the time of her suicide. The extent of her indebtedness is evident from the fact that she had approximately a debt repayment liability of ₹6,000 per month. The multiple loans happened on two counts. First, the deceased client had provided multiple IDs to MFIs, which resulted in CB reports not reflecting the true picture of her credit profile. Second, the credit institutions also did not provide full information available with them while making credit inquiry—something referred to as 'inquiry softening'. Provision of partial information probably did not match the records fully, enabling the institution to lend. Field practices show that such instances keep happening, as institutions pursue high growth, short-circuiting the systems, and this leads to various malpractices such as

- High targets for field staff, which do not take into account issues such as overpenetration and concentration in concerned geographies.
- Pressure on staff to meet huge targets, leading to collusion with a few members/leaders of joint liability group (JLG) to form groups. The tendency to rely on these center leaders for quickly achieving volume leads to issues such as dominance and pipelining of loans.
- Reduction of time spent on CGT as well as group meetings after disbursement—focus being on improving efficiency.
- Inquiry softening while seeking information from CBs.

This is not to highlight a few instances of adverse practices, or to critique the system, as it is well acknowledged that establishing a foolproof system for millions of clients takes time but only to caution against sole reliance on CBs at present. What is worrying is the fact that the field practices of MFIs have given a go by to the traditional loan approval process, incorporating the cash flow analysis of the client, and they currently rely solely on CB data. This has happened at a time when there are several gaps in CB reporting, as well as the fact that loan sizes have gone up, aggravating the risks. Wherever cash flow analysis continues to be a part of loan appraisal, the practices do not reflect rigor and are seen more as paper compliance by the field staff. It is not uncommon to see cases of several clients in a branch, with exactly the same figures of income, expenses, and loan-limit assessment. The MFIs need to realize that till the gaps in CB reporting are filled through capture of data from all relevant institutions, and e-KYC-based authentication of client identity, CB checks can only serve as an additional source of information to supplement the appraisal process. Many people believe that MFIs are well aware of this aspect, and it is a question of 'growth' over 'knowledge'. This suggestion does seem credible, as practitioners would be much more informed than others.

SUMMING UP

Chapters 2 and 3 outlined the continued journey of the MFIs toward responsible finance, aided by supportive regulation and industry initiatives. Despite functioning under one of the most elaborate regulatory rules globally, the industry has not only demonstrated adherence to them but also voluntarily gone ahead on several counts, such as the ceiling of ₹60,000 on maximum indebtedness as against regulatory limit of ₹1 lakh. Collection practices have improved vastly, institutions have adopted the additional requirement of CSR despite already being a double bottom line industry, transparency in communication is at global best, product diversity along with movement toward cashless economy is taking roots, and client grievances are being accorded priority. These numerous initiatives taken in last six years ensure smoother movement of the sector back to its client-centric roots. These gains are critical, as with 35 million outreach to poorer segments of the society, microfinance institutions are a key player in India's quest for universal financial inclusion. Thus,

it is extremely important that practices which move the sector away from client centricity are avoided. Microfinance continues to be in policy spotlight, and it will remain so, as it deals with vulnerable sections of the society. Any slippage now risks tightening of regulation, and it will lead to loss for clients, as seen even today in AP and Telangana. Over the years, the regulatory framework has changed from being forbearing to supportive, comforted by sector's adherence to responsible finance, and nothing should be done to reverse that.

However, as discussed in this chapter, there are signs of weak spots emerging. The chase of growth at a frenetic pace is not leading to a wider spread but concentration in top 50 or -80 districts out of 676 districts in India. The repeated instances of client distress keep popping up at regular intervals to remind the sector that all is not well. While these may be isolated incidents, there are important lessons in them. The most critical lesson is that extending credit beyond the capacity of clients only adds to distress and can give only short-term growth. This has been demonstrated time and again in microfinance, as well as in the wider financial sector, and so the microfinance sector needs to rectify the trend of competing in the same market. There are enough financially excluded pockets and regions, to which the sector should spread. Profitability is on the rise as discussed in Chapter 2, and this buffer should be used to go to financially excluded areas—even at a cost, initially. This is the right time for the sector to go beyond seeing client centricity from a compliance perspective and integrate it as the core working philosophy. On the product side, while product diversity is welcome, and needs to be scaled up, a trend of retailing consumer goods is being seen. This needs to be checked. Credit appraisal also seems to be getting diluted and is being replaced just by adherence to CB checks. This move, when the CB reporting suffers from gaps, is likely to lead to a higher risk and credit overload for clients. A client-centric approach also requires the industry to deliberate whether increasing the period of repayment frequency is what the clients want or it is merely a method to increase productivity. Field staff motivation and mission commitment are important in ensuring client centricity, as it is they who interact with the clients. The investments in staff capacity-building, especially field staff, seem to be lagging behind, with focus on ramping up the productivity. This paradigm of growth needs to be reversed, and investors and bankers have a critical role in facilitating this change.

The financial landscape is changing fast, and in the near future, MFIs will have to compete with banks downscaling, SFBs, and schemes like PMJDY. Banks will have an edge in being able to offer wider variety of services, and the comparative advantage of MFIs will continue to be their expertise in relationship-based last mile lending. The future of microfinance lies in strengthening client centricity, and in being more responsive to the client, rather than chasing growth. The trust reposed in them by policy and regulation should not be allowed to diminish.

ANNEXURE 5.1
State-wise Details of Portfolio and Clients—MFIN Member NBFC-MFIs

State	Total Portfolio (₹ Cr)			No. of MFI	No. of Clients (lakhs)	
	2010	2015	2016		2015	2016
NORTH						
Haryana	48.77	421	1165	14	2.86	4.91
Himachal Pradesh	5.96	NA	NA	NA	NA	NA
Punjab	5.98	NA	988	10	NA	5.62
Chandigarh	0.23	NA	NA	NA	NA	NA
Rajasthan	346.56	705	1259	14	5.58	7.54
Delhi	346.42	365	582	8	2.12	5.56
Bihar	493.55	1534	2921	21	12.06	19.31
Uttar Pradesh	890.14	3071	5645	19	21.16	31.27
Uttrakhand	47.8	342	593	11	2.29	3.31
Sub-Total	2185.41	6438	13153	97	46.07	77.52
EAST						
NE	308.99	356	813	10 (Assam)/ 5 Tripura	3.25	5.66
Jharkhand	175.03	385	898	17	3.34	5.66
Odisha	1200.41	1649	3141	13	13.90	21.35
West Bengal	2106.28	1659	3075	14	16.87	21.91
Sub-Total	3790.71	4049	7927	44	37.36	54.58
WEST						
Chhattisgarh	211.82	445	877	17	4	5.86
Goa	7.83	NA	NA	NA	NA	NA
Gujarat	216.22	1028	2064	19	9.12	12.34
Maharashtra	967.14	3362	6329	32	25.74	37.11
Madhya Pradesh	593.81	2254	4084	27	18.35	28.05
Sub-Total	1996.82	7089	13354	95	56.93	83.36
SOUTH						
Andhra Pradesh	5210.71	78	82	5	1.27	1.15
Karnataka	1897.69	4109	7165	24	27.38	38.23
Kerala	159.83	1150	2434	10	6.70	12.230
Tamil Nadu	2387.09	5080	8687	19	44.44	56.50
Pondicherry	15.53	113	193	10	0.92	1.220
Sub-Total	9670.85	10530	18561	68	80.71	109.33
TOTAL	**17643.81**	**28106**	**52995**	**304**	**221.07**	**324.79**

Notes: 1. States with less than 5 NBFC-MFIs data is not disclosed by MFIN.
2. As Bandhan has been removed from 2015 figures, figures reported in last year report are different.

ANNEXURE 5.2
Top 80 Districts with NBFC-MFIs Portfolio

State	District—MFIN	No. of NBFC-MFIs	Portfolio (₹ Billion)
KA	BANGALORE	17	14.53
TN	COIMBATORE	20	6.42
KA	MYSORE	16	6.16
MH	NAGPUR	20	5.97
MH	PUNE	20	5.85
TN	CHENNAI	21	5.44
TN	KANCHEEPURAM	20	5.31
MP	INDORE	25	4.75
TN	THIRUVALLUR	21	4.7
TN	THANJAVUR	16	4.58
TN	CUDDALORE	17	4.47
TN	MADURAI	16	4.33
UP	SAHARANPUR	12	4.24
KL	THRISSUR	9	4.11
KA	BELGAUM	18	4.08
KL	PALAKKAD	11	4.04
TN	TIRUCHIRAPPALLI	19	3.86
MH	KOLHAPUR	21	3.84
WB	NORTH TWENTY FOUR PARGANAS	36	3.83
KA	TUMKUR	18	3.81
BR	PATNA	15	3.65
MH	AMRAVATI	20	3.53
MH	THANE	22	3.52
TN	SALEM	22	3.43
TN	TIRUNELVELI	14	3.41
GJ	AHMADABAD	19	3.33
KL	ALAPPUZHA	7	3.11
TN	ERODE	23	3.08
MH	SOLAPUR	18	3.06
TN	NAGAPATTINAM	14	3.05
TN	VELLORE	20	3.01
MP	JABALPUR	24	3
WB	KOLKATA	10	2.97
MH	MUMBAI	22	2.93
BR	MUZAFFARPUR	14	2.92
TN	DINDIGUL	18	2.91
KA	MANDYA	12	2.89
TN	THIRUVARUR	17	2.88
TN	VILUPPURAM	18	2.84
MP	SAGAR	20	2.83

State	District—MFIN	No. of NBFC-MFIs	Portfolio (₹ Billion)
WB	SOUTH TWENTY FOUR PARGANAS	36	2.82
BR	BEGUSARAI	11	2.78
KA	HASSAN	15	2.78
UP	MEERUT	9	2.78
MH	NASHIK	21	2.71
UP	ALLAHABAD	13	2.71
UP	BULANDSHAHR	9	2.69
UP	GORAKHPUR	13	2.68
WB	BARDDHAMAN	14	2.67
KA	DAVANAGERE	18	2.59
UP	AGRA	11	2.57
KL	KOLLAM	6	2.54
MH	YAVATMAL	18	2.51
TN	NAMAKKAL	18	2.5
TN	THENI	15	2.47
UP	VARANASI	15	2.44
OR	KHORDHA	12	2.43
WB	MURSHIDABAD	12	2.38
MH	AURANGABAD	15	2.33
KL	THIRUVANANTHAPURAM	8	2.28
OR	GANJAM	13	2.25
TN	TIRUPPUR	19	2.25
UP	GHAZIABAD	14	2.25
WB	HAORA	10	2.24
RJ	JAIPUR	13	2.24
KA	DHARWAD	17	2.24
TN	KANNIYAKUMARI	11	2.2
MP	BHOPAL	20	2.2
OR	CUTTACK	12	2.19
MH	AHMADNAGAR	16	2.19
UK	HARDWAR	10	2.18
MH	SANGLI	21	2.16
MH	JALGAON	18	2.09
MP	UJJAIN	24	2.08
BR	SAMASTIPUR	14	2.08
TN	VIRUDHUNAGAR	17	2.07
KA	CHAMARAJANAGAR	12	2.07
TN	PUDUKKOTTAI	16	2.05
KA	CHITRADURGA	18	2.02
KA	BELLARY	18	2

Source: CRIF High Mark.

ANNEXURE 5.3
NBFC-MFIs Portfolio and Clients Handled per Loan Officer

S. No.	MFI	FY 2011–12		FY 2014–15		FY 2015–16	
		GLP per Loan Officer (₹, Lakh)	Clients per Loan Officer	GLP per Loan Officer (₹, Lakh)	Clients per Loan Officer	GLP per Loan Officer (₹, Lakh)	Clients per Loan Officer
1	Janalakshmai	41.0	353	61.9	384	140.7	592
2	SKS	16.2	312	89.9	787	121.4	733.3
3	Ujjivan	37.6	438	84.7	568	134.4	761
4	Equitas	60.8	1,002	96.4	1,031	107.5	898
5	GFSPL	65.5	433	73.5	434	100.6	477
6	Satin	36.1	345	155.5	866	121.2	686
7	L & T Finance#	64.6	1,431	68.8	644	106.6	847
8	ESAF	32.9	403	82.7	461	112.7	565
9	Gramavidiyal	30.3	476	93.1	794	99.3	653
10	Utkarsh	34.9	492	74.9	626	123.4	870
11	Spandana*	49.6	631	59.1	557	74.2	668
12	Suryoday	66.9	733	84.2	706	110.5	695
13	Sonata	32.5	426	68.9	471	70.9	405
14	SVCL	26.2	375	68.4	540	74.0	463
15	Asirvad	29.8	651	108.7	881	93.1	577
16	Annapurna	16.1	230	76.3	643	72.9	493
17	FFSL*	75.1	1,018	112.6	722	110.3	718
18	Arohan	9.8	195	67.1	564	59.2	479
19	Muthoot	36.0	408	79.2	517	56.2	274
20	Fusion	58.2	578	82.8	620	75.8	554
21	Share*	74.2	760	31.5	348	31.5	272
22	Madura#	114.7	1,716	56.9	489	70.8	527
23	RGVN			78.2	773	165.3	1030
24	BSS			108.8	603	117.7	548
25	Disha	52.1	563	81.3	723	80.6	515
26	Intrepid			56.3	569	126.6	954
27	Belstar	35.1	379	77.8	679	86.1	657
28	VFS	25.2	397	38.9	486	72.5	541
29	Chaitanya	34.3	373	39.6	278	45.9	277
30	Saija	5.2	124	63.6	568	56.4	435
31	Margdarshak	22.3	303	67.2	533	59.3	465
32	Jagaran	4.3	432	41.1	507	59.8	468
33	Midland			66.2	819	125.2	1143
34	Vedika			49.2	269	99.1	451
35	Light			77.8	356	79.1	395
36	ASA	13.9	245	24.8	395	30.8	354

S. No.	MFI	FY 2011–12		FY 2014–15		FY 2015–16	
		GLP per Loan Officer (₹, Lakh)	Clients per Loan Officer	GLP per Loan Officer (₹, Lakh)	Clients per Loan Officer	GLP per Loan Officer (₹, Lakh)	Clients per Loan Officer
37	Samasta	31.1	401	47.4	380	96.7	558
38	Svatantra			37.1	383	45.9	292
39	Namra	16.1	259	43.1	537	57.7	486
40	M Power	21.9	199	59.1	449	102.9	639
41	Pahal			55.9	565	69.8	511
42	Hindusthan			33.4	219	58.4	307
43	Varam	33.9	774	187.2	1,013	106.5	632
44	Adhikar	29.8	629	74.1	578	63.8	554
45	Sambandh			119.5	855	19.0	243
46	Navachetna	14.1	228	65.7	523	58.4	268
47	Uttarayan			32.9	317	50.3	401
48	Nirantara			70.4	414	81.1	505.2
49	Svasti	19.0	243	56.7	437	63.4	381
50	IDF			53.9	513	56.7	388
51	Shikhar			59.6	614	75.8	607
52	Sahayog	22.5	178	27.4	246	21.2	174
53	Sarvodaya	5.4	89	15.7	236	15.5	200
54	MSM			56.3	597	64.6	458
55	Nightingale			75.1	795	74.6	777
56	Agora	10.4	86	28.8	282	58.1	409

Source: MFIN Micrometer.

ANNEXURE 5.4
Top 80 Districts with Highest Microlending (JLG) Portfolio and Extent of Multiple Loans

State	District	Portfolio Rank	GLP—March 16 (Bn)	Clients with > 2 loans
KA	BANGALORE	1	15.04	1.59
WB	NORTH TWENTY FOUR PARGANAS	2	12.11	0.73
WB	SOUTH TWENTY FOUR PARGANAS	3	10.57	0.51
MH	PUNE	4	8.31	5.13
MH	NAGPUR	5	8.28	8.67
TN	COIMBATORE	6	7.98	4.14
WB	MURSHIDABAD	7	7.95	0.58
WB	NADIA	8	7.95	0.8
WB	HUGLI	9	7.59	0.68
WB	BARDDHAMAN	10	7.56	0.97
TN	THANJAVUR	11	7.31	4.1
WB	HAORA	12	7.22	0.91

(Continued)

(Continued)

State	District	Portfolio Rank	GLP—March 16 (Bn)	Clients with > 2 loans
WB	KOCH BIHAR	13	7.13	0.35
KA	MYSORE	14	7.02	4.4
WB	JALPAIGURI	15	7.01	0.44
MP	INDORE	16	6.23	8.35
KA	BELGAUM	17	6	6
TN	KANCHEEPURAM	18	5.98	1.71
BR	PATNA	19	5.92	3.7
TN	CUDDALORE	20	5.84	1.18
UP	SAHARANPUR	21	5.62	2.43
MH	KOLHAPUR	22	5.61	9.84
TN	CHENNAI	23	5.57	0.86
TN	MADURAI	24	5.42	2.39
TN	SALEM	25	5.32	2.05
WB	KOLKATA	26	5.31	1.79
TN	TIRUCHIRAPPALLI	27	5.28	3.46
TN	THIRUVALLUR	28	5.08	1.66
MH	AMRAVATI	29	4.97	7.56
WB	UTTAR DINAJPUR	30	4.94	0.48
MH	THANE	31	4.93	3.53
KL	PALAKKAD	32	4.74	5.79
KL	THRISSUR	33	4.71	4.43
TN	TIRUNELVELI	34	4.68	2.2
KA	TUMKUR	35	4.6	3.07
MH	SOLAPUR	36	4.49	5.29
TN	ERODE	37	4.33	2.99
WB	MALDAH	38	4.27	0.84
BR	MUZAFFARPUR	39	4.26	2.46
GJ	AHMADABAD	40	4.13	4.08
BR	SARAN	41	4.09	5.37
MH	MUMBAI	42	4.06	4.7
TN	VILUPPURAM	43	4.05	0.78
AS	NAGAON	44	4.02	0.11
MH	AHMADNAGAR	45	4.01	4.93
BR	BEGUSARAI	46	3.93	2
KL	ALAPPUZHA	47	3.89	2.17
TN	NAGAPATTINAM	48	3.88	1.02
WB	PURBA MEDINIPUR	49	3.82	0.47
RJ	JAIPUR	50	3.79	4.48
TN	THIRUVARUR	51	3.79	1.6
MH	YAVATMAL	52	3.76	4.56

(Continued)

(Continued)

State	District	Portfolio Rank	GLP—March 16 (Bn)	Clients with > 2 loans
UP	GORAKHPUR	53	3.75	7.15
AS	KAMRUP	54	3.74	0.85
TN	TIRUPPUR	55	3.7	2.92
KA	HASSAN	56	3.66	3.46
MP	JABALPUR	57	3.65	6.99
TN	VELLORE	58	3.65	0.82
UP	BULANDSHAHR	59	3.64	2.01
MP	SAGAR	60	3.64	7.45
UP	ALLAHABAD	61	3.63	6.97
UP	VARANASI	62	3.62	9.04
TN	DINDIGUL	63	3.6	1.85
AS	KAMRUP METROPOLITAN	64	3.54	2.35
MH	NASHIK	65	3.51	2.05
TN	NAMAKKAL	66	3.43	2.43
KA	MANDYA	67	3.39	4.12
OR	KHORDHA	68	3.33	2.38
OR	GANJAM	69	3.3	0.82
OR	CUTTACK	70	3.3	1.32
WB	DARJILING	71	3.29	0.65
KL	THIRUVANANTHAPURAM	72	3.23	1.06
AS	SONITPUR	73	3.23	0.09
MH	SANGLI	74	3.23	7.41
KL	KOLLAM	75	3.23	1.87
BR	SAMASTIPUR	76	3.21	1.69
WB	BIRBHUM	77	3.14	0.45
UP	MEERUT	78	3.13	0.77
MH	JALGAON	79	3.1	2.21
MH	AURANGABAD	80	3.08	3.01

Source: CRIF High Mark.

NOTES AND REFERENCES

1. *MFIN MicroMeter* (17).
2. http://thewire.in/18937/why-microfinance-is-becoming-a-bad-word-all-over-again, accessed on October 1, 2016.
3. http://www.livemint.com/Opinion/Gn7z2lGvfvwgoyjxByRHpO/Murmurs-of-a-fresh-crisis-in-the-microfinance-sector.html, accessed on October 1, 2016.
4. http://www.livemint.com/Money/BwyLY3cntN-rJiKNRCXB6NP/Signs-of-froth-in-microfinance.html, accessed on October 1, 2016.
5. Misra, Alok. 2015. "Emerging Risks in MFI Model: Let the Leaves Not Wilt". In *Responsible Finance India Report 2015: Client First: Tracking Social Performance Practices*. New Delhi: SAGE Publications.
6. The analysis is based on NBFC-MFIs (MFIN members) because of their 90% market share as well as data availability.
7. Excludes Delhi and Puducherry.
8. Based on the analysis of own portfolio, excluding off-balance sheet portfolio.
9. *MFIN MicroMeter* (17).
10. Figure 5.6 has 18 institutions as Muthoot and Spandana have been excluded from the analysis as Muthoot has shown very low figures due to organizational restructuring and Spandana has been stagnant since AP crisis.

11. MFIN has 56 members, top 20 plus 26 other members.
12. Srinivasan, N. 2011. *Microfinance India: State of Sector Report 2011*. New Delhi: SAGE Publications.
13. 2016. Microfinance Market Outlook: Developments, Forecasts, Trends. Zurich: responsAbility.
14. 2016, January. *Microfinance Institutions: Industry Outlook and Performance of Microfinance Institutions*. ICRA Limited, India.
15. RBI circular no. DBR.No.CID.BC.60/20.16.056/2014-15 dated January 15, 2015.
16. 2011, September. "Credit Reporting at the Base of the Pyramid- Key Issues and Success Factors". Access to Finance Forum. CGAP and IFC.
17. Misra, Alok. 2015. *Responsible Finance India Report: Client First: Tracking Social Performance Practices*. New Delhi: SAGE Publications.

SBLP: Time to Mainstream RF Agenda

6

Chapter

6.1 GRASSROOTS INNOVATION: THE ORIGIN OF SBLP

The microfinance movement in India started in the 1990s, and since then it has been dominated by two main approaches. The MFI model, originating from development-focused NGOs doing credit intermediation, has changed drastically over the last 20 years to be dominated by profit NBFC-MFIs. However, the initial design of JLG-based lending has remained intact—recently, the MFI model is seeing a shift toward individual loans, as higher loan sizes decrease the efficacy of the joint liability concept. As discussed in Chapters 2 and 3, the MFI model has also come under a very tight regulatory oversight in order to ensure that it remains client-centric. The other approach, SBLP, originated by NABARD as the apex agency for rural finance, is a homegrown model, building synergistic relationship between existing informal groups of the poor and banks. This synergistic relationship between SHGs and banks has been aptly summed up by the ex-chairman of NABARD, Y.S.P. Thorat[1].

> The essential genius of NABARD in the SHG–Bank program was to recognise this empirical observation that had been catalysed by NGOs and to create a formal interface of these informal arrangements of the poor with the banking system. This is the beginning of the story of SHG–Bank linkage program.

Since its launch in 1992, the SBLP has come a long way, with outreach of savings-linked SHGs touching 79 lakhs by March 31, 2016, of which 46.73 lakh SHGs have outstanding loans to the tune of ₹51 billion[2]. Considering an average of 13 members per SHG, the total outreach translates to nearly 100 million savings-linked clients, almost three times the coverage of NBFC-MFIs.

The designs of both the programs have key differences, owing to original thinking as well as regulation. MFIs do retailing of wholesale loans obtained from banks to their clients organized in JLGs. There is no concept of savings, as MFIs cannot accept deposits, the recent change allowing them to collect deposits as BC has not taken off, and credit remains the focus. SBLP, on the other hand, is built on savings-first-and-credit-later model. The savings and credit being from banks, the banking regulation covers SBLP. As against the preset loan products of MFIs, the SBLP model provides loan to the group, allowing it the flexibility to decide the loan amount, tenure, and interest rate among members. The SHG was conceived as a strong client-centric approach, and it was hoped that the democratic nature of groups would check control by any dominant individual. Realizing that banks will find it difficult to handhold groups and follow up, the SBLP model has a key role for the self-help promoting agency (SHPA), which acts as the bridge between the group and the bank. NABARD as a promoter of the concept has been providing refinance support to banks, revolving fund (RF) assistance, providing grants to SHPAs for group formation and linkage, and training bankers and other stakeholders. The design of the program in the beginning had the following key pillars: (a) savings first, (b) credit in proportion to savings, (c) flexibility to the group in inter-loaning, (d) no interest subsidy, and (e) establishing SHG lending as a business case for banks. These features make it highly client-centric, as the driver of growth is supposed to be community.

While these essential features broadly remain the same but for interest rate[3], the philosophy/objective has evolved over the years. The policy circular of NABARD to banks in 1992 launching the pilot project listed the following objectives:

1. To evolve supplementary credit strategies for meeting the credit needs of the poor.
2. To build trust and confidence between bankers and rural poor.
3. To encourage thrift and credit banking among sections hitherto excluded from the formal sector.

It shifted to economic empowerment of rural poor[4], and then in 1999, in another publication, 'Microfinance & NABARD: Role & Perspectives', the vision became broader by referring to empowerment of poor. The term 'economic empowerment' is substituted here by 'overall empowerment'. By 2008, it shifted in line with global discourse to financial inclusion and this year's publication says, "[T]he SBLP programme besides credit and savings provides wholesome social and economic justice to the excluded and deprived section of the society"[5]. Amidst such omnibus, overlapping, and differing objectives, the underlying common principle seems to be financial inclusion, with high focus on clients' needs over a preset design. As such, the responsibility of SBLP to be operating in accordance with tenets of responsible finance is much higher. Twenty-four years since its launch, SBLP has seen major changes which have changed the operational design substantially.

6.2 QUANTITY, SGSY, AND NOW NRLM/NULM: KEY CHANGES OVER TIME

Although these changes were touched on in the last year's report, it is necessary to mention them, as these have changed the SBLP drastically. The first change relates to the people's movement turning into a numbers game. In the initial years, the realization that organizing groups requires time and resources, as also stricter observance of operational norms, led to a slow growth—which was very much in line with program philosophy. After 12 years, with significant resource commitment by NABARD, the program had only ~1 million credit-linked SHGs. Between 2004 and 2010, the numbers grew to 4.8 million credit-linked SHGs. The target-based approach,

pushed by the government and NABARD, saw a frenetic rush to link more and more SHGs, ignoring quality. The numbers game went to the extent wherein token amount of credit was being provided to groups to count as credit-linked—various studies have commented on this. The quality deterioration of this phase is now showing up, with a lag in rise of NPAs and stagnant numbers. From a high of 4.8 million credit-linked SHGs in 2010, the numbers dipped to 4.1 million by March 31, 2014 and have now inched upward to 4.6 million by March 2016. It can be inferred that the numbers game played during 2004–10 has seriously dented the program, and experts proffer various reasons, ranging from disinterest of bankers to apathy among SHGs, to lack of quality SHPAs. However, it is a good sign that growth has halted, giving time for building quality. But, is this pause changing things for good the subject of analysis in this chapter?

The other critical change which has even more wider ramifications—both positive and negative—is the use of SHGs by other credit programs. It started with Swarnjayanti Gram Swarozgar Yojana (SGSY) of the Government of India in 1999, and since 2011, its rechristened avatar National Rural Livelihoods Mission (NRLM) termed Aajeevika in Hindi.

6.2.1 What Has Changed in SBLP under Various State Government Programs, SGSY, and Now NRLM

It needs to be emphasized that SBLP, with passage of time, has become an umbrella program, which subsumes diverse interventions at the state and national levels, using the central design of linking SHGs with banks. The Government of Tamil Nadu, using the SHG model, launched its Mahalir Thittam[6] program in 1989 in Dharmapuri district, with the assistance of International Fund for Agricultural Development (IFAD). Later it was extended to all districts, with funding from the state government. It is dubbed as a socio-economic empowerment program for women and is implemented by Tamilnadu Corporation for Development of Women Ltd. It adds on elements such as RF support, capacity-building, livelihoods, and formation of federations of SHGs. In erstwhile, undivided AP, the Society for Elimination of Rural Poverty (SERP) was established by the government to facilitate poverty reduction through social mobilization and improvement of livelihoods of rural poor in AP. Now with state reorganization, it is divided into AP SERP and Telangana SERP, for implementing Indira Kranthi Patham (IKP). Stree Shakthi[7], another SHG-based program, was started by the Government of Karnataka in 2000–01, and it is being implemented throughout the state to empower rural women and make them self-reliant. Kudambshree[8] was started by the Government of Kerala in 1998. The common theme running along these state government initiatives is using the SHGs for economic and social empowerment, but the critical changes introduced by these initiatives relate to interest rate subsidy, provision of initial capital support, adding on federations and livelihood programs, and also organizing groups along poverty status like below poverty line (BPL) groups. While these programs, often funded by donors such as the World Bank, United Nations Development Programme (UNDP), and IFAD, did create a strong SHG movement in the respective states, they also contributed to diluting the design features, keeping SHGs free from subsidy, providing credit in proportion to savings, and keeping it focused on financial inclusion. For example, the IKP has built in community-based livelihoods as part of its package, and the aims are diverse, ranging from developing new tools and equipment for reducing drudgery to women farmers, to managing RF for decentralized extension system, leading to multiple livelihood options models to be managed by communities on their own.

Parallel to the state government's initiative, the central government launched SGSY in 1999, which was an improvement over the earlier Integrated Rural Development Programme (IRDP). The core approach adopted in SGSY to mitigate the problems faced under IRDP of low repayment rates was the concept of back-end subsidy—release of subsidy at the end of a loan term. The scheme was implemented by District Rural Development Agencies (DRDAs)/Zilla Parishads through Panchayat Samitis, with active involvement of Panchayats. The SGSY experiment lasted a decade or so, and the groups formed through state machinery were found to be weak, often interested only in availing subsidy, compromising the sustainability of livelihoods. While the reasons from IRDP to SGSY remained more or less similar, demonstrating that formation of groups and providing them credit requires time and resources, interest rate subsidy is not the panacea, as SBLP started with the maxim 'timely credit

is more important than cost of credit'. Along with the fact that state machinery is ill suited to do this community work, the learnings have not been fully heeded. The result has not been to go back to the original design but add newer dimensions. Perhaps the state has found SHGs a useful grassroots-level structure to channel its development programs.

The poor performance of SGSY led to its reformulation as NRLM. Using the SHG route, NRLM has built in several important features, which enhance its appeal, and it is important to describe them, as NRLM now accounts for ~40% of SHGs reported under SBLP. The core values which guide all the activities under NRLM are (a) inclusion of the poorest and meaningful role to the poorest in all the processes, (b) transparency and accountability of all processes and institutions, (c) ownership and key role of the poor and their institutions in all stages—planning, implementation, and monitoring, and (d) community self-reliance and self-dependence.

NRLM implementation is in a mission mode by the Ministry of Rural Development and lists shifting from the present allocation-based strategy to a demand-driven strategy, continuous capacity-building, imparting requisite skills, and creating linkages with livelihoods opportunities for the poor as its core design. Realizing the deficiencies in earlier programs, NRLM also places priority monitoring against targets of poverty outcomes. The objective under the program is as follows:

> At least one woman member from each identified rural poor household, is to be brought under the self help group (SHG) network in a time bound manner. Special emphasis is particularly on vulnerable communities such as manual scavengers, victims of human trafficking, particularly vulnerable tribal groups (PVTGs), persons with disabilities (PwDs) and bonded labour[9].

NRLM has following pillars: (a) universal social mobilization, (b) participatory identification of poor, (c) provision of community funds, (d) financial inclusion, (e) livelihoods, and (f) dedicated support structure. On financial inclusion, NRLM does follow the SBLP model, with a slight tweak. It also envisages group formation to be followed by savings and inter-loaning and credit linkage with banks in 9 to 12 months after group formation. However, unlike the original SBLP approach, and in line with other state government initiatives, it has a provision for three types of funding support to member organizations. RF of ₹10,000–15,000 is available to SHGs after three months as a corpus. Grant of RF is contingent on SHGs following 'Panchasutra' (regular meetings, regular savings, regular inter-loaning, timely repayment, and up-to-date books of accounts). As of September 2016, 6.29 lakh SHGs have been provided the RF[10]. It also provides community investment fund (CIF) as seed capital to SHG federations at cluster level, to meet the credit needs of the members, through the SHGs/village

organizations. Total 4.32 lakh federations have been provided CIF. There is also a provision for vulnerability reduction fund (VRF) to SHG federations at village level to address vulnerabilities such as food security and health security; however, no data is available on funds disbursed under this.

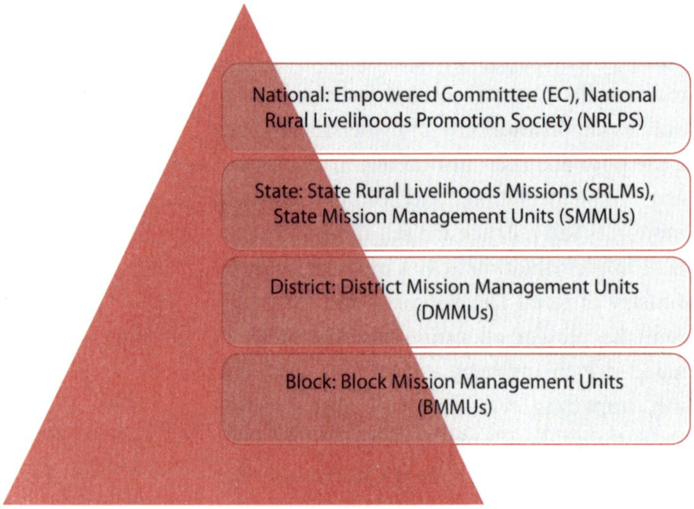

As livelihoods promotion, promotion of SHG federations and people's collectives, is a key strategy of NRLM, it has put in place dedicated resource teams at various levels (Figure 6.1). At the district level, the structure is led by a district mission manager (DMM), hired from open market on contract or on deputation from government, and includes functional specialists in social inclusion, financial inclusion, livelihoods, and capacity-building. The reach of NRLM to subdistrict level, consisting of a block mission manager (BMM) and three–five spearhead teams, is impressive and overcomes the issue of resource allocation under SBLP. SBLP depends on the initiative of bankers and SHPAs, while NRLM has put in place a dedicated support structure from national level to subdistrict level. The results are obvious, with NRLM reporting coverage of 493 districts and 31 lakh SHGs having been financed by banks. The confidence of banks on SHGs covered under NRLM is high, as they feel that with the support structure, the delinquency will be lower.

It is an ambitious program, which covers a host of activities woven around SHGs, and the range of activities is well depicted in a World Bank document[11] on the subject (Figure 6.2). The support structure being created is both at community level and at NRLM unit level. Interest subvention is provided to banks so that the cost of credit to SHGs remains at 7%. However, as in addition to this, state governments provide additional interest rate subvention, the interest rates on bank lending to SHGs remain in the range of 0–7%, completely distorting the market for other players like MFIs.

The grand design and intent is sought to be monitored through its web portal[12], which gives detailed reports. A perusal of the reports available on the website shows that like SBLP, the reporting is focused on operational and financial numbers, such as number of villages covered, SHGs formed, funding assistance, bank loan provided, and NPA position. Almost no information is available on aspects like financial literacy, livelihood promotion, work done on federations, and support provided for marketing. The mid-term review of NRLM[13]

Figure 6.1 NRLM Support Structure

Source: www.nrlm.gov.in, accessed on October 3, 2016.

National: Empowered Committee (EC), National Rural Livelihoods Promotion Society (NRLPS)

State: State Rural Livelihoods Missions (SRLMs), State Mission Management Units (SMMUs)

District: District Mission Management Units (DMMUs)

Block: Block Mission Management Units (BMMUs)

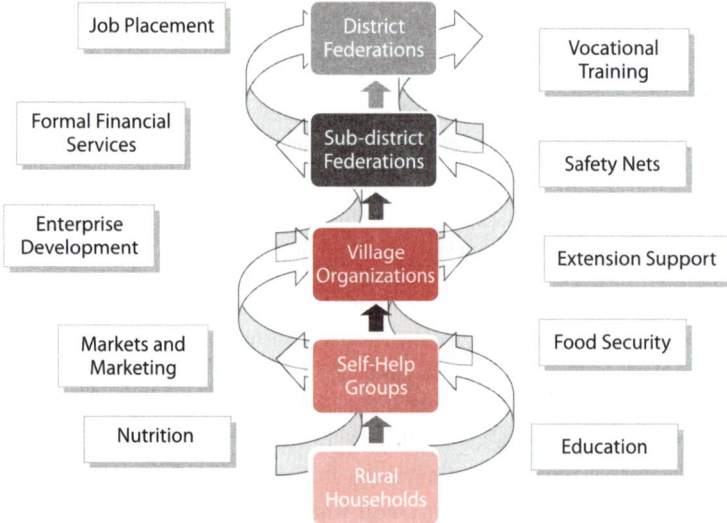

Figure 6.2 NRLM Design

Source: http://siteresources.worldbank.org/INDIAEXTN/Resources/india-NRLM-overview.pdf, accessed on November 3, 2016.

done last year also had negligible mention of livelihood services, market linkages, or innovations. The report primarily talks about the number of SHGs mobilized, trainings, savings, loans, RF, and capital support provided to SHGs and federations. The source of information on its progress is limited to these reports, as well as some press reports. It is hoped that having put in place an impressive structure, other needed services such as livelihood support and market linkages will be provided in the same "mission mode" approach and it will not be relegated to financial assistance.

Thus, the SBLP umbrella so to say at present is comprised of different national- and state-level programs, with sometimes overlapping roles. NABARD, in its annual report on SBLP, includes outreach under all these programs, and hence it has been used for analysis. During the last year, there have been constructive linkages built between NRLM and NABARD to have a synergistic relationship.

6.3 PROGRESS UNDER SBLP- GREEN SHOOTS?

Comprised of different types of interventions as discussed above, SBLP has emerged as a significant component of financial inclusion for the poor and the excluded. However, as described above, after reaching a peak of 4.8 million credit-linked SHGs in 2010, the program has struggled to meet that number. Even after five years of NRLM, the number of SHGs credit-linked by March 31, 2016, at 4.67 million, is below the 2010 level. However, the stagnation in savings-linked SHGs has been reversed, with the current outreach at 7.9 million touching the peak figures. Assuming 13 members per SHG, the savings outreach of SBLP is 102 million and credit outreach translates to 60 million clients (State-wise figures of savings and credit linkage in Annexure 6.1).

In the data presented in Table 6.1, figures for 2015 have changed from what was reported in the

Table 6.1 **SHG–Bank Linkage Programme—Key Highlights over the Years**

Particulars	2010	2011	2012	2013	2014	2015	2016
No. of SHGs with Outstanding Bank Loans	4,851,356	4,786,763	4,354,442	4,451,434	4,197,338	4,486,018	4,672,621
Of which in Southern Region	2,582,112	2,706,408	2,355,732	2,415,191	2,221,038	2,389,972	2,543,219
Share of Southern Region (%)	53	57	54	54	53	53	54
NPA % under SHG Loans	2.9	4.7	6.1	7.1	6.8	7.4	6.5
Share of SGSY/NRLM Groups (%)	26	27	28	27	23	41	47
Share of Women's Groups (%)	80	83	84	84	81	83	86
Loans Disbursed to SHGs during the Year (₹ Billion)	144.53	145.48	165.35	205.85	240.17	303	373
Average Loan Disbursed during the Year per Group (₹)	91,081	121,625	144,048	168,754	175,768	169,608	203,495
Total Bank Loan Outstanding to SHGs (₹ Billion)	280.38	312.21	363.41	393.75	429.27	515	571
Average Loan Outstanding per SHG (₹)	57,794	65,224	83,457	88,455	102,273	115,295	122,242
Incremental Groups with O/S Loans (Million)	0.63	(–)0.06	(–)0.43	0.1	(–0.25)	0.29	0.18
Incremental Loans O/S (₹ Billion)	45.9	33.53	57.22	30.35	35.52	86.18	55.74
No. of SHGs with Savings Accounts with Banks (Million)	6.95	7.46	7.96	7.32	7.42	7.69	7.90
Total Savings of SHGs with Banks (₹ Billion)	61.99	70.16	65.51	82.17	98.97	110.59	136.91
Average Savings of SHGs with Banks (₹)	8,915	9,402	8,230	11,229	13,321	14,661	17,324

Source: NABARD.

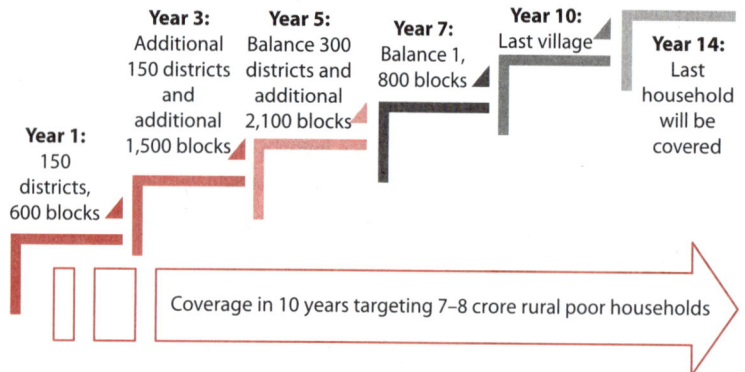

Figure 6.3 NRLM Coverage Plan

Source: www.nrlm.gov.in, accessed on October 3, 2016.

previous report, as NABARD has revised the provisional data for 2015. From the panel data, two key things emerge. First, the NRLM is gradually taking over the SBLP, accounting for 47% of the credit-linked SHGs and the way it is expanding in mission mode, soon it will account for almost full share. According to the NRLM website (Figure 6.3), the program was expected to reach 300 districts by the fifth year, that is, 2016 but it has already reached that figure. The second aspect relates to the ever-increasing loan size, with average loan outstanding per SHG touching ₹1,22,242. Quite a substantial part of this increase is attributable to NRLM. Finally, the reported figures of NPA for March 2016 have shown a decline of almost 100 basis points, which is a welcome step. The growth in numbers after the decline of 2014, arrest of NPAs, and increase in loan sizes has led NABARD to say, "Efforts of NABARD during the year had paid off and can be seen in the turnaround made. It is heartening to share that green shoots are visible in all aspects of the movement as compared to last year"[14]. However, a deeper analysis of the macro data presented in subsequent sections shows that critical issues continue to persist, despite the efforts of NABARD and NRLM. Moreover, the data reported under the program also have limitations, as often the data change with time and source, and often the data points reported differ across time periods, making comparison difficult. For example, the number of NRLM groups credit-linked as on March 31, 2016 is 2.19 million, while the NRLM portal puts the figure of NRLM norms-compliant SHGs at 1.78 million and total SHGs at 3.8 million.[15] On differing data points,

while NABARD reports NPA position as obtained from banks, NRLM reports the number of overdue accounts. The digitization pilot being undertaken by NABARD (discussed later) has shown that numbers can be misleading. Field practitioners opine that even nonexistent SHGs are there in the database, and SHGs with changed name are counted twice, as old records are not deleted. The point is that the SBLP data quality remains a grey area, and the full digitization of records, as and when completed, will show the real picture. However, considering the massive outreach and involvement of multiple agencies and governments, the sheer collection of data at national level in itself is a daunting task.

The SBLP (all channels included) data as well as the NRLM data are limited to operational and financial performance. The responsible finance indicators, such as outcomes at client level, product diversity, poverty outreach, and so on can be gathered through occasional studies, as well as field interactions with SHG members and other stakeholders. The analysis presented is based on these sources, with the focus being on client centricity.

6.3.1 Geographical Outreach—Remains Highly Skewed

Despite changes in operational metrics, and new initiatives, one thing which has remained static is the regional skew in SBLP outreach. Its relationship with responsible finance lies in the fact that financial inclusion outreach programs such as SBLP including NRLM should focus on regions with higher exclusion. A skewed outreach toward states/regions with higher human development index (HDI) rankings needs to be balanced, if not reversed, in favor of less developed states. Although the skew has reduced since 2001, when southern region accounted for 70% share, it has remained stagnant at around 55% for the last 10 years (Table 6.2). The strategic approach adopted by NABARD in mid-2000 for the expansion of SBLP in 13 priority states has also not yielded results beyond a point. NRLM's increasing share of credit-linked SHGs has also not helped, and significantly, it is in fifth year of operation.

While it is appreciated that this is a legacy issue, and can take time to address, it would be comforting if the current activity in terms of group formation, savings, and credit linkage would be more

Table 6.2 Regional Share in Number of SHGs Credit-linked (2010–16)

Region/Year	2010	2011	2012	2013	2014	2015	2016
Northern	3.10	3.10	4.90	4.80	4.40	3.94	3.31
Northeastern	2.80	3.10	3.70	3.20	3	2.75	3.23
Eastern	21.20	23.10	22.60	22.90	23.30	23.84	24.20
Central	10.30	7.50	8.10	8.10	10	9.77	9.31
Western	9.40	6.60	6.60	6.60	6.40	6.05	5.52
Southern	53.20	56.50	54.10	54.30	52.90	53.64	54.43

Source: NABARD.

Table 6.3 Regional Share in SHGs Provided Credit during 2015–16

Northern	2.08
Northeastern	1.42
Eastern	22.52
Central	4.60
Western	6.14
Southern	63.24

Source: NABARD.

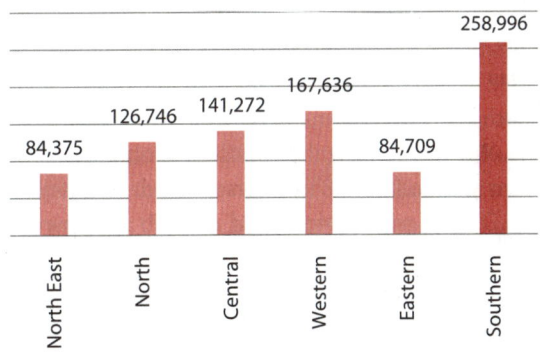

Figure 6.4 Average Loan Size to SHGs during 2015–16 (in ₹)

Source: NABARD.

geared toward states with less penetration. However, the analysis of the disbursement pattern to SHGs shows that the skew is getting worse (Table 6.3). Total 64% of SHGs which received bank credit during the last year are from southern region. If the credit disbursement continues in this pattern, then it will further increase the regional imbalance.

The situation seems to be more imbalanced, when seen with share in loan portfolio outstanding with SHGs. While the southern region accounts for ~55% share in number of SHGs credit linked, its share in total loan outstanding is much higher, at 75%. The eastern region, which accounts for ~25% of credit-linked SHGs, in comparison, has only 12% share of outstanding loans. This further aggravates the skew as the southern region has higher number of SHGs, plus the quantum of loans being provided there is much larger than in other parts of the country. What it says is that 75% of bank credit under SBLP has gone to 7 southern states and other 27 states receive only 25% of bank credit.

From a responsible finance angle, it has resulted in a situation, where in some parts of the country, the SHG members receive adequate credit, while in most other states, there is severe underfinancing. Figure 6.4 shows that the difference in average loan size disbursed to SHGs in southern states is higher

than 200% over eastern and northeastern states. The second-highest region is western, where too the average loan size to SHGs during 2015–16 was 60% of that in southern states.

Chapter 5 showed that in the case of MFIs, regional imbalance has been substituted by state- and district-level concentration. Here, in the case of SBLP, concentration exists at both regional and state levels. District-level data in the case of SBLP are not publicly available. The imbalanced growth of SBLP exhibits both concentrations, with top 10 states accounting for 90% share of outstanding loans (Table 6.4).

However, there is a silver lining that traditionally less activity states like Assam and Bihar figure in the list of top-10 states. The other notable positive feature is that in Bihar, 96% of SHGs with savings accounts have also been credit linked. This being the highest for the country, even surpassing the credit linkage rate in AP and Telangana, makes it quite remarkable.

From both public policy perspective and responsible finance angle, it will be worthwhile for NABARD and NRLM to commission a study on the reasons for this lopsided growth. Interaction with industry

Table 6.4 Top 10 States with SHGs Savings and Credit Linked

States	Savings-linked SHGs (Lakhs)	Savings (₹ Billion)	SHGs with Loan O/S (Lakhs)	Loan O/S (₹ Billion)	% of SHGs Credit Linked
Karnataka	9.62	14.42	6.32	74.74	65.70
Andhra Pradesh	9.01	41.45	8.02	172.20	89.01
Tamil Nadu	8.52	9.20	4.32	63.59	50.70
West Bengal	8.31	15.35	5.84	37.79	70.28
Maharashtra	7.89	8.57	2.08	16.97	26.36
Telangana	5.42	14.91	4.92	98.63	90.77
Odisha	4.86	4.85	2.13	18.83	43.83
Uttar Pradesh	3.63	3.82	2.17	15.25	59.78
Assam	3.33	1.11	1.07	6.60	32.13
Bihar	2.78	3.60	2.67	10.02	96.04
Total Top 10	63.37	117.28	39.54	514.62	62.40
Other 24 States	**15.66**	**19.63**	**7.18**	**56.57**	**45.85**
Total	79.03	136.91	46.72	571.19	59.12

Source: NABARD.
Note: Bold figures signify the low shares of other states.

experts brought out a common point for this, with almost everybody saying that the SBLP needs strong promotional support to SHPAs, and the growth of SHGs is strongly related to this factor. In all the southern states, the state governments have invested heavily in building SHG movement with initial donor support, and the current outreach figures mirror that. NABARD's support for SHPAs has been there since the start of the program, and the range of SHPAs included are diverse: from NGOs, to banks, to individual rural volunteers. However, the quantum of support has always been a controversial topic, with SHPAs considering it as too small, and NABARD arguing that the support is to be seen as incremental to SHPAs existing work. The analysis of assistance provided by NABARD since start shows that by March 31, 2016, it had sanctioned ₹535 crore for formation and credit linkage of about 1 million SHGs. As against this, the amount disbursed is mere ₹170 crore.

The regional spread of NABARD's promotional assistance to SHPAs shows that NABARD has been conscious of providing larger share to states other than southern states, who received only 7% of assistance, and largest chunk went to eastern and western regions (Figure 6.5). However, the promotional assistance has no correlation with the growth of SBLP, and that is perhaps accounted by two factors. First, the amount is small compared to the program size (only 7.6 lakh SHGs promoted with NABARD assistance as against 79 lakh SHGs in the country).

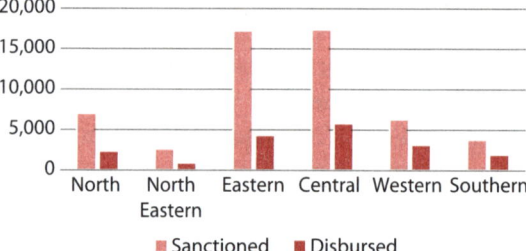

Figure 6.5 Regionwise Promotional Assistance to SHPAs by NABARD (Cumulative, ₹ Lakhs)

Source: NABARD.

Second, the quantum of assistance and focus on credit linkage have dampened the actual release, as against the sanctions granted. A recent circular of NABARD[16] pegs the assistance to NGOs per SHG at ₹5,000, and only 30% of the sanctioned amount is provided before credit linkage. The balance 70% is conditional on achievement of two credit cycles and completion of audit. The average amount provided to SHPAs per SHG formation and credit linkage works out to ₹2,000. C.S. Reddy, CEO Mahila Abhivruddhi Society, opined that the assistance should be front heavy, as against the end heavy pattern of now, the reason being that the SHPAs spend more time and resources in group formation and in encouraging thrift than in credit linkage. Moreover, the credit linkage depends on bankers, and SHPAs have no control on their decisions. As against this, the state governments with strong SHG movement have provided much higher support, and that seems to be a reason for this regional imbalance. However, the thin presence of quality SHPAs in many states is also an important factor, and considering this, NABARD has expanded the ambit of eligible agencies/people to act as SHPA. This is not to argue for state government/donor support, as that has also to be tested with cost benefit analysis, but to show that it has been a factor in regional skew.

6.3.2 Appropriate Products: Adequacy of Credit, Savings Linkage, and Products

The SBLP has a distinct advantage over MFIs, as it can provide savings service to groups and that is the main pillar of the program. From responsible finance perspective, there are two aspects which need analysis. It is important to see if clients of SBLP are getting credit in proportion to savings, as well as the adequacy of credit. The other point is credit type to see if the program has been able to diversify product suite.

The program design requires groups to save with banks, as also use it for inter-loaning. According to NABARD, around one-third of the savings of SHGs is with banks, and the rest is used for internal lending. Although the assumption is questionable, as there are no robust studies to provide evidence, if taken true, it implies that SBLP members have savings of ₹41,000 crore which is almost 70% of outstanding credit. A recent study by Mahila Abhivruddhi Society (MAS) for NABARD[17] found that the amount of members' savings with the SHGs ranges between ₹5,000 and ₹2,00,000, with an average of ₹51,680. As banks consider the amount available with them for providing credit, the ratio of savings with banks to credit provided is presented in Table 6.5.

The figures show that on the yardstick of savings to credit norm of 1:4 ratio, SBLP is doing well. Although the outstanding loan amount for all

credit-linked SHGs has remained around four–five times of savings, if ~40% of SHGs not having loans are taken out, then the savings to credit ratio goes much beyond the prescribed norm. This shows that while 40% SHGs have no loans, others have loans much in excess of four times of group savings. Furthermore, there are issues with the aggregate data, as the link between savings and credit varies across states, and agencies like cooperative banks being the most conservative—though they should have been at the forefront, considering their grassroots operations. Another factor that needs to be considered for revitalizing the movement is to harness the full power of SHG savings. If the entire savings of SHGs is considered, including the amount with the groups, then the ratio of credit to savings drops to 140%. It is imperative that the savings of SHGs should be made to work for them. A higher proportion of SHG savings with banks will lead to higher credit flow and possibly can address the issue of lower credit flow. Field practices show that SHGs are not comfortable parking higher share of their savings with banks, as often the savings are not allowed to be withdrawn freely until the loan is completed. If this issue can be tackled, then it will lead to much higher savings with banks. During the last two years, the spread of PMJDY has led to a paradoxical situation for SHGs, with members having individual savings account, preferring to save individually to group account. It remains to be seen as to how the program will tackle this emerging scenario, as this along with the requirement of individual credit reporting can erode group dynamics.

The adequacy of credit provided, as mentioned above, has an important bearing on SBLP. Groups getting lower than needed credit develop a sense of disillusionment and turn to other lenders. It makes little sense for groups to be underfinanced, as substantial time is spent on group formation and

Table 6.5 Savings and Loans of SHGs (2009–16)

	2009	2011	2012	2013	2014	2015	2016
No. of SHGs with Savings Accounts with Banks	6,950,000	7,460,000	7,960,000	7,320,000	7,420,000	7,697,000	7,903,002
No. of SHGs with Outstanding Bank Loans	4,851,356	4,786,763	4,354,442	4,451,434	4,197,338	4,468,180	4,672,621
Percentage of SHGs not Credit Linked	30.20	35.80	45.30	39.19	43.40	41.80	40.87
Amount of SHG Savings with Banks (₹ Billion)	61.99	70.16	65.51	82.17	98.97	110.59	136.91
Amount of Loan O/S against SHGs (₹ Billion)	280.38	312.21	363.41	393.75	429.27	515.45	571.19
Ratio of Credit to Savings (%)	452	445	555	479	434	466	417.2

Source: NABARD.

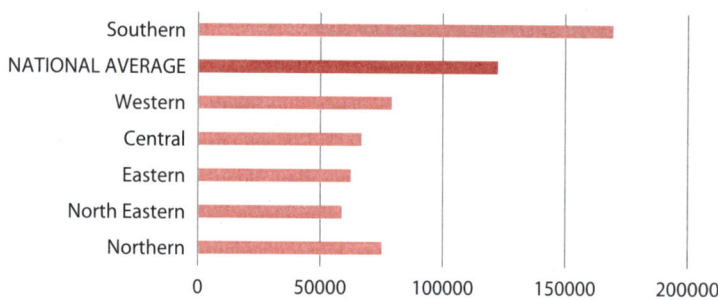

Figure 6.6 Average Loan Outstanding per SHG as on March 31, 2016 (₹)
Source: NABARD.

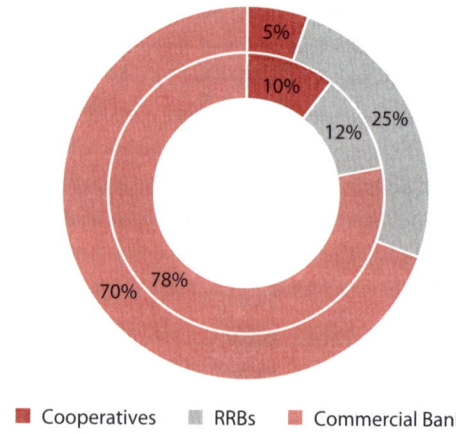

■ Cooperatives   ■ RRBs   ■ Commercial Banks

Figure 6.7 Share of Agencies in Savings and Loan Amount (March 2016) (Inner Pie Savings, Outer Loans)
Source: NABARD.

handholding till credit linkage. The analysis of loan outstanding amount per SHG shows that though the all-India average has jumped to ₹122,242, there are regional and institutional differences. Figure 6.6 shows that other than the southern region, the average loan outstanding per group is roughly half of national average. Assuming 13 members per SHG, the amount of loan outstanding across all regions, except southern, is approximately ₹5,000. Considering the loan sizes of other microlenders, including MFIs, this is highly inadequate and leads to clients seeking other sources of financing. A responsible finance provider needs to ensure that the needs of the clients are fully met from one source, avoiding the need to borrow from multiple sources. Inadequate finance is not only troublesome for the client but also uneconomical for the lender, as lower loan size raises the operational cost.

Agency-wise, while for commercial banks, average loan outstanding per SHG is higher than the national average, and for regional rural banks, slightly lower than average, cooperative banks are an outlier, with their average loan outstanding to SHGs at 52% of national average. Along with bringing group savings of members to bank accounts, deepening the outreach through cooperative banks needs to be addressed on priority to improve the credit availability to the groups. The weakness of cooperatives is further accentuated by the fact that while they account for 10% of SHGs savings, their share in loan outstanding is mere 5% (Figure 6.7). It is heartening that RRBs are doing the best among agencies in terms of savings to loan ratio.

On the product side, there has not been any innovation, and the practice of giving a standard loan to the group with a tenure of one–two years continues. The innovation part is left to the groups, as the SBLP design allows the flexibility to the group to

allocate amount and decide tenure and rate of interest among members. This is indeed an ideal concept, which is akin to wholesale lending to a community organization, and if it works well, then it should be the ideal for microfinance. Interaction with bankers and practitioners reveals that the dominant practice is to divide the amount equally, so rates of interest are same across members and the loan purpose and tenure too. C.S. Reddy, CEO of MAS, who has been working with SHGs extensively for two decades, agreed with this and said, "loan eligibility has become loan entitlement"[18] and this has eroded the flexibility given by the program. Training of the groups to build in the required flexibility according to member need and loan utilization purpose has been missing and requires strong focus.

However, the nature of loan given by banks has changed over the years, from a primarily term loan to a cash credit facility. The cash credit facility was introduced to give flexibility to the group in withdrawing the money whenever needed, but what has happened is that groups tend to withdraw the entire amount in one go, rendering it similar to term loan. Furthermore, in any areas, banks do not allow the group to withdraw the entire amount in one go, forcing the groups to withdraw in three to four installments—the reason being, it shows up as the account being operated regularly! The purpose and intent behind this was great, but in absence of proper borrower education, it has only ended up creating issues for the groups. Banks are more comfortable with cash credit account as NPA regulations for cash credit accounts provide them more leeway over term loan accounts[19].

Both of the above aspects, that is, flexibility in loans depending on members needs and purpose, as well as efficient operation of cash credit facility, require intensive training and handholding, to achieve their full potential of being client-centric.

After a long time, there has been some progress in piloting microinsurance and pension products, which are equally important services required by the poor. It was reported last year that NABARD, in association with Religare Health Insurance Pvt Limited, introduced an affordable and customized micro-insurance pilot scheme covering 1,000 SHG members and their families in Alwar District of Rajasthan and 2000 SHG members and their spouses in Ramgarh. During the last year, NABARD sanctioned a pilot project on micropension to International Network of Alternative Financial Institutions (INAFI). The project is being implemented in the tribal district of Dungarpur in Rajasthan. It has various components, including financial education of SHG members, workshops for NGOs, and technical workshops for finalizing the pension product. It targets coverage of 1,000 SHG members through micropension products. These are important initiatives, as the poor often face health issues, leading to income and livelihood shock as well as uncertain old age in absence of social protection. Coming after nearly 25 years, these efforts need to be scaled up. The PMJDY umbrella schemes do provide insurance and pension products at nominal cost, and it will be worthwhile to explore possibility of linking SHGs with these schemes in collaboration with the Government of India. It will require tweaking of the schemes, as at present these are offered to individuals and not to groups.

6.3.3 Is the Pricing Responsible?

Considering the fact that banks lend to SHGs directly, the rate of interest under SBLP has implied that the rates (ranging from 10–12%) are much lower than what is charged by other microlenders. The implementation of interest subvention scheme by various state governments as well as under NRLM has implied that actual rates range from 0–7% across states. As against this, other micro-lenders rates range from 20–26%. Providing loans at subsidized rates has been a key policy objective in many countries, despite the evidence that lower than viable rates lead to higher exclusion, as lending institutions shy away from lending, as well as unviability of lending

institutions. Under SBLP, these aspects have been covered, as governments provide the gap between actual lending rate and the rate at which loans are provided to the SHGs by way of interest subvention. Thus, the banks viability is not compromised and there is no disincentive to lend. But at the same time, this introduces a market distortion impact. In the same market and same client segment, there is a marked difference in rate of interest between SBLP and other players. Borrowers who cannot obtain loans under SBLP, or whose needs are not fully met, have to borrow from other players at much higher lending rates. This creates a moral hazard, as one set of borrowers have preferential rates, and often leads to client distress. This is a very complex issue, but if the intention of public policy is to lower the cost of borrowings, it should cover all borrowers from a similar segment.

The other part of SBLP pricing is that the actual cost incurred by the group is much higher than the nominal rate charged by the bank. The cost goes up on account of delays in sanctioning loans, paper work, opportunity cost of time lost in pursuing loans, and in some cases, graft. Various studies in the past have commented on this. NCAER[20], in its study (2011) took sample of borrowers of bank, SBLP and MFIs, and computed actual cost to the client. The report found that considering costs other than the interest rate, clients had to pay maximum for bank loans, followed by SBLP and MFI. For a ₹1,000 loan, client had to bear an additional cost of ₹30 in the case of direct loan from banks, ₹24 if the loan was availed as SHG member and ₹13 in the case of loan from MFIs. This additional cost component included wage loss due to time spent in getting the loan, travel cost, document charges and bribes.

This year, the study conducted by MAS (referred to above) across seven states covering 432 SHGs provides similar conclusion. The study reports that the time taken for SHGs for obtaining credit (seen as time between submission of loan application and disbursement) varies between 1 and 52 weeks, with an average of 4.37 weeks. Nearly one half of the SHG got credit linkage within a week, 28% of SHG got linkage between 3 and 4 weeks, nearly one-fifth of SHGs got linkage between 1 and 2 months and small number of SHGs got linkage between 2 and 6 months. This contrasts starkly with the less than a week, and in many cases, 2 days turnaround time, in the case of MFIs. The time spent in pursuing bank

Table 6.6 Amount Spent to Get the Current Loan Under SHGBLP (% of SHGs)

S. No.	Amount in ₹	3–6 Years (N = 194)	6–9 Years (N = 85)	9–12 Years (N = 62)	12–15 Years (N = 53)	15+ Years (N = 38)	Total (N = 432)
1	< 500	52.1	49.4	41.9	26.4	31.6	45.1
2	500–1,000	20.6	24.7	32.3	34.0	18.4	24.5
3	1,001–1,500	9.8	10.6	8.1	13.2	31.6	12.0
4	1,501–2,000	7.2	7.1	9.7	9.4	5.3	7.6
5	> 2,000	10.3	8.2	8.1	17.0	13.2	10.6
	Total	100	100	100	100	100	100

Source: MAS Study, 2016.

loan by SHGs has a cost element and includes indirect costs such as food expenses, travel, stationary, photographs, documentation fee, service fee paid to federations, bookkeeper charges, and so on. The study reports that 10% of SHGs spent >₹2000 in securing a bank loan and the average amount for a sample of 432 SHGs is ₹1,031 per SHG (Table 6.6).

The report finds that the amount spent to get a bank loan depends on the state/area, distance to the bank, loan size, SHG age, bank, and SHPA. Thus, the policy objective of providing low-cost credit to SBLP clients is not only distorting the market for other similar clients, but also not fully achieving its goal. The key lies in improving processes through the value chain, starting from quality of SHGs to building capacity of SHPAs and sensitizing the banks on the need to expedite the credit appraisal.

6.3.4 Prevention of Over-Indebtedness: What Does Higher NPA Level Show?

Normally, rise in nonperforming loans in microfinance is associated with excess debt, affecting the repayment capacity of the borrower. However, SBLP performance shows a paradoxical situation, with low per member credit but still rising overdues. As indicated previously, the national average loan outstanding per SHG is ₹1,22,242, and most of the states have a much lower figure than the average outstanding. Moreover, the savings linkage under SBLP also provides it with cushion, as the credit given is in proportion to the savings.

The NPA levels under SBLP matched that of MFIs, but started moving upwards since early 2000, touching a high of 7.4% as of March 31, 2015. Though the slight increase in NPA was reported way back in 2002, it is worrisome that over time it has kept inching upwards to reach 7.4% by March 2015. The NPAs registered a 1% decline as of March 31, 2016 but

continue to be a cause of concern as this is despite relaxed NPA norms under cash credit account. The problem for clients is getting compounded as rising NPAs make banks more conservative in sanctioning loans, further aggravating the situation.

The NPA position is similar across agencies (cooperatives/regional rural banks/commercial banks) but has regional/state dimensions. An analysis of states with high NPAs along with states with high loan outstanding per SHG shows that there is no correlation between size of credit and NPA. (Tables 6.7 and 6.8). It shows that states with highest NPA under SBLP have much smaller average loan outstanding, while states with highest average loan outstanding have much lower NPAs. Andhra Pradesh and Telangana have average loan outstanding in excess of ₹200,000 and are highly saturated states in terms of SBLP penetration, but still their NPAs are around 3%. What is worrying is that 20 States have now NPA in double digits. However, the data clearly suggests that the reason lies somewhere else, other than loan size.

Table 6.7 Top 10 States with NPA

State	NPA	Average Loan O/S (₹)
Tripura	34.07%	40,035
Meghalaya	28.31%	74,189
Rajasthan	25.08%	66,440
Orissa	24.93%	88,060
Manipur	24.56%	45,314
Chandigarh	24.02%	93,881
New Delhi	21.52%	89,512
Puducherry	20.78%	120,333
Uttarakhand	20.18%	56,895
Uttar Pradesh	20.11%	70,256

Source: NABARD.

Table 6.8 NPA in States with Highest Loan O/S

State	NPA	Average Loan O/S (₹)
Andhra Pradesh	3.23	214,663
Telangana	2.6	200,087
Goa	4.04	170,891
Tamil Nadu	10.86	146,895
Mizoram	5.86	137,453

Source: NABARD.

Table 6.9 Repayment Rate from SHGs to Bank (% of SHGs)

S. No.	RR (in %)	AP	ASM	KNT	MHR	ODS	UP	Total
1	< 75	9.7	8.3	2.8	9.7	34.7	33.3	16.4
2	76–99	29.2	26.4	5.6	0.0	27.8	22.2	18.5
3	100	61.1	65.3	91.7	90.3	37.5	44.4	65.0
	Total	100.0	100.0	100.0	100.0	100.0	100.0	100.0

Source: MAS study of 432 SHGs, 2016.

NRLM in its fifth year of operation also shows similar position with respect to overdues, and this is despite the extensive support structure put in place under NRLM. The data reported shows that, as of September 2016[21], 33% of SHG loan accounts were overdue, and the overdue amount constituted 16% of loans outstanding. This compounds the issue, as despite the support structure, RF assistance, and interest rate subvention, the recovery position remains poor (state-wise details of NPA in Annexure 6.2).

As mentioned in last year's report, bankers feel that it is not possible for them to do follow up and this should be the responsibility of SHPAs, while SHPAs tend to dilute their role after credit linkage. The 2016 MAS study also supports this finding, by reporting that the handholding support to SHGs from the SHPAs reduces substantially once the donor support/promotional assistance ends, leaving the groups unable to own, manage, and control their institutions. Further, roping in of diverse SHPAs, ranging from NGOs and individual volunteers to government agencies, without much coordination on having a basic understanding on quality aspects, is leading to formation of groups with an eye on loans and subsidies. C.S. Reddy, CEO, MAS, opined that there is a big gap between the huge outreach of the program, compared with availability of quality SHPAs, and it is time to incubate resource SHPAs or strengthen existing SHPAs and ensure that the handholding support continues beyond a limited time period.

The seven state study done by MAS also throws pointers on the repayment problem (Table 6.9). The states covered in the study shows extreme variance in NPA levels. While Andhra Pradesh, Maharashtra, and Karnataka have very low NPAs, the other three states, namely, Odisha, Uttar Pradesh, and Assam have high NPAs. The findings of the study validate the position reported by NABARD,

except in Andhra Pradesh, where, surprisingly, 10% SHGs have less than 75% repayment rate.

In Odisha and Uttar Pradesh, one third of SHGs have less than 75% repayment rate. A deeper analysis of the profile of SHGs and reported repayment rate throws up interesting insights. The repayment rate is positively correlated with SHG vintage (repayment rate is high in 12–15 year SHGs) as also with SHGs having repeat linkages (92%) rather than fresh linkages (84%). However, the report also finds that SHGs having loans with multiple agencies have a higher repayment rate, which begs the question on genuineness of repayment—Is it due to rotation of funds, borrowing from one to repay another? No clear pointers on this have been captured in the study report.

Coming to the causes of nonrepayment of loans, the study analyzed both willful and nonwillful reasons and, strikingly, the findings show that the default is mainly associated with health and livelihood issues (Figure 6.8; as the SHGs gave multiple reasons, total is not 100%). However, there are state-specific reasons for default. In the three states with higher delinquency, political promises of waiver is the major reason in AP (12 out of 16 SHGs); less availability of work (7 out of 12 SHGs) and ill-health

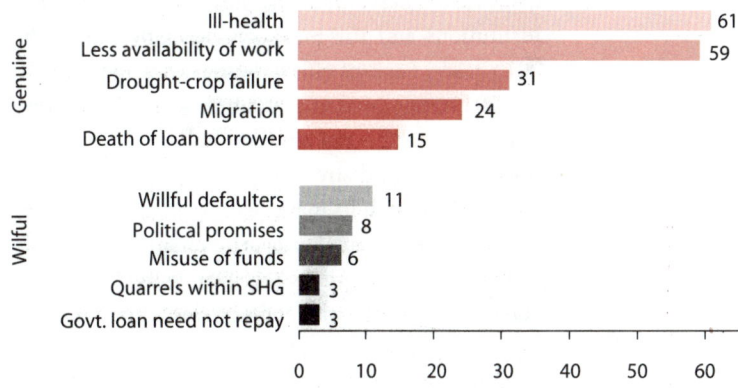

Figure 6.8 Reasons for Defaulting (% of SHGs)

Source: See Note 16.

(5 out of 12 SHGs) in Assam; less availability of work (18 out of 28 SHGs), crop failure (10 out of 28 SHGs), and willful default (11 out of 28 SHGs) in Odisha; and ill-health (82%) and less availability of work (48%) in UP. Thus, there are multiple state-specific reasons for default and there is no common pattern, other than the clear pointer that nonwillful default is the dominant reason. The report does not go into analyzing the efficacy of self-help in defaulting groups in cases such as migration of few group members or ill health.

The meta-data shows that loan size has no relation with NPAs and the MAS study shows that the primary causes of nonrepayment of loans relate to ill health and livelihood challenges like drought. The study findings, seen with near 100% repayment rate of similar client segment in same area but borrowing from different sources like MFIs, is a topic requiring further empirical study. This has important connotations for responsible microfinance, and policymakers need to analyze this dichotomy.

6.3.5 Grievance Redressal: Needs to be Accorded Top Priority

Having an effective grievance redressal channel is an important pillar of responsible finance. This enables clients to register their issues for remedial action, and its importance gets enhanced due to the fact that often the policies and field practices differ. Effective grievance redressal, besides enabling clients to voice their issues, also acts a feedback mechanism for the institution. Based on the feedback, institutions can do design or policy corrections to match the expectations of clients. In Chapters 2 and 3, the increasing importance attached to grievance redressal framework in the MFI model was discussed. These initiatives have come from both institutions and the industry association after the 2010 crisis. Lack of effective grievance redressal in pre-2010 period led to a situation where MFIs were unable to see the gap between policy and practice, leading to client distress.

The SBLP, with its massive outreach, continues to depend on the formal grievance channel applicable to banks, which implies registering the issue with banks, and in the case of nonresolution, upscaling the complaint to the banking ombudsman appointed by the RBI. It has severe limitations. First, it only covers the banking transaction part related to savings and credit, while group dynamics under SBLP and the role of SHPA entail so many other issues, such as poor support provided by SHPA or domination of the group. Second, in a scenario when the typical microfinance client is not comfortable in transacting directly with banks, it is difficult to assume that he/she will register a complaint with the bank. The perennial need for credit, coupled with scarcity of it, makes it even worse; clients fear that by making complaints, they will only worsen the situation. Globally, for such clients, it is necessary to have a toll-free number to register their problems, and in order to overcome the hesitation, it is necessary that complaints go to a place where their identity will be protected and yet remedial action will be taken. At present, the common grievances of SHGs relating to issue of subsidy and reported cases of financial cuts in releasing them, delays in sanctioning loans, or underfinancing relate to the bank, while lack of adequate support and guidance relate to SHPAs. The growing NPAs under the program can also have an indirect link to absence of grievance redressal; clients unable to register a complaint due to genuine reasons might drop out of the program. A regionwise toll-free number covering the functioning of both banks and SHPAs needs to be put in place. In fact, it can be integrated with the digitization work currently underway. Further, turnaround time for complaint resolution, escalation matrix, and education of clients on using the channel also needs to be put in place. With NRLM broadening the ambit of the program to include formation of higher-level structures, livelihoods, and collectives, the need for a robust grievance redressal channel has become much more pressing. This issue has been repeatedly mentioned in previous editions of this report, but has not received the attention.

6.4 DIGITIZATION OF SHG RECORDS: HUGE IMPLICATIONS FOR RESPONSIBLE FINANCE

The previous sections outlined various issues with the SBLP, especially data quality and timeliness. In the absence of a credible and automated database, the present system is dependent on annual data published by NABARD, and the local level real time financial data availability is available with the bank branch concerned. Aspects of group dynamics, such as loans at member level, internal savings, and so on, are known only to the group, or to the SHPA.

The availability of data in microsilos, and questions on validity not only constrain the macro analysis, but also make the banks more cautious. It seems all this is going to change with the digitization work initiated by NABARD during 2014–15. This much-needed initiative by NABARD is commendable, and has also been hastened by the regulatory guidelines requiring submission of SHG data to credit bureaus—which in the absence of digitization is not possible, as at present banks do not have individual member level information. The Aditya Puri Committee[22] (2014), set up by the RBI to look into credit information data reporting, in its report suggested that it is critical that lenders (banks) should consider prior borrowings from SBLP and MFIs, and hence it is needed that banks may capture and provide credit related information of individual borrowers within the SHG to the credit bureaus. This has been followed by an RBI policy circular this year[23] mapping out a phase-wise approach for coverage of SHG member data. Realizing the challenges, a phased approach has been adopted, but, importantly, the information requirements include both credit and noncredit information. In the current phase of one year, it mandates that the collection and reporting of credit information with respect to SHG members will be restricted to the members of those SHGs that take bank loans exceeding ₹1,00,000. However, noncredit information has to be collected for all SHGs. The digitization process will enable this information to be available on real time. These initiatives are set to positively influence the architecture of responsible finance for microfinance. At present, a program with 7.9 million SHGs translating to ~100 million clients is outside the purview of credit bureaus, and that erodes the efficacy of credit appraisal of other players like MFIs. With significant

borrower overlap, the present situation has the distinct potential to lead to overindebtedness. Hopefully, all this is going to change with digitization, the RBI guidelines, and Aadhaar-based KYC.

The process of digitization has been covered in detail in last year's report[24]. It started with a pilot in two districts (Ramgarh in Jharkhand and Dhule in Maharashtra), which has since been completed. The project covers mapping of the existing SHGs in the district (bank-wise and branch-wise), covering all SHGs including SGSY/NRLM-promoted SHGs. In the pilot, SHPAs were trained on collecting SHG-wise/member-wise data. Extensive data points were captured and based on that financial statements can be generated automatically, besides giving an insight into intragroup dynamics. Critically, to instill confidence of banks in SHG quality, the system has been designed so that it can produce SHG grading based on NABARD–SHG grading tool. In the pilot, the tablet-based software developed by Leaps & Bounds was used, but the project envisages integrating it with an android-based phone application. The validated data (after data capture it is signed off by the group) is then uploaded through a customized software in a central server. Banks, based on their location, will be given access to information on SHGs in their area. NABARD has launched a web portal[25] for hosting the SHG data under the digitization project. The process flow is given in Figure 6.9. The model allows for offline data entry, which is a useful feature, considering the connectivity issues in rural areas.

Post successful completion of the pilot, and the improvement seen in SHG ecosystem in these pilot districts (Box 6.1), NABARD has extended the pilot in phase to 22 districts in 20 states. As the pilot covers even North Eastern states and hills, the second

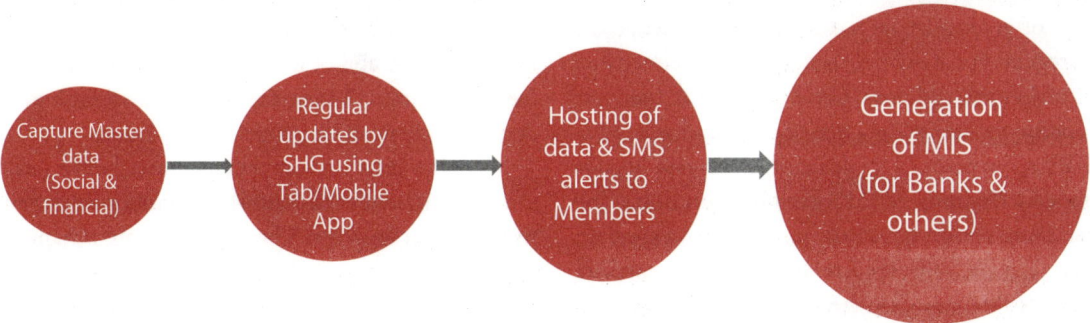

Figure 6.9 Digitization Process Flow
Source: MCID, NABARD.

Box 6.1 Effect of Digitization in Ramgarh and Dhule

Number of credit-linked SHGs jumped from 340 to 1006 in Ramgarh from pre-digitization to post-digitization.

Similar pattern seen in Dhule with credit-linked SHGs going up from 1424 to 2254.

The increase in linked SHGs comprises both first time linkages and repeat linkages.

Banks have increasingly used the grading reports generated by the system for lending decisions.

Availability of credit and noncredit information has fostered greater understanding about SHGs among bankers.

Real time SMS alerts of transactions has increased trust of clients.

Source: Status of Microfinance in India 2015–16, NABARD.

phase implementation will provide critical indicators on the level of effort, costing and feasibility. Based on the feedback of second phase digitization, NABARD plans to cover all districts in the third phase. At present, the cost of digitization is being borne by NABARD, and in the last year's report the cost implications and training of SHPAs to undertake the work were highlighted as possible roadblocks. However, NABARD Chairman opined that NABARD is willing to make the initial investment, and the hope is that seeing the utility of the process, users like banks will willingly pay for it. The expected cost per district is likely to come down to roughly ₹1 crore based on economies of scale[26].

While the benefits of digitization are immense, ranging from standardized records at group level, real time data availability to banks, uploading of member-level data to credit bureaus, and generation of grading reports, the crucial challenge lies in regular update of the data and also maintenance of tablets/smartphones. Once the pilot is over, and funding for doing data verification and upload to SHPAs dwindles, it is difficult to foresee regular updates. Training of SHG members on doing this can be an option but in any case groups, especially new groups, will require handholding support. Both NRLM and NABARD should devise a concrete plan to ensure that the data updates continue,

by allocating resources for it and also identifying agencies/SHPAs who will do it. In the past, experiments of this nature, like "Computer *Munshi*", faded away after the pilot, and this needs to be avoided.

6.5 CLIENT-LEVEL OUTCOME: EVIDENCE ON SOCIAL EMPOWERMENT

The SHG program is predicated on building synergy between banks, SHPAs, and people's associations, to build economic and social capital. NRLM in its mission also talks about "monitoring against targets of poverty outcomes". In fact, the building of social capital and women empowerment are the dominant themes of SBLP. Considering the absence of any MIS incorporating indicators on these aspects, the evidence for social impact comes from studies conducted from time to time. This year, a major study covering 7 states and 432 SHGs was conducted by MAS for NABARD (referred earlier). The draft findings of it provide valuable information on these aspects (key factsheet of the study in Annexure 6.3).

The study measured empowerment of women SHG members on aspects such as self-confidence, access to family resources, control over SHG and other loans, mobility, decision-making, and discussion of problems with other members. The broad indicators have been further sub-divided into several parameters, and to assess change associated with SHG membership, a before and after comparison has been done. The study findings show a significant increase in parameters under self-confidence. About 97% of SHG members feel more confident in approaching the bank now, as against 20% earlier and, similarly, 71% women have gained confidence on account of their association with the group, to raise issues in public meeting like gram panchayat. A high increase is seen across other parameters under this, such as confidence to speak to visitors and ability to sign. Such a clear positive outcome under all measures provides enough evidence for the positive impact on this front.

Access to family resources is another key indicator, as traditionally the control of women over family resources has been low. The study measured changes under this indicator on women members, say, in sale of small quantity household produce, raising loans, and medical expenses of the family. Traditionally,

Table 6.10 Control of SHG and Other Loans (% of SHG Members)

S. No.	Amount of Control	Use of Earnings of IGA		Use of SHG Loan		Use of Personal Savings	
		Before	Present	Before	Present	Before	Present
1	Total	2.2	16.9	3.6	17.4	5.4	24.2
2	Major	4.6	18.3	8.6	42.7	14.8	36.7
3	Equal	21.6	49	31.6	33.8	27.3	33.1
4	Minor	47.9	11.5	43.4	6.1	41	6
5	No control	23.6	4.4	12.8	0	11.5	0
	Total	100	100	100	100	100	100

Source: MAS study of SHGs, 2016.

in rural settings, while women contribute equally in production, their role in procurement of raw materials and sale of finished goods or cultivated produce has been low. The study finds that 23.6% of women members now play a major role in sale of household produce, as against 9% earlier. Control over medical expenses is key, as women members take care of children but often do not have the power to decide on health and food expenses. About 36% of women now play a major or an equal role in deciding medical expenses, as against 13% before becoming a SHG member. Control of resources by male members in household also extends to use of loans taken by the SHG members. It has often been reported that women members act as a loan-pipelining conduit for male members of the household and their role is limited to availing the loan. As this significantly erodes the ability of women to control household resources, the study examined this across three dimensions: (a) use of resources generated out of income generating activity, (b) use of SHG loans, and (c) use of personal savings (Table 6.10).

The study findings show marked increase across all the three dimensions with 94% of women having equal, major, or total control of savings, and similar percentage on other two dimensions is 84% and 92% respectively. This reflects that almost all SHG women members are either controlling use of savings and loans, or being consulted as an equal partner. The SHG membership has also enabled women members across other indicators of mobility and decision-making. Considering the all-round impact, it is logical to infer that women's role in public meetings and participation in political activities would also have increased. However, the study

findings reveal that while there has been a positive movement under these, the shift is not so marked as compared to other indicators. Out of 864 sample SHG members, the percentage of women who contested for political office rose from 14% to 16% but, significantly, the number of members who "contested on family interest and others" pressure' has declined. The ability to raise voice in gram sabha/panchayat assumes importance, as most government schemes are channeled through the village bodies. The study reports that SHG members' participation and voices in gram sabha has increased from 27% to 56%. More importantly, there is a significant increase in the percentage of SHG members who raise their voice in gram sabha meetings.

The study also examined the financial/economic side of changes, looking into savings behavior, positive and negative consequences of taking credit, asset purchase, and earnings from income-generating activities. As SBLP has a strong savings focus, the report analyzed whether members savings have increased after becoming SHG members. Around 50% of members reported increase in savings, an equal number had no change, and 3% reported decrease in savings. The SHG members have an average of ₹18,004 as household savings, and continue to prefer banks as the preferred institution to save. About 51% of members' savings is with banks, followed by SHGs (27%) and post office (6%). Nearly one third of household savings with the group indicates that members perceive the benefits of using it for availing loans, as well as the flexibility of withdrawal over banks. The economic impact has not been captured as before and after, hence, it is difficult to see the economic impact. However, some proxy measures, such as use of loan for income-generating activities, income, and asset ownership can be analyzed. It is surprising that only 27% of members used the loan for income-generating activities, which implies that majority of SHG loans are being used for household needs. This contrasts with the MFI sector, wherein, as per regulation, 50% of loans by an institution should be for productive purposes, and the same is checked through loan utilization checks. The report does not go into reasons for low use of credit for income-generating activities, and it would have been useful to examine whether it is due to low amount of credit or due to other factors.

The lower use of credit in income-generating activities is reflected in current household income and asset-ownership pattern. Households (27%) who took up IGA reported an average monthly income of ₹4,623. The average income is highest is cases of flower business, bakery, poultry, and hotel business and lowest in the case of garment shops, petty/grocery shops, vegetable vending, tailoring, honey bee business, milk collection and selling, and sheep/goat rearing. No distinct pattern is seen across service, trade, and agri-activities, as well as between farm and nonfarm activities. Still, the average income reported from IGA is significant, considering that the program targets poorer sections of the society. The study findings would have been more relevant if the share of this additional income in total household income would have been captured, and analyzed with similar data for nearly 70% members who did not use the loan for income generating activities. On assets side, about two-thirds of SHG member households have procured one to six assets of different forms after becoming SHG members, which shows that asset purchase cannot be correlated with income from productive use of credit. The nature of assets purchased shows a marked preference for income generating assets, with 40% members reporting purchase of livestock, and only 10% reported purchase of household appliances. The findings are comforting, as the asset purchase pattern shows that despite a high percentage of members who did not use the loan for productive purposes, the asset purchases are geared toward raising income.

The findings show a very positive impact on women empowerment across all indicators, but the economic impact is not clear, as the report does not provide information on changes in overall household income and asset ownership, though it is acknowledged that there are limitations in capturing economic impact without a baseline study.

SUMMING UP

The SBLP is going through an interesting phase. The savings and credit linkage activity is picking up after a period of stagnation and negative growth, NRLM is emerging as the main player accounting for 40% of SHGs, which is likely to significantly increase, digitization of SHG records has started and evaluation of SBLP impact on women members shows powerful impact on women empowerment. At the same time, the program also shows a lot of weaknesses from the perspective of clients. Persistence of regional skew implies that clients in poorer parts of the country remain less covered, high overdues is making the bankers more conservative, thereby aggravating the existing underfinancing in all regions except southern region, product innovation has not changed, except the nature of credit facility, and in a multi stakeholder environment, clients do not have access to a customer friendly grievance redressal mechanism. The program's design features have also been compromised, with introduction of interest rate subsidy and provision of funds to groups under NRLM. The issues of bankers' conservatism about SHG lending and data quality are likely to improve drastically with digitization, but other issues of product innovation and grievance redressal channel require priority action by NABARD in conjunction with NRLM. Work on devising a way to link SHG members with insurance and pension schemes of the government, and making group savings leverage a higher amount of credit also need policy attention. Considering a negative or no correlation between loan amount and overdues, there is need to study as to whether the rise in overdues is related to quality of SHPAs, or geographical context, or some other variable.

Various studies, including this years' study by MAS, have shown that SBLP has a strong impact on women empowerment and household finances. It will be useful to integrate reporting on social outcomes in the digitization project, through simplified reporting template. This will enable regular update on some key outcomes at client level, while a deeper analysis can be done through studies. Once the digitization project is extended to Pan-India in its final phase, it will become increasingly difficult to integrate client-level outcome metrics. A program listing building of social capital as its primary objective needs to accord priority to it. Globally, outcome based funding is the new norm in development finance. If the issues narrated in the chapter are acted on, the responsible finance agenda will get a definite fillip.

STATEMENT - II - A

ANNEXURE 6.1

Progress under SHG—Bank Linkage Programme—Savings and Credit of SHGs with Banks

		(Amount ₹ lakh)				
		Savings Linkage		**Credit Linkage**		**Percentage of SHGs Credit-linked**
S. No.	**Region/State**	**No. of SHGs**	**Savings Amount**	**No. of SHGs**	**Savings Amount**	
NORTHERN REGION						
1	Chandigarh	225	127.85	211	198.09	93.78
2	Haryana	42921	15891.44	18912	20512.89	44.06
3	Himachal Pradesh	44185	3411.12	18261	11165.80	41.33
4	Jammu & Kashmir	8386	2410.50	3641	2504.54	43.42
5	New Delhi	3668	535.87	558	499.48	15.21
6	Punjab	29971	3978.20	15034	15843.16	50.16
7	Rajasthan	264119	18659.06	98107	65183.06	37.14
	Total	**393475**	**45014.04**	**154724**	**115907.02**	**39.32**
NORTH EASTERN REGION						
1	Assam	333686	11128.22	107137	66031.12	32.11
2	Arunachal Pradesh	4617	417.33	408	365.44	8.84
3	Manipur	13620	356.98	2063	934.84	15.15
4	Meghalaya	8196	937.77	1573	1167.00	19.19
5	Mizoram	8072	497.14	2156	2963.48	26.71
6	Nagaland	11432	698.20	3348	2963.25	29.29
7	Sikkim	1542	396.42	632	618.55	40.99
8	Tripura	48658	4594.27	33543	13429.05	68.94
	Total	**429823**	**19026.33**	**150860**	**88472.73**	**35.10**
EASTERN REGION						
1	A & N Islands (UT)	4475	660.49	623	550.57	13.92
2	Bihar	278608	36006.37	267338	100247.52	95.95
3	Jharkhand	99326	9558.45	64999	36693.41	65.44
4	Odisha	486686	48587.72	213871	188335.18	43.94
5	West Bengal	831011	153538.75	584071	377939.91	70.28
	Total	**1700106**	**248351.78**	**1130902**	**703766.59**	**66.52**

(Continued)

(Continued)

S. No.	Region/State	Savings Linkage		Credit Linkage		Percentage of SHGs Credit-linked
		No. of SHGs	Savings Amount	No. of SHGs	Savings Amount	
CENTRAL REGION						
1	Chhattisgarh	160461	16046.37	81328	29843.38	50.68
2	Madhya Pradesh	248618	24831.13	118926	97288.19	47.83
3	Uttar Pradesh	363979	38206.29	217159	152568.12	59.66
4	Uttarakhand	42595	5024.88	17384	9890.65	40.81
	Total	**815653**	**84108.67**	**434797**	**289590.34**	**53.31**
WESTERN REGION						
1	Goa	7541	1543.95	1791	3060.65	23.75
2	Gujarat	221350	18414.23	48187	30669.01	21.77
3	Maharashtra	789158	85745.68	208141	169731.90	26.38
	Total	**1018049**	**105703.86**	**258119**	**203461.56**	**25.35**
SOUTHERN REGION						
1	Andhra Pradesh	901517	414561.96	802227	1722082.57	88.99
2	Karnataka	962446	144242.13	632437	747474.74	65.71
3	Kerala	272859	62907.18	177880	213125.28	65.19
4	Lakshadweep	2	0.10	2	1.50	100.00
5	Puducherry	14763	4089.71	4833	5815.72	32.74
6	Tamil Nadu	852034	92003.16	432893	635902.06	50.81
7	Telangana	542275	149130.09	492947	986323.36	90.90
	Total	**3545896**	**866934.33**	**2543219**	**4310725.23**	**71.72**
	Grant Total	**7903002**	**1369139.01**	**4672621**	**5711923.47**	**59.12**

(Amount ₹ lakh)

ANNEXURE 2

Non-Performing Assets of Banks against SHGs—Position as on March 31, 2016

(Amount ₹ lakh)

S. No.	Region/State	Public Sector Commercial Banks			Private Sector Commercial Banks			Regional Rural Banks			Cooperative Banks			Total		
		Loan Amount OS against SHGs	Amount of Gross NPAs against SHGs	NPA as %age to Loan OS	Loan Amount OS against SHGs	Amount of Gross NPAs against SHGs	NPA as %age to Loan OS	Loan Amount OS against SHGs	Amount of Gross NPAs against SHGs	NPA as %age to Loan OS	Loan Amount OS against SHGs	Amount of Gross NPAs against SHGs	NPA as %age to Loan OS	Loan Amount OS against SHGs	Amount of Gross NPAs against SHGs	NPA as %age to Loan OS
Northern Region																
1	Chandigarh	198.09	47.58	24.02%	0.00	0.00	0.00%	0.00	0.00	0.00%	0.00	0.00	0.00%	198.09	47.58	24.02%
2	Haryana	10674.42	2101.09	19.68%	2402.40	0.00	0.00%	6847.00	284.00	4.15%	589.07	440.00	74.69%	20512.89	2825.09	13.77%
3	Himachal Pradesh	4050.91	427.98	10.57%	296.54	0.00	0.00%	2332.00	262.00	11.23%	4486.35	831.48	18.53%	11165.80	1521.46	13.63%
4	Jammu & Kashmir	786.49	47.88	6.09%	674.49	3.16	0.00%	1011.71	43.47	0.00%	31.85	15.98	50.17%	2504.54	110.49	4.41%
5	New Delhi	495.42	107.48	21.69%	0.00	0.00	0.00%	0.00	0.00	0.00%	4.06	0.00	0.00%	499.48	107.48	21.52%
6	Punjab	10275.47	836.09	8.14%	2342.40	0.15	0.01%	2345.38	192.84	8.22%	879.91	200.00	22.73%	15843.16	1229.08	7.76%
7	Rajasthan	20087.22	9366.71	46.63%	19414.91	805.25	4.15%	9859.54	4042.20	41.00%	15821.39	2134.54	13.49%	65183.06	16348.70	25.08%
	Total	**46568.02**	**12934.81**	**27.78%**	**25130.74**	**808.56**	**3.22%**	**22395.63**	**4824.51**	**21.54%**	**21812.63**	**3622.00**	**16.61%**	**115907.02**	**22189.88**	**19.14%**
North Eastern Region																
1	Assam	32169.03	5299.24	16.47%	45.21	0.87	1.92%	32930.60	2982.16	9.06%	886.28	441.20	49.78%	66031.12	8723.47	13.21%
2	Arunachal Pradesh	237.97	37.39	15.71%	1.21	0.00	0.00%	60.10	25.54	42.50%	66.16	20.31	30.70%	365.44	83.24	22.78%
3	Manipur	415.26	183.13	44.10%	0.00	0.00	0.00%	517.28	44.16	8.54%	2.30	2.30	0.00%	934.84	229.59	24.56%
4	Meghalaya	242.00	102.49	42.35%	0.00	0.00	0.00%	674.83	138.41	20.51%	250.17	89.50	35.78%	1167.00	330.40	28.31%
5	Mizoram	83.38	22.70	27.22%	0.00	0.00	0.00%	1440.05	137.61	9.56%	1440.05	13.26	0.92%	2963.48	173.57	5.86%
6	Nagaland	781.01	217.89	27.90%	0.54	0.29	53.70%	2.32	0.15	6.47%	2179.38	224.53	10.30%	2963.25	442.86	14.95%
7	Sikkim	595.43	32.66	5.49%	0.00	0.00	0.00%	0.00	0.00	0.00%	23.12	0.00	0.00%	618.55	32.66	5.28%
8	Tripura	4005.01	1198.17	29.92%	0.00	0.00	0.00%	6709.00	2871.00	42.79%	2715.04	506.51	18.66%	13429.05	4575.68	34.07%
	Total	**38529.09**	**7093.67**	**18.41%**	**46.96**	**1.16**	**2.47%**	**42334.18**	**6199.03**	**14.64%**	**7562.50**	**1297.61**	**17.16%**	**88472.73**	**14591.47**	**16.49%**
Eastern Region																
1	A & N Islands (UT)	55.47	6.64	11.97%	0.00	0.00	0.00%	0.00	0.00	0.00%	495.10	73.06	14.76%	550.57	79.70	14.48%
2	Bihar	46389.44	9317.36	20.09%	4495.10	0.53	0.00%	49362.98	3962.23	8.03%	0.00	0.00	0.00%	100247.52	13280.12	13.25%

(Continued)

(Continued)

S. No.	Region/State	Public Sector Commercial Banks			Private Sector Commercial Banks			Regional Rural Banks			Cooperative Banks			Total		
		Loan Amount OS against SHGs	Amount of Gross NPAs against SHGs	NPA as %age to Loan OS	Loan Amount OS against SHGs	Amount of Gross NPAs against SHGs	NPA as %age to Loan OS	Loan Amount OS against SHGs	Amount of Gross NPAs against SHGs	NPA as %age to Loan OS	Loan Amount OS against SHGs	Amount of Gross NPAs against SHGs	NPA as %age to Loan OS	Loan Amount OS against SHGs	Amount of Gross NPAs against SHGs	NPA as %age to Loan OS
3	Jharkhand	28971.44	4474.19	15.44%	356.13	0.00	0.00%	7236.39	970.42	13.41%	129.45	0.00	0.00%	36693.41	5444.61	14.84%
4	Orissa	71759.41	19436.54	27.09%	19725.65	16.29	0.08%	83268.65	25365.17	30.46%	13581.47	2141.00	15.76%	188335.18	46959.00	24.93%
5	West Bengal	103353.62	9580.48	9.27%	5754.38	0.00	0.00%	178439.24	9450.67	5.30%	90392.67	4246.77	4.70%	377939.91	23277.92	6.16%
	Total	**250529.38**	**42815.21**	**17.09%**	**30331.26**	**16.82**	**0.06%**	**318307.26**	**39748.49**	**12.49%**	**104598.69**	**6460.83**	**6.18%**	**703766.59**	**89041.35**	**12.65%**
	Central Region															
1	Chhattisgarh	9280.58	1664.75	17.94%	1357.49	2.89	0.21%	18620.00	1107.00	5.95%	585.31	87.26	14.91%	29843.38	2861.90	9.59%
2	Madhya Pradesh	31528.52	6211.04	19.70%	40540.83	209.12	0.52%	23973.80	3434.63	14.33%	1245.04	135.63	10.89%	97288.19	9990.42	10.27%
3	Uttar Pradesh	66349.53	12084.40	18.21%	18342.98	37.33	0.00%	67354.88	18425.50	27.36%	520.73	140.66	27.01%	152568.12	30687.89	20.11%
4	Uttarakhand	4107.68	671.18	16.34%	1005.96	0.00	0.00%	2531.36	533.90	21.09%	2245.65	791.29	35.24%	9890.65	1996.37	20.18%
	Total	**111266.31**	**20631.37**	**18.54%**	**61247.26**	**249.34**	**0.41%**	**112480.04**	**23501.03**	**20.89%**	**4596.73**	**1154.84**	**25.12%**	**289590.34**	**45536.58**	**15.72%**
	Western Region															
1	Goa	1479.17	77.52	5.24%	582.48	1.12	0.19%	0.00	0.00	0.00%	999.00	44.92	4.50%	3060.65	123.56	4.04%
2	Gujarat	18486.21	1367.86	7.40%	4989.95	60.30	1.21%	5543.75	362.58	6.54%	1649.10	463.78	28.12%	30669.01	2254.52	7.35%
3	Maharashtra	56640.57	9252.69	16.34%	70166.94	715.51	1.02%	28562.50	2864.13	10.03%	14361.89	3514.22	24.47%	169731.90	16346.55	9.63%
	Total	**76605.95**	**10698.07**	**13.97%**	**75739.37**	**776.93**	**1.03%**	**34106.25**	**3226.71**	**9.46%**	**17009.99**	**4022.92**	**23.65%**	**203461.56**	**18724.63**	**9.20%**
	Southern Region															
1	Andhra Pradesh	1218187.02	42692.94	3.50%	374.76	21.98	5.87%	484370.18	12447.16	2.57%	19150.61	383.02	2.00%	1722082.57	55545.10	3.23%
2	Karnataka	456497.29	8084.31	1.77%	73704.04	504.17	0.68%	131371.68	5132.99	3.91%	85901.73	1947.08	2.27%	747474.74	15668.55	2.10%
3	Kerala	152312.42	8940.50	5.87%	10646.58	248.19	2.33%	24795.00	745.00	3.00%	25371.28	1511.02	5.96%	213125.28	11444.71	5.37%
4	Lakshadweep	1.50	0.00	0.00%	0.00	0.00	0.00%	0.00	0.00	0.00%	0.00	0.00	0.00%	1.50	0.00	0.00%
5	Puducherry	3486.53	1072.32	30.76%	0.00	0.00	0.00%	1597.84	54.73	3.43%	731.35	81.64	11.16%	5815.72	1208.69	20.78%
6	Tamil Nadu	318281.54	50876.16	15.98%	177443.50	3575.90	2.02%	54415.11	5469.57	10.05%	85761.91	9143.89	10.66%	635902.06	69065.52	10.86%
7	Telangana	587632.96	20097.28	3.42%	0.00	0.00	0.00%	384761.33	5080.27	1.32%	13929.07	428.87	3.08%	986323.36	25606.42	2.60%
	Total	**2736399.26**	**131763.51**	**4.82%**	**262168.88**	**4350.24**	**1.66%**	**1081311.14**	**28929.72**	**2.68%**	**230845.95**	**13495.52**	**5.85%**	**4310725.23**	**178538.99**	**4.14%**
	Grand Total	**3259898.01**	**225936.64**	**6.93%**	**454664.47**	**6203.05**	**1.36%**	**1610934.50**	**106429.49**	**6.61%**	**386426.49**	**30053.72**	**7.78%**	**5711923.47**	**368622.90**	**6.45%**

ANNEXURE 6.3
**Key Fact Sheet of the Study "Impact and Sustainability of Self-help Group—Bank Linkage
Programme in India by APMAS for NABARD, 2016"**

Title of the Study: Impact and Sustainability of SHGBLP in India		
A. SHGBLP in India—At a Glance as on March 2016 (Source: NABARD)		
• Number of SHGs having savings accounts with bank (in lakhs)	:	79.03
• Average amount of funds in SHG SB account (in ₹) per SHG	:	17,324
• Number of SHGs having loan outstanding with banks (in %)	:	51
• Average loan per SHG (₹ in lakh)	:	2.03
• Nonperforming assets (NPAs) (in %)	:	6.45
B. Sample Covered		
• Number of states (AP, AS, KA, MH, OR, UP)	:	6
• Number of districts	:	12
• Number of SHGs	:	432
• Number of SHG member households	:	864
C. Profile of SHGs		
• ST and SC groups (% of SHGs)	:	4 & 18
• Other SHGs (% of SHGs)	:	78
• Average age of SHG (in years)	:	7.76
• Average size of SHG (no. of members)	:	11
• SHGs reported dropouts (% of SHGs)	:	56
• Average distance to bank (in Kms)	:	6
D. Savings		
• Average savings per month per member (in ₹)	:	84
• Average savings per SHG (in ₹)	:	51,679
• Average savings per member (in ₹)	:	4,527
• SHGs withdrawn and distributed savings (in %)	:	39
• Average amount of funds in SHG bank account (in ₹)	:	31,641
• SHGs using own funds for internal lending (% of SHGs)	:	69
E. Meetings		
• SHG meetings—monthly (% of SHGs)	:	56
• SHG meetings—weekly/fortnightly (% of SHGs)	:	38
• Average percentage of meetings conducted in the past 6 months	:	89
• Members' attendance in meetings (% of members)	:	82
F. Book Keeping		
• Books are kept with the SHG leaders (% of SHGs)	:	81
• Books written by SHG members (% of SHGs)	:	71
• SHGs pay honorarium to book writers (% of SHGs)	:	19
• Average monthly honorarium to book writers per SHG (in ₹)	:	82
G. Leadership		
• Leadership rotation in SHGs (% of SHGs)	:	41
• Number of women SHG members elected for local bodies	:	39
• SHGs have the norms of fines and penalties (% of SHGs)	:	60

(Continued)

(Continued)

Title of the Study: Impact and Sustainability of SHGBLP in India		
H. Grades of SHGs		
• A-grade (% of SHGs)	:	68
• B-grade (% of SHGs)	:	24
• C-grade (% of SHGs)	:	8
I. Credit Access to SHGs (Current Loans)		
• Average loan under SHGBLP (₹ in lakhs)	:	1.99
• Average loan from federations (in ₹)	:	70,514
• Average loan from NGO-MFIs (in ₹)	:	91,797
• Average time taken to get bank loan (in weeks)	:	4
• Average amount spent to get bank loan (in ₹)	:	1,031
J. Repayment Rate		
• Average loan repayment rate from SHGs to banks (in %)	:	88
• SHGs reported active defaulters (% of SHGs)	:	35
• Average amount of overdue per SHG (in ₹)	:	11,952
K. Profile of SHG members		
• ST and SC members (in %)	:	7 & 26
• Literacy levels (in %)	:	73
• Female-headed households (in %)	:	16
• Incidence of migration (% of households)	:	17
L. Women Empowerment (% of Members) B-Before/P-Present		
• Confidence to approach bank—B/P	:	20/97
• Use of SHG loans—equal and above role—B/P	:	44/94
• To attend SHG work outside the village—go alone—B/P	:	7/63
• Decision-making on daughter's marriage—equal role	:	57
• Casting of own vote—independently—B/P	:	51/87
• Work burden increased—B/P	:	23/57
• Husband sharing the household work increased—B/P	:	16/27
• Women taking up nontraditional activities—increased—B/P	:	10/51
• SHGs involved in social activities	:	65
• Sending both son and daughter to same school	:	52
• Positive attitude of men toward women (% of members)	:	66
M. Access to Development Programmes (% of HHs)		
• Households accessed to PDS/ration card	:	88
• Households benefited with PMJDY	:	34
• Households participated in MGNREGS	:	41
• Household involved in Swachh Bharat Mission	:	44
• Households having functional toilets	:	63
N. Impact at Household Level		
• SHG women having individual savings bank A/c (% of members)	:	88
• SHGs' savings against total household savings	:	27

Title of the Study: Impact and Sustainability of SHGBLP in India		
• Households having 100% of their loan from SHGs (% of HHs)	:	64
• Households having taken up economic activity	:	27
• Average monthly income from economic activity (in ₹)	:	4,623
• Households purchased livestock	:	40
• Household reported improvement in income	:	90
• Repaid household old debts	:	37

NOTES AND REFERENCES

1. Thorat, Y.S.P. 2006. "Microfinance in India: Sectoral Issues and challenges." In *Towards a Sustainable Microfinance Outreach in India: Experiences and Perspectives*, 27–42. Mumbai: NABARD, German Technical Cooperation (GTZ), and Swiss Agency for Development and Cooperation (SDC).

2. *Status of Microfinance in India 2015–16*. Mumbai: NABARD.

3. Most states now offer interest rate subvention to banks on SHG lending.

4. NABARD (National Bank for Agriculture & Rural Development). 1997. *Micro-Finance Innovations and NABARD*. Mumbai: DPD-NFS, NABARD.

5. *Status of Microfinance in India 2015–16*. NABARD, 2.

6. http://www.tamilnadumahalir.org/sample-sites/mahalir.html, accessed on October 5, 2016.

7. http://dwcdkar.gov.in/index.php?option=com_content&view=article&id=260%3Astree&catid=224%3Aflash&lang=en, accessed on October 5, 2016.

8. http://www.kudumbashree.org, accessed on October 5, 2016.

9. http://aajeevika.gov.in/content/universal-social-mobilization, accessed on October 5, 2016.

10. http://nrlm.gov.in/outerReportAction.do?methodName=showIndex, accessed on October 5, 2016.

11. http://siteresources.worldbank.org/INDIAEXTN/Resources/india-NRLM-overview.pdf, accessed on October 5, 2016.

12. http://www.nrlmbl.aajeevika.gov.in, accessed on October 5, 2016.

13. *Aajeevika (NRLM)—Mid-Term Assessment Report*. National Mission Management Unit, National Rural Livelihoods Mission, RL Division, Ministry of Rural Development Government of India.

14. *Status of Microfinance in India 2015-16*. NABARD, 4

15. http://www.nrlmbl.aajeevika.gov.in/NRLM/UI/Reports/GeoWiseNRLMCompStatusReport.aspx, accessed on October 5, 2016.

16. Circular No. 263/MCID-07/2015, dated December 18, 2015. Available at: http://www.sa-dhan.net/Resources/Circular%20MFI%20as%20SHPI.PDF, accessed on October 5, 2016.

17. *Impact and Sustainability of Self Help Group Bank Linkage Programme in India*. MAS, Study commissioned by NABARD.

18. Interaction with the author on July 19, 2016 in Hyderabad.

19. RBI circular defines overdue cash credit account as "An account should be treated as 'out of order' if the outstanding balance remains continuously in excess of the sanctioned limit/drawing power. In cases where the outstanding balance in the principal operating account is less than the sanctioned limit/drawing power, but there are no credits continuously for 90 days as on the date of Balance Sheet or credits are not enough to cover the interest debited during the same period, these accounts should be treated as 'out of order.'"

20. 2011. *Assessing the Effectiveness of Small Borrowing in India*. New Delhi: NCAER.

21. http://www.nrlmbl.aajeevika.gov.in/NRLM/UI/Outstanding/BankOverdues.aspx, accessed on October 5, 2016.

22. *Report of the Committee to Recommend Data Format for Furnishing of Credit Information to Credit Information Companies*. RBI. Available at: https://rbi.org.in/scripts/PublicationReportDetails.aspx?UrlPage=&ID=763, accessed on October 5, 016.

23. RBI circular No. DBR.CID.BC.No.73/20.16.56/2015-16, dated January 14, 2016. Available at: https://rbi.org.in/scripts/NotificationUser.aspx?Id=10227&Mode=0, accessed on October 5, 2016.

24. Misra, Alok. *Responsible Finance India Report 2015*, An Access Publication, 79–81. Available at https://in.sagepub.com/en-in/sas/responsible-finance-india-report-2015/book251469, accessed on October 5, 2016.

25. www.eshakti.nabard.org, accessed on October 5, 2016.

26. Interaction with the author on September 9, 2016 in New Delhi.

New Initiatives and Strengthening Responsible Finance

The financial sector landscape has undergone a paradigm shift in the last two–three years. The changes have been focused on ensuring universal financial inclusion through harnessing varied channels and technology. From the creation of institutions such as MUDRA and SFBs to the implementation of programs such as PMJDY, these initiatives are today playing a major role in the financial inclusion space, in addition to the existing arrangements in the form of MFIs and SBLP. The policy for financial inclusion has moved from being bank-led to a blended approach, combining the strengths of each channel. While SFBs have yet to start operations in their new avatar, MUDRA and PMJDY have gained sufficient traction to merit an analysis of their role. Similarly, as part of the policy rethink on greater acceptability of channels other than banks, the RBI is in the process of coming out with guidelines for P2P lending.

As MFIs followed by SHGs continue to lead the market in extending financial services to the poor, their responsible performance accounts for a major part of the report. However, as these new initiatives have the potential to significantly impact the future of financial inclusion landscape, this chapter examines the performance of MUDRA, PMJDY, and two P2P players from the clients' perspective—how have things changed for the clients with the coming of these institutions and programs. The second part of the chapter presents action points for strengthening responsible finance, based on the review in earlier chapters. While the focus of the action points is on improving the outcomes at the client level, it is acknowledged that only financially viable and operationally robust institutions can provide client-centric services in the long run.

7.1 MUDRA: HAS IT LIVED THE PROMISE?

The establishment of MUDRA in 2014 was primarily geared to give a fillip to the financing of micro-units or micro-enterprises, as well as to provide credit guarantee to lenders in this space[1]. However, following the budget speech, there were policy announcements concerning MUDRA, which expanded the role to areas such as covering SBLPs as well as MFIs and critically added other aspects to its work area namely (a) regulation, (b) accreditation/rating, (c) laying down responsible finance practices, and (d) technology solutions[2]. However, after the initial year, things have settled down, and it is clear that MUDRA will focus on accelerating credit flow to small entrepreneurs and micro-units, with few additional roles (Figure 7.1)

Besides the refinance and credit guarantee role, MUDRA has now two developmental roles, of being a technology enabler and facilitating sector development through skill development, financial literacy, and institution development.

From a conceptual standpoint, MUDRA's stepping in to accelerate credit flow to micro-units is a very laudable and responsible objective. Indian small and medium enterprises (SME) sector is a highly important part of the Indian economy, which provides employment to nearly 80 million people and contributes about 8% to GDP, and makes up for 45% to the total manufacturing output and 40% of India's exports[3]. However, the contribution is more from SMEs than from micro-enterprises. Despite their important role in the economy, the SME sector suffers from various constraints, with

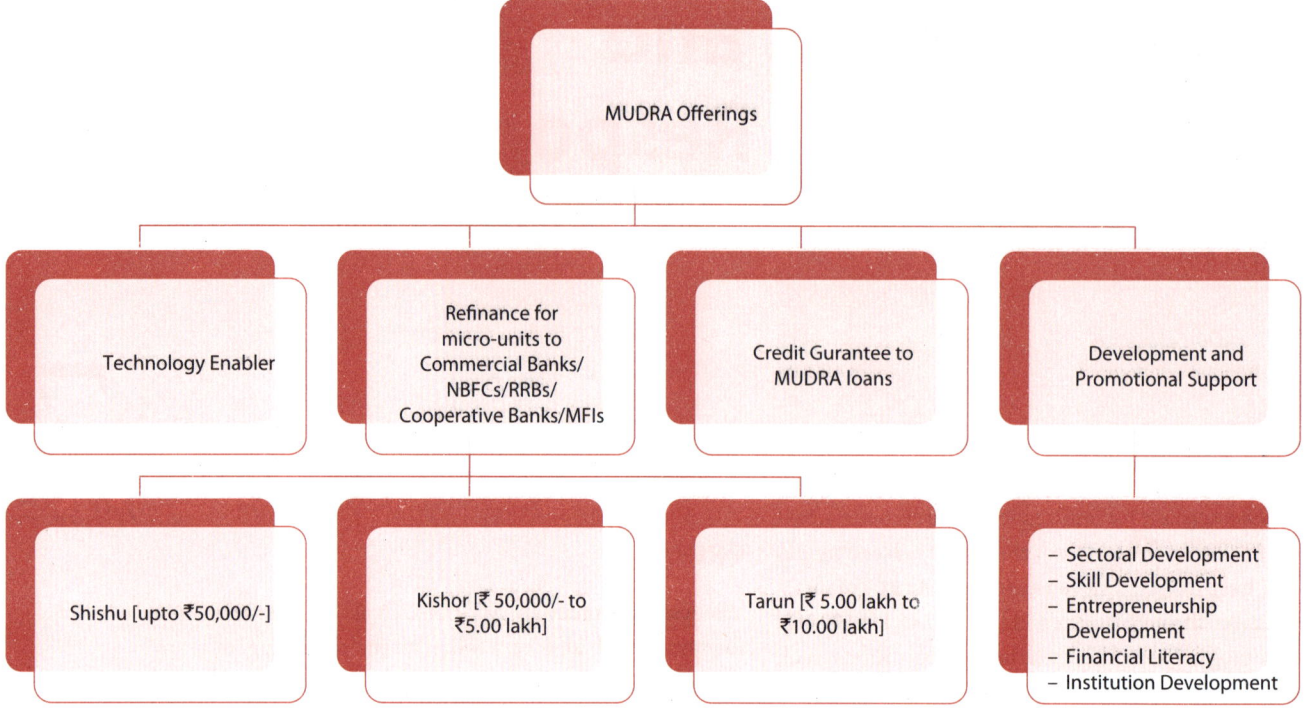

Figure 7.1 MUDRA Functions

Source: MUDRA website.

credit being a key one. IFC in its report[4] on women in SMEs in India says that there are nearly three million micro-, small, and medium enterprises with full or partial female ownership. Majority of women businesses are in services sector (78%), and these women-owned enterprises contribute 3.09% of industrial output, employing over eight million people. The women ownership is skewed toward smaller-sized businesses, with 98% of women-owned businesses being micro-enterprises—the target market defined for MUDRA. The report also highlights the financing gap, by stating that 90% of credit requirements of women-owned small businesses are met through informal sources, and pegs the credit gap at ₹6.37 trillion. The key issues faced by women businesses relate to being in the service sector, inability to offer traditional collateral, and information asymmetry. The establishment of MUDRA has the objective of developing the ecosystem for lending to micro-units, accelerating credit flow, and providing comfort to bankers in the form of credit guarantee. Considering the huge credit gap in the sector, more so in the case of women enterprises, along with their role in the economy, MUDRA's work has huge implications for furthering responsible finance.

7.1.1 Building Up the Ecosystem: Good Progress in Bridging Information Gap

During last one year, SIDBI (MUDRA being a wholly owned subsidiary of SIDBI) has done significant work in improving the ecosystem for lending to SMEs, in congruence with the Stand-Up India initiative of the government. Under the Stand-Up India scheme, bank loans ranging from ₹10 lakh to ₹–1 crore have to be given to one scheduled caste or scheduled tribe entrepreneur, and one woman entrepreneur by each bank branch. The Stand-Up India platform is being managed by SIDBI and a portal, Standupmitra[5], has been set up to help the entrepreneurs put up greenfield enterprises. The portal is aligned to accept MUDRA loans also.

One of the critical challenge faced by entrepreneurs relates to the information gap about credit schemes, technical support agencies, bank branches and training centers in their area of operation. It is commendable that in a short span of one year this portal has been built, and it contains all the information an entrepreneur needs and much more (Figure 7.2). Through the portal, an entrepreneur can have access to a pool of more than 17,000 hand-holding agencies hosted on the portal. The access to the portal has been extended to the entire banking

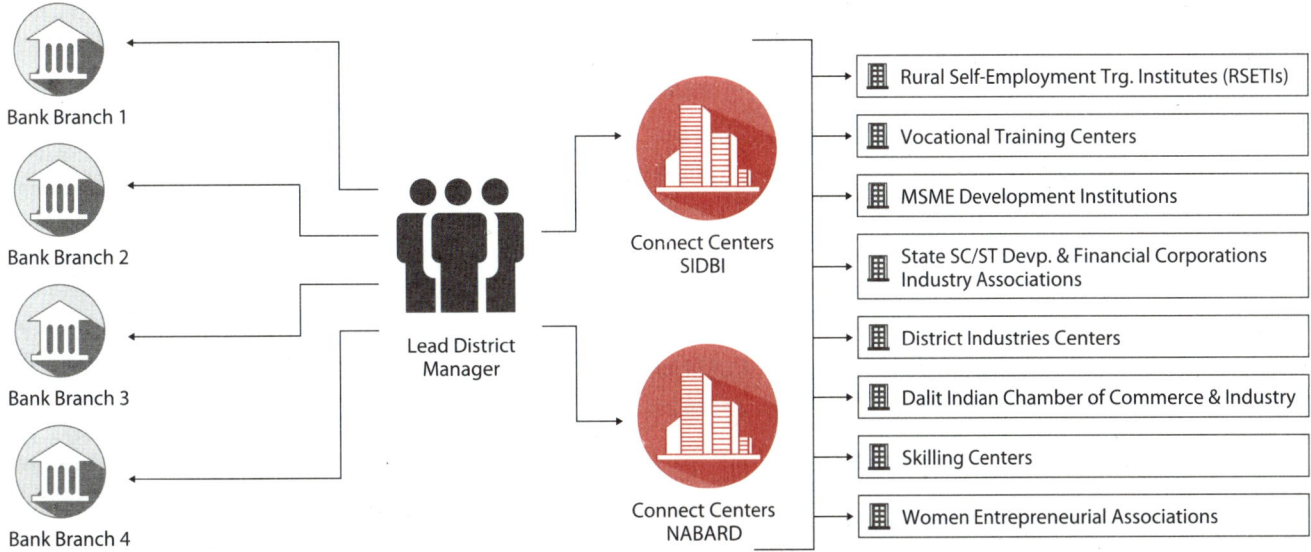

Figure 7.2 Stand-up India Ecosystem

Source: https://www.standupmitra.in/

network in India through an e-market place. The eligible entrepreneur can apply online, by means of a standardized application form, from any corner of the country, and the applicants have the facility to track their application. Any bank, which has been indicated by the applicant as a preferred bank, can pick up the application for sanction.

This is a game changer in the lending and support ecosystem, with availability of Pan-India information at the click of a mouse, drastically bringing down information sourcing costs. Availability of e-application reduces paperwork and provides for a transparent decision-making process. SIDBI's CMD, Sri K. Shivaji, in his interaction with the author, spoke of trying to change the game from being a "lenders market" to a "borrowers market". The intention is that, based on the loan application, banks will now make counter offers and it is the borrower who can choose the bank which he/she wants to associate with.

Further, to help the beneficiaries, several model schemes have been uploaded on the site. Though at present, the loan applications are for Stand-Up India scheme, the wealth of information available can be used by all entrepreneurs, and it is expected that soon this will become a marketplace for SME lending. The innovative design of the portal and its functionality is in line with the mission of Digital India. Transparency, availability of appropriate products, and addressing concerns of clients are key aspects of responsible finance, and this site addresses all these

aspects. On similar lines, ab Udyami Mitra website has been developed, wherein all categories of enterprises can apply for a loan, including MUDRA loans.

7.1.2 MUDRA 'Funding the Unfunded': Need to Focus on Ecosystem Building Over Credit

Within the aegis of PMMY, MUDRA has created products to meet the credit needs of micro-entrepreneurs. The loan products have been named 'Shishu', 'Kishor', and 'Tarun' to signify the stage of growth/development and funding needs of the beneficiary micro-unit/entrepreneur. At present, there are three types of loans:

- **Shishu:** covering loans up to ₹50,000.
- **Kishor:** covering loans above ₹50,000 and up to ₹0.5 million.
- **Tarun:** covering loans above 0.5 million and up to 1 million.

According to the strategy, more focus is given to Shishu category units, and then to Kishor and Tarun categories. The loans are geared to meet the funding requirements of micro-entrepreneurs for business, equipment, and working capital. Along with accelerating the credit flow for micro-units, another objective of MUDRA is to bring down the rates of interest through its refinance at lower rates.

The report card for PMMY for 2015–16 shows impressive numbers, with banks, RRBs, and MFIs providing loans of ₹1,32,954 crore under the three schemes, surpassing the target for the year. The

Table 7.1 Key Statistics of PMMY during 2015–16

Number of accounts financed under PMMY	34,880,924
Of which by banks	11,086,497 (32%)
Of which by MFIs	23,794,427 (68%)
Total amount disbursed under PMMY (in ₹ Crore)	1329.547
Of which by banks	87,050 (65%)
Of which by MFIs	45,904 (35%)
Average loan amount disbursed by banks	79,000
Overall average amount disbursed under PMMY	38,000
Number of new entrepreneurs financed	12,474,668
Number of women entrepreneurs financed	27,628,265

Source: Review of performance of PMMY, MUDRA.

Table 7.2 MUDRA's Financial Assistance under PMMY

	₹ Crore	Rate of interest
Cumulative financial assistance to banks	2,891.42	6.72%
Cumulative financial assistance to NBFC-MFIs	741	9.45% 11.95% based on rating
Cumulative financial assistance to RRBs	239.25	6.72%

Source: MUDRA.

report card says that lending by banks to this segment grew by 70% during 2015–16, as compared to the previous year. Table 7.1 provides a few key statistics of PMMY during 2015–16.

The impressive figures clearly show that MFIs contribute 68% of the loan accounts, though their share in amount disbursed is smaller, at 35%, owing to smaller loan sizes. The dominance of MFIs is evident, with MFIs accounting for 86% of women entrepreneurs and 50% of new entrepreneurs financed. However, numbers reported under PMMY have no relation with the funding made available through MUDRA, on account of its limited resource base. As on July 31, 2016, MUDRA has an equity of ₹750 crore and borrowings from RIDF shortfall of ₹5000 crore. The cumulative disbursement since inception made by MUDRA to MFIs and banks forms a mere 3% of the disbursement made under PMMY in 2015–16.

Not only is the financial assistance provided by MUDRA insignificant to boost credit flow, the lower rates of interest have also not been able to lower the rates to clients. Though according to the MUDRA website[6], banks availing MUDRA refinance have to lend at base rate/MCLR for lending to micro-units, and RRBs and cooperatives have been given

an interest cap of 3.50% over and above MUDRA refinance rate. In the case of NBFC-MFIs, there is an interest cap of 6% over and above MUDRA refinance. However, there is no mechanism to check this, and the author could verify that in the case of NBFC-MFIs, there is no such mechanism. Moreover, the implementation of this cap would result in a piquant situation, with a few borrowers getting loans at lower rate of interest compared to the majority, which goes against responsible pricing, as well as market dynamics. Moreover, with mere 3% assistance, MUDRA at present does not have the capacity to influence interest rates.

The logical question which arises from the above is whether the lending claimed under PMMY is attributable to MUDRA or a natural growth of business by banks and NBFC-MFIs. The product design remains the same in the field, and the only change offered relates to renaming of loans as Shishu, Tarun, or Kishor, based on the loan size. In the case of NBFC-MFIs, as their entire lending is under "Shishu", the entire portfolio is booked under PMMY, with token refinance assistance, and the same is the case with banks. Thus, the role of MUDRA in influencing credit flow to micro-units by way of refinance is negligible to say the least, which is logical, as there are enough funders for NBFC-MFIs, and banks have liquidity at their disposal. Even if the fund size of MUDRA grows in future, it will only act to replace other sources of credit. In last year's report, it was suggested that the role of MUDRA lies in "MUDRA can serve the cause of funding the unfunded better, if its focus shifts from credit, to building a supportive eco-system through its work in regulation, credit guarantee mechanism and financial education."[7] Focus on credit is neither required, nor will be useful.

While some steps have been taken by MUDRA during the last year on these lines such as credit guarantee scheme and ecosystem building, it is yet to take up any significant initiative under its functions of being a technology enabler and supporting financial education. In terms of building the ecosystem, MUDRA organized a credit campaign from September 1 to October 2, 2015. The campaign culminated in mega credit camps in different locations in the country from September 25 to October 2, 2015, and the focus of these camps was especially on "Shishu" loans. Further, MUDRA carried out a month-long publicity campaign, on behalf of department of financial services, through print media and radio. The other thing done by MUDRA relates to launch of MUDRA card (discussed in Chapter 2), which can also be seen as its role of being a technology enabler. MUDRA card is a co-branded card with the lending bank offering hassle-free credit to small borrowers, allowing loan withdrawal on demand. Mudra Card is on RuPay platform of NPCI, and is operable on ATMs and POS machines. In order to stimulate its use, MUDRA is providing refinance and credit guarantee for loans granted under MUDRA Card. About 517,000 cards for ₹1477 crore credit limit have been issued during first year.

7.1.3 Credit Guarantee Scheme—A Step in Right Direction

It was mentioned in last year's report that a major bottleneck faced by micro-units in availing loans from banks relates to bankers' risk perception. The enhanced risk perception is borne out of unavailability of clear collateral, gaps in financial and operation information, and costs of follow-up. However, the case with MFIs is different as they lend through group guarantee, substituting physical collateral with social, and lower their risks through smaller loan sizes. Micro-units requiring loan amounts ranging from ₹100,000–500,000 are the most affected by this risk aversion, and fall between the cracks of MFI's maximum amount and banks' minimum amount[8]. Offering credit guarantee is one way of addressing this situation and such a scheme was announced by the finance minister during his 2015–16 budget speech. In response to that, a Mudra Credit Guarantee Fund has been operationalized with a corpus of ₹3,000 crore, of which ₹500 crore was received as the first installment. The scheme started on April 18, 2016, and provides for coverage of all eligible MUDRA loans. The extent of guarantee provided under the scheme covers 50% of the amount in default, after excluding first loss of 5% to be borne by the lending institution. The fee gap been kept at 1% per annum of sanction amount, with a provision for additional risk premium on the basis of percentage of NPA and/or claim payout ratios. By August 2016, 26 institutions have enrolled under the scheme. While this is a right step, the present corpus is too little to cover the sector, and will require additional resources.

Role for MUDRA to Strengthen Responsible Finance

As analyzed above, MUDRA has to move away from refinance function and focus on building the ecosystem through expanding credit guarantee scheme, promoting financial literacy for clients, helping lending institutions develop products suited to clients, and helping NGO-MFIs transform to suitable legal forms for financial intermediation. Financial literacy has not received the attention it deserves, as NBFC-MFIs are constrained for margin, and banks do not have the reach and orientation. Various issues associated with clients, such as over indebtedness, and opting for illegal companies and chit funds to deposit their money, can be tackled by proper financial literacy. MUDRA can support the institutions by way of funding the training, as well as in designing training modules, with a clear outcome-based measurement. Product innovation is another critical aspect, which needs attention from responsible finance angle. While issues such as transparency, responsible pricing, and grievance redressal are being addressed by regulation and SRO, appropriate product design, being part of the aspirational agenda, depends on institutions for action. The rush for growth and pressure for margins has ensured that product design has been relegated to the background and MFIs are mainly offering similar group loan products. MUDRA can think of working with MFIs to develop products suited to context, help the MFIs with meeting the funding requirements for the product design, and piloting as well as developing a supportive ecosystem. At present, there is no incentive for institutions to invest in product design, and one way of incentivizing them can be lower rates of bank funding. MUDRA can take the lead in this dialogue between banks and MFIs.

Equally important is the need to help NGO-MFIs continue their responsible microfinance, which at present is threatened by banks' reluctance to lend to them. There are no signals for reintroduction of the microfinance bill, which could bring legitimacy to NGO-MFIs, and the present context offers them two options—either get transformed as NBFC-MFI or become a banking correspondent. Many of these NGO-MFIs have localized operations and, coupled with long years of operation, a strong connect with clients has been developed. It is imperative that these institutions should not be allowed to wither away. MUDRA can play a critical role in this sphere.

In last year's Responsible Finance report, it was suggested that MUDRA can fill the regulatory vacuum by being the regulator for NGO-MFIs, but as things have transpired, it is clear that MUDRA will not have a role in regulation. Thus, the role of MUDRA can be to help NGO-MFIs decide their strategic option and help them to follow the chosen path. Sa-Dhan, as the SRO with primarily member base of NGO-MFIs can be an ideal partner in this initiative.

7.2 PRADHAN MANTRI JAN DHAN YOJANA: IMPRESSIVE OUTREACH, BUT CRITICAL ISSUES REMAIN

The launch of PMJDY in 2014 and its success in extending the reach of financial services to all has been phenomenal. As of end of August 2016, 23.93 crore savings accounts have been opened under the scheme, and the amount of deposits held in these accounts has swelled to ₹41,789 crore. These numbers have belied the naysayers who did not believe that these numbers could be achieved anytime soon, and more so, the amount of deposit in these accounts. PMJDY, however, is not merely about opening savings account but multiple financial services. It has six pillars:

- Universal access to banking facilities.
- Providing basic bank account with OD facility and RuPay debit card to all households.
- Financial literacy program, to increase uptake of financial products.
- Credit guarantee fund to mitigate risks on account of OD facility extended to these accounts.
- Micro-insurance for all account holders under PMJDY.
- Pension schemes like Swavalamban for the unorganized sector.

While all these elements have been put in operation, according to the mission document, the initial emphasis is on first three aspects. The wide popularity of the scheme rests to a large extent on extensive promotion of the scheme as making available financial services at low-cost and the expectation that in future all government payments will be routed through PMJDY accounts. As the banking network has limited reach and manpower, the extensive reach of the program has been possible on the backbone of BCs or Bank Mitras (BMs)—both these terms are used interchangeably. As of date, there are 126,000

BMs on the ground, either as individual BMs or as customer service points of corporate BCs.

From a responsible finance angle, the PMJDY performance can be assessed on two counts. First, are the customers getting what is promised under the scheme, and second, is the BM structure viable and will it be able to provide the services sustainably in future? The second point is also critical, as unless a robust and viable BM structure is in place, customers will not be able to avail of the services. The assessment of PMJDY comes from two studies. MicroSave[9] conducted a nationwide study of PMJDY in December 2015, and it covered 1,627 BMs across 42 districts in 17 states. This was the third in a series of assessments done by MicroSave. The other study was conducted by PwC[10] for Poorest State Inclusive Growth Programme (PSIG), being implemented by SIDBI and funded by UK Aid. This study was focused on one state—Madhya Pradesh—and covered 350 BMs across 16 districts. Both studies provide useful insights into performance of PMJDY from two different perspectives; one is broad and at a national level, while the other is a deep dive in one state. Before discussing the findings, it must be mentioned that it is acknowledged that grounding of a nationwide scheme which is a game changer takes time, and improvements will happen over time.

7.2.1 Customer Experience: Improving, Need to Focus on Quality Now

The first aspect which a customer requires is ease of opening accounts, and the scheme provides for simplified KYC norms. According to the Micro-Save study, it takes an average of nine days to open a PMJDY account. Further, the study found that 14% of customers could not open accounts due to multiple reasons, such as insistence on Aadhaar as KYC and nonacceptance of self-attested proof. While nine days is the average time, the maximum time reported to be taken is two months. Once the account has been opened, the customers are supposed to be provided with a RuPay debit card and PIN for ATM transactions, and be considered for an OD facility. The debit card provides the customer with flexibility to draw cash from ATMs, and absence of it ties the customer to the BM for transactions. The MicroSave study reports that only 42% of customers had received the RuPay debit card, while in the PwC study, almost 80% of the customers had received the debit card, showing a wide difference across states. The delay in distribution of RuPay debit cards is attributable to delivery, infrastructure, and usage problems. Typically, banks either organize a camp to distribute the cards or take the help of BMs to personally deliver the cards. The other related problem is that the customer has to visit the bank branch for card activation, and bank branches suffer from weak infrastructure and low staff capacity to handle the PMJDY business. Further, it is reported that in many cases banks discourage RuPay card distribution, fearing possibility of misuse or fraud by illiterate customers. Low availability of RuPay-card-enabled devices with BMs forces clients to change password at ATMs, which is considered cumbersome, as customers are not used to ATM transactions. Some customers, to avoid this, request the BM to do it for them, which can lead to malpractices. However, these issues can be attributed to unfamiliarity with new technology, and the situation is likely to improve as customers gain experience with ATM transactions and higher availability of RuPay-enabled devices with BMs.

The availability of OD facility linked to the PMJDY account was considered to be a major attraction for opening of PMJDY accounts. The scheme provides for an OD facility of ₹5,000, and to raise awareness about this, ministry of finance had instructed all banks to send text messages to all customers about this facility. However, the MicroSave study finds that only 7% of PMJDY account holders have received an OD facility, and the average amount is paltry at ₹815. This has led to lot of consternation among customers on account of not reading the fine print associated with the facility. First, the popular perception was that the OD amount is interest-free and available to everyone, while the rules require activity in savings account for six months, to be eligible for OD, and banks charge 11/12% rate of interest on the OD amount. Second, the study finds confusion caused by promotion of MUDRA loans, as customers feel that under MUDRA loan they can get a much higher amount. These twin factors are affecting the demand side, with 80%[11] of the customers refusing to take the OD facility offered by the bank. On the supply side, banks are also conservative in granting the OD facility, fearing NPAs, even after submission of documents by the BMs. This is a classic case of raising expectations and then not being able to meet them. While the rules for grant of OD facility and charging of interest are fair, it would have been

prudent to announce it clearly rather than showcase it as a right for each customer.

Despite these issues, there are positives associated with PMJDY at client level. The primary motivation of clients to open PMJDY accounts is to save, and that is a very positive outcome. In the MicroSave study, 38% clients indicated zero-balance requirement as the driving force for opening an account, and a further 8% opened the account for saving in close proximity of their habitat. In the PwC study, 80% of customers indicated savings as the primary reason for opening of accounts. PMJDY also had a positive impact on gender, and reaching the poorest. The MicroSave study reports that among the customers having their first bank account under PMJDY, 36% are female. The PwC study reports a similar figure of 27%. The outreach of PMJDY to poorer sections of society is vindicated by the fact that the average monthly income of PMJDY customers is ₹4,701, which is lower than the national poverty line[12]. (Figure 7.3)

This shows the depth of financial inclusion achieved under PMJDY. While the depth of outreach across all categories is BPL, it is more so in the case of rural and women customers.

Having seen the outreach, from the perspective of clients, it is critical to examine as to whether they appreciate the services provided by BMs, and what is the usage pattern of these accounts. The usage is particularly important, as it was feared that most of the accounts may soon become dormant.

Over three rounds of studies, MicroSave has tracked the views of customers on use of BMs. The latest round shows that 88% of customers prefer BMs for opening of accounts and transactions. The PwC study also corroborates this, by reporting more than 90% customers reposing faith in BMs, and reflects the growing trust for BMs. For clients, availability of BMs to do transactions is a key factor.

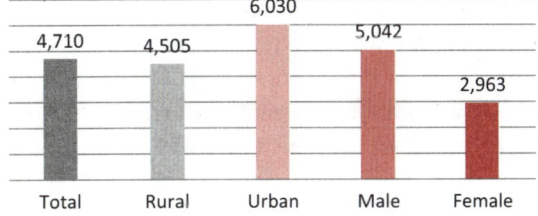

Figure 7.3 Average Monthly Income (₹) of PMJDY Customers

Source: PwC Study, 2015.

The MicroSave study shows that while the traceability of BMs has improved due to availability of list of BMs on PMJDY website, the transaction readiness remains at level similar to second wave assessment in mid-2015. Of the total 1,627 BMs covered in the study, 50 (3%) could not be traced, 165 (10%) were dormant, and 128 (8%) were not able to do transactions. The inability to do transactions was on account of multiple reasons, such as faulty machine, nonavailability of machine, and connectivity issues. Put together, 21% of BMs could not provide services, and this is a worrisome, especially as in absence of widespread use of RuPay debit cards, customers remain dependent on BMs. Lack of interoperability across BMs prevents them from using other active BMs, other than their BM. The reasons for high dormancy of BMs are analyzed in the next section.

On the usage side, the data is encouraging. The MicroSave study reports that 28% of accounts are dormant (no activity in the account for last three months), which is in line with figures reported by PMJDY website for zero-balance accounts at 24%. The PwC study reports 18% accounts as inactive, though it uses a higher time period of six months to define inactive accounts. Differing reasons have been attributed for this. One major aspect relates to duplicate accounts. The MicroSave study shows that 31% of customers have multiple accounts, and many of them more actively use accounts other than PMJDY for their needs. PMJDY accounts of such customers are likely to be inactive, but this begets the question as to why these accounts have been opened. The study provides answer by indicating that while some customers expected freebies under PMJDY account, many other accounts were opened primarily for incentive, as BMs compensation remains tilted toward account opening. The PwC study also analyzed reasons for inactivity, and came up with a totally different perspective. Total 62% of inactive accounts are due to lack of money with the customer and another 32% use the account only for receiving subsidy, and once the subsidy amount is withdrawn, the account remains inactive. However, with proper awareness, the trend of zero-balance accounts is declining (Figure 7.4). The MicroSave study points out that banks also use tricks like depositing a token amount of ₹10 in accounts to reduce the percentage of zero-balance accounts. Such practices, seen along with duplicate accounts, are typical of a target driven approach,

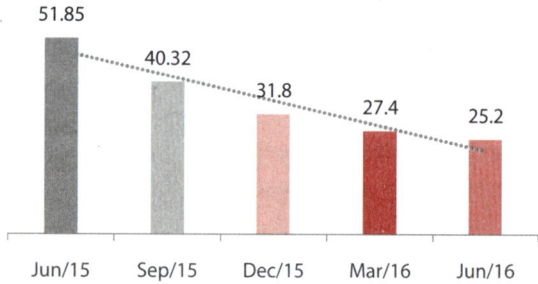

Figure 7.4 Trend in Zero-balance Accounts (%)
Source: Presentation by Director, DFS at MDI in July 2016.

and having achieved the numbers, PMJDY should move to qualitative aspects, such as financial literacy, ensuring transaction readiness of BMs, and instilling a sound grievance redressal mechanism. While the PMJDY mission has set up 2 national-level and 36 state-level toll-free numbers for registering grievances, the study shows that awareness of these numbers remains low. Aside from customers, among BMs, only 59% were aware of the call center. Absence of a widely disseminated system to help customers with their queries and grievances is likely to lead to customer dissatisfaction, especially in the current phase focusing on OD, insurance, and pension facility. These are complex financial products and BMs are not in a position to adequately answer the customer queries. Financial literacy needs to be accorded priority and this can be done through the suggested role for MUDRA. This is the time to consolidate the gains and focus on qualitative issues.

7.2.2 Is the BM Structure Viable?

While the customer experience is improving, though there are issues to be addressed, the entire scheme rests on the edifice of BMs. In absence of BMs, it is not possible to imagine that banks will be able to manage this volume of customers, and more so reach them—access is the key. Even where bank branches are in close proximity to customers, those requiring small-value transactions are not comfortable in going to the branch. It is critical that the structure of BMs remains viable, and keeps growing. Both studies previously referred to analyzed the position of BMs, and the findings show that the structure is not viable at present. BM dormancy[13] is going up, with the MicroSave study reporting 10% dormancy up from 8% in the earlier round. Most of the dormant BMs attribute dormancy to poor handholding support from the bank, or the corporate BC. The MicroSave study rightly points out,

> BM dormancy hampers customers' trust in the entire BC model. When a customer opens a bank account at the BM, s/he is the only touch point that the customer has for all his financial needs. The customer trusts the BM, before trusting the entire channel and back-end machinery. BM dormancy can thus hamper customers' trust on financial inclusion as whole.

It is believed that BMs will take up this activity in conjunction with their other activities, like a grocery store, but over time, seeing the potential, many have taken this activity on stand-alone basis. The PwC study of BMs in Madhya Pradesh reports that 22% of BMs are involved in other economic activities to support their income, and only 5% of BMs are women, while the MicroSave study shows that 37% of BMs have alternate business. Thus, the scenario looks more like BM being the primary activity for male member of the household. The reasons for being a BM vary from social recognition and stable source of income, to association with a bank. A BMs' income from being an agent depends on number of accounts handled, daily footfalls, volume of transactions, and commission structure.

The MicroSave study finds that, on an average, a BM has 949 PMJDY customers and receives an average daily customer footfall of 27, with large variations across the spectrum (Figure 7.5). What

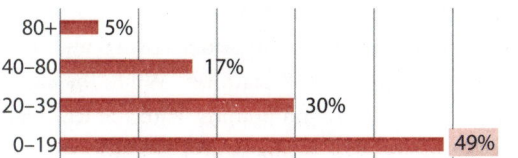

Figure 7.5 Daily Customer Footfall at BMs
Source: PMJDY Wave III Assessment, MicroSave.

is alarming is that almost half of BMs report less than 19 customers daily. A CGAP report[14] on agent network suggests that agents working exclusively as agents need 50–150 customers daily for viability. The footfalls have not improved with time, and the MicroSave study shows that many agents used OD facility as bait for opening accounts. Customers, after realizing that OD is difficult to get, plus carries interest, have gone dormant, affecting the viability of BMs. The PwC study findings show that each BC had on an average 2,335 customer accounts, with 40% women accounts. Though the number of customers per BM reported by MicroSave and PwC is quite different, surprisingly, both studies show similar findings in the case of the more critical aspect—the value and number of transactions. This information is more critical, as transactions define the income of BMs.

The MicroSave study finds that average number of transactions done per month by BMs is 301, which is a substantial improvement over last round's number of 209. The PwC study finds that BCs on an average do 33 transactions per day, which translates to 330 transactions in a month. This is what determines the revenue for BMs. At present, there are three compensation models for the BMs—fixed, fixed plus variable, and only variable. With account opening having reached saturation level, which contributed to a major chunk of BM's revenue, the income source has now changed to transactions. Both these studies report that there is high level of dissatisfaction with the income, and the analysis shows that BM's income remains far below the level required. In the MicroSave study, 35% of BMs were "highly unsatisfied' with the income but 98% are willing to continue in the business, expecting positive changes. The cost and income structure reported in both studies is summarized in Table 7.3.

The figures are not comparable, as the MicroSave study has divided BMs based on technology, while

Table 7.3 Cost and Income Structure of Bank Mitras

	MicroSave Study		PWC Study	
	Micro-ATM/POS	Laptop	Rural	Urban
Average one time fixed cost	36,968	67,715	75,000	75,000
Average monthly expense	2,617	3,249	4,300	6,500
Total average monthly cost^	3233	4374	5550	7750
Average monthly income#	3,995 to 5,775		4,000	5,400

Notes: ^ [Monthly expense plus one time fixed cost amortised over 60 months].
3,995 for fixed income model, 4,415 for variable income model and 5,775 for mixed model.

the other study has gone by location of BMs. However, both throw strong pointers to average monthly income of BMs being in the range of ₹4,000–4,500, which is marginally higher or lower than their expenses on the activity. Certainly, anybody investing around ₹50,000 in a business will not be satisfied with breakeven, and this is the reason for high level of dissatisfaction, which must be addressed. The expected income level indicated by BMs, at ₹13,303, is far above the current income levels. The problem of lower income is further compounded by delays in compensation by banks/corporate BCs, as well as lack of transparency. MicroSave study states:

> BMs receive a lump sum amount in their account, without any break-up of paid commission. This leaves them unsure of the linkage of monthly transactions to the commission earned, and keep track of monthly earning. In situations where BMs are being managed by BCNM, BMs raised concerns whether BCNMs are implementing commission structure appropriately.

Some BMs reported receiving commissions with a delay of three to six months.

Considering the tenuous viability of BMs, the MicroSave study has suggested changing the commission structure's emphasis from account opening to transactions, as well as routing of all G2P payments through the PMJDY account. The PwC study has also suggested a revised commission structure for agents. However, how these accounts affect the viability of banks has not been analyzed in both studies, and any increase in commission has to be seen from banks' angle also. Many bankers feel that even the current commission structure is not profitable for them. A more effective option will be to increase the traction of these accounts through G2P payments. This needs to be addressed at the soonest, as dormancy of BMs will lead to loss of faith in the system for customer.

The above findings from the field throw up significant imperatives to be addressed. Massive outreach has been achieved, and the more difficult task of increasing the depth of services awaits. While there are many operational issues requiring attention, from clients' point of view, there are three actionable issues. Financial literacy has emerged as a major requirement, with many wrong notions being associated with PMJDY and its basket of services, and these misinformed notions are gradually leading to disillusionment. The financial education drive has not even fully covered the BMs, not to speak of clients. There is an urgent need for streamlined training of BMs, and through them, training of their customers, which can involve the Financial Literacy and Counselling Centres (FLCC). Second, banks have to ensure that alternative arrangements are made, in case the BMs become dormant. This can be done through more white-label ATMs, or working speedily on an interoperable ecosystem across BMs, so that, in the case of BM's dormancy, clients can transact at other BMs or ATMs. Finally, a composite dialogue between banks, BMs, and technical agencies should be held to resolve the issue of BM's viability, as at present levels of income, this is not a sustainable activity. PMJDY has changed the financial inclusion landscape of India, and the operational and policy issues emerging from studies should be addressed on priority. No other financial inclusion initiative in the country has more potential than PMJDY.

7.3 P2P: THE NEW PLAYER ON THE BLOCK

In the wide spectrum of financial sector, P2P platforms have emerged globally in the last 10 years or so. Microfinance sector has also seen global P2P players, like the much widely known Kiva, as well as national players. The basic operating principle of P2P players remain the same, that is, connecting individual lenders and borrowers through their intermediation—basically bridging the information gap, and ensuring credit underwriting and processes through the P2P platform. While the sector has grown by leaps and bounds, with the RBI placing the global P2P business at 4.4 billion pounds, the sector is still at a nascent stage in India. The reason why it is being covered in the report is the fact that there are P2P players in India, working on linking microfinance clients with social capital. Till now, they have operated without any clear regulatory purview, but the release of a consultation paper on P2P lending by the RBI[15] has instilled hope that they will covered by a regulatory structure and be able to grow. RBI has acknowledged the role of P2P lending by stating, "Although nascent in India and not significant in value yet, the potential benefits that P2P lending promises to various stakeholders (to the borrowers, lenders, agencies etc.) and its associated risks to the financial system are too important to be ignored".

Regulation of P2P has wide variance globally, and central bankers have struggled to devise a common strategy. In Japan and Israel it is not allowed, whereas France and Germany treat it as banks. Overall, there are five regulatory models, and the other models are (a) treating P2P platforms as an intermediary and (b) being exempt from regulation for lack of regulatory definition. The P2P has grown immensely in China, and the central bank there has still kept it exempt from regulation. Indian situation was also same, exempt from regulation, but the consultation paper has raised hopes that the model will soon fall under regulation. The consultation paper analyzes the pros and cons of regulating the activity. Key cons being (a) regulatory structure for a nascent sector may stifle innovation, (b) regulation may put the stamp of legitimacy on the sector, and (c) the sector is too small for causing any systemic issues. The pros are: (a) P2P can soften lending rates and bring competition to the sector, (b) any systemic surprises can be avoided in future, and (c) absence of regulation might lead to unhealthy practices and harm the clients. The adverse consequences listed sound too familiar to the situation in microfinance industry from the 1990s to 2010, and the post-2010 regulation by the RBI has been a reaction to the crisis. As such, it seems the pros seem much more realistic, and it is imperative that the P2P sector is brought under regulation, to allow for its orderly growth, and to avoid surprises.

The consultation paper rightly favors regulation, and has suggested that P2P platforms can be defined as NBFCs under section 45I(f)(iii) of the RBI Act, by issuing a notification in consultation with the Government of India. Post this, the RBI can issue directions on capital adequacy, governance, reporting requirements, customer interface, and other matters (Box 7.1). As per sound practices, the RBI has sought feedback on key issues such as (a) should there be regulation, (b) is the proposed regulation adequate, (c) does the proposed regulation cover all risks, and (d) any other issues missed in the paper. Prominent P2P lenders operating in microfinance space (Rang De and MicroGraam) have welcomed this initiative and given their suggestions to the RBI.

While the suggested framework seems fine, this being a nascent industry, the RBI will have to ensure

---

Box 7.1 Suggested Regulation for P2P

- Direct transfer of money from lender to borrower, avoiding deposit provisions
- No assured return
- No cross-border transactions
- Minimum capital of ₹20 million
- Registration as company—NBFC
- Robust governance and business-continuity plan
- Abide by fair practice code applicable to other lenders

Source: RBI consultation paper.

---

that the regulation remains light touch in terms of business rules, thereby not stifling innovation, but being firm on consumer protection from the beginning. The consultation paper suggests that rules for NBFC-MFIs in terms of transparency and appropriate collection practices can be applied to P2P platforms, and this is a welcome step. However, preventing global funding may stifle the growth, as much of social capital flows from outside India. KYC norms and reporting requirements should be able to take care of any money laundering concerns, rather than applying a blanket ban. Another aspect which comes to the fore is that many social P2P platforms in India are not for profit (Section 8 companies), and the regulation should allow for their coverage under the regulations.

7.3.1 Rang De and MicroGraam[16]: Lending Model and Potential

Both Rang De and MicroGraam are two well-known P2P lending platforms operating in microfinance space, with the objective of provide affordable microloans to rural Indians who do not have access to credit, that can enable them to improve their lives. Both offer an online lending platform that empowers rural entrepreneurs with access to loans from socially minded investors. On their website, individuals can log on and choose the borrowers to whom they wish to lend. The focus of Rang De is on first-time borrowers, that is, individuals who haven't had access to credit from formal financial institutions before. However, considering that microfinance loans require field-level outreach for disbursal and monitoring post-disbursement, both of these organizations have introduced a change from typical P2P lending model

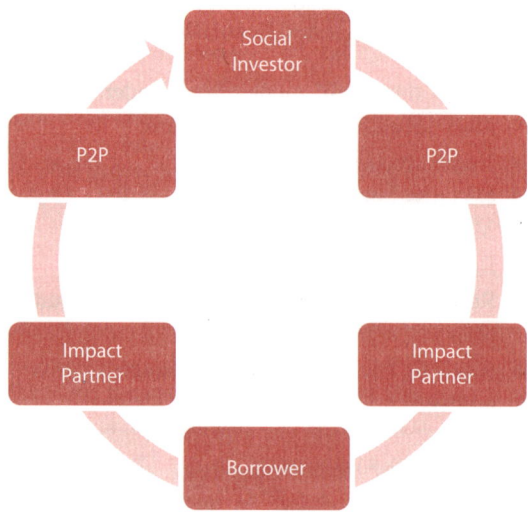

Figure 7.6 P2P Lending Model
Source: Author.

(Figure 7.6). The concept of partner organizations, which are typically NGOs, community organizations, and development agencies working in the field act as another intermediary between P2P and borrower. These partner organizations go through an accreditation process conducted by the P2P platform. Rang De also carries out regular field audits at partner locations, to verify that the partner is maintaining high standards of integrity and lending principles. The audit comprises examination of the partner's financial and field processes, as well as interaction with the borrowers, to verify that the impact partner is not overcharging the borrowers, or behaving in a manner detrimental to the interests of the borrowers. It has also prescribed that its partner organizations adhere to the RBI guidelines for MFIs on transparency, grievance redressal, and appropriate collection practices. MicroGraam's executives also make field visits to ensure that partner organizations are abiding by rules and clients' interests are taken care of.

What differentiates these two players from typical MFIs, from the responsible finance perspective, is their ability to meet clients' need in terms of product flexibility and rates of interest. Unlike the set repayment frequency and loan size/term of MFIs, in this model, the client can decide the terms in consultation with the partner organization. The rates of interest at client level are also much lower than MFIs (Table 7.4) and it is seen that the major differential between MFI cost structure and these two P2P platforms is in the cost of funds and profit margin.

As MFIs like BFIL are now lending at 19.75%, the interest-rate advantage of P2P lenders is thinning, though majority of the MFI sector is still lending at around 24–25%, which gives P2P platforms a distinct edge. However, their main appeal lies is flexibility on products. Despite these advantages, the growth of both organizations has been modest. Rang De has facilitated more than 50,000 loans worth approximately ₹45 crores, and reached out to individuals in 17 states across India, since its formation in 2008. MicroGraam has facilitated nearly 14,000 loans worth ₹20 crore since inception. Both have reported 99% recovery rate, in line with the MFI industry. The key reasons for lack of their growth despite positive features, nonprofit orientation, and product flexibility has been lack of regulatory clarity, deterring investors, especially wholesale/high-net-worth individuals, as well as dearth of quality partner organizations. While the expected RBI guidelines based on the consultation paper will address the regulatory vacuum, the challenge of quality partner organizations will continue to constrain growth.

Rang De has thought of an alternate strategy to overcome this constraint, which it calls "inorganic model of growth," as against current "organic growth model", reliant on partner organizations. It feels that the recent developments in the technology and regulatory fronts provide Rang De with the

Table 7.4 Cost and Lending Structure of Rang De and MicroGraam

	Investor	Partner Organization	P2P	Rate of Interest for Clients
MicroGraam (Declining)	7.5%	6 to 7%	2.5%	16% to 18%
Rang De (Flat)	2%	0 to 5.5%^	2%	9% to 18% declining

Source: Information obtained for the report from Rang De and MicroGraam.
Notes: ^ depends on loan type, in agriculture loans it is 0%, micro-enterprise 2%, and business 5.5%.
Rang De also has a contingency charge of 0.5–1% depending on loan for credit underwriting.

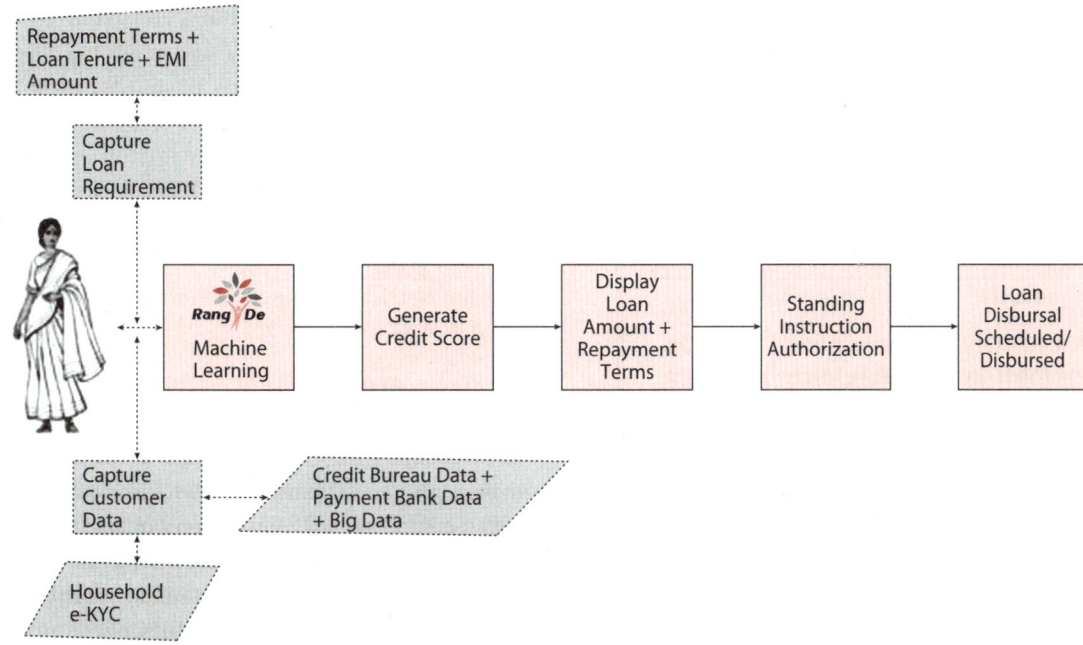

Figure 7.7 Proposed Credit Process of Rang De
Source: Rang De.

opportunity to explore inorganic growth and overcome the limitations of impact partners. It is thinking of tying up with a payment bank to facilitate P2P lending, using innovative platforms such as UPI, e-KYC, and IndiaStack, to get access to rich data about the communities that Rang De would like to work with. It plans to partner with a payments bank, to develop machine learning algorithms, and to derive credit scores based on empathy and multiple data sources (financial data and nonfinancial data), and the role of impact partner will be that of referring clients. The use of big data on clients' past history will enable the model to replace social collateral with data-based credit score. Customers requiring a loan will have to undergo financial literacy training through the digital kiosk, to be set up at the payments bank, and then apply for a loan. Post-this, through the machine, clients can apply for the loan, and their eligibility will be checked through machine-based algorithms and built-in CB checks. Leveraging the power of technology, Rang De expects to achieve a breakthrough in scale and pricing: It expects the lending rate to fall in single digits. The model looks theoretically sound but its regulatory acceptance, as it will use a payments bank and the question of monitoring repayment, as well as follow-up with clients remains unclear.

The moot point in touching upon P2P lending is the fact that they hold potential for future, in leveraging social capital, technology, and product flexibility to offer another choice to microfinance clients. The RBI guidelines on P2P lending will enable these new initiatives to scale up. However, to strengthen responsible finance, the regulations relating to client protection, as applicable to NBFC-MFIs, should be applied on P2P lenders also.

7.4 MICROFINANCE (MFIs AND SBLP): STRENGTHENING RESPONSIBLE FINANCE

The earlier sections of this chapter discussed the current performance of new initiatives, and suggested steps to strengthen their impact as well as ensure that they promote responsible finance. In addition to these new initiatives, the MFIs and SBLPs, with an outreach of around 120 million clients, continue to occupy the preeminent position in microlending. The enormity of their contribution, in ensuring financial inclusion of the excluded, becomes more evident when compared with similar segment outreach of banks, who have 29 million loan accounts with credit facility less than ₹25,000 (which is comparable with microfinance)[17]. The microfinance sector has actively moved toward responsible finance supported by regulation and self-initiative, and this movement toward client centricity needs to be maintained and strengthened. The review of both MFIs and SBLPs in previous chapters shows certain gaps, as well as the need for proactive measures. Action on these points will further their adherence to responsible finance. These issues have been mentioned in previous chapters but summarized here for easy reference.

7.4.1 Policy and Operational Issues to Promote Responsible Microfinance

Moving from CSR to Shared Value Approach (MFIs)

The microfinance sector is a double bottom line industry, whereby both financial and social performance are accorded primacy. The MFIs have demonstrated this by having social goals, passing on efficiency gains to the clients and improving in social governance as well as providing credit plus services in some cases. While the concept of SPM still has gaps and needs to be worked on, the MFIs are faced with resource constraint. The situation prevailing is that while on one hand MFIs are subject to regulatory cap on pricing, on the other, they have no control over cost of debt and equity. This leaves them with tight-margins, and less legroom to invest in SPM and credit-plus activities—though it is acknowledged that by their core operations also they create social capital. Investors and lenders have not provided any incentive for SPM. To add to this, depending on size and turnover, the CSR provisions are applicable to NBFC-MFIs, and going by the growth being seen in the sector, majority of them will soon attract CSR provisions. It needs to be understood that CSR is not SPM, and is more suited for mainstream companies, whose primary objective is to maximize profits. MFIs are a good example of the new thinking on CSR, moving to shared value, wherein the idea is to create economic value in such a way that it also creates value for the society, by addressing its needs and challenges. In the case of MFIs, investments in monitoring social goals, providing financial literacy training, and similar activities are examples of this, and this requires resources. It will be useful if the policy can recognize this approach, and make it applicable to MFIs—the need is to define measurement metrics for creating shared value. If this approach substitutes CSR provisions, it will have a double effect. On one hand, it will free up resources. On the other, it will

enable the sector to think more concretely about social goals, and monitoring and reporting them, and it will translate into higher value creation for its clients. To illustrate, MFIs at present are hesitant to expand to remote areas, fearing cost escalation. If this could be captured in shared-value creation metrics, it can lead to coverage of excluded areas. This approach is in complete alignment with SPM, and it does not restrict institutions who want to go beyond it and do CSR also.

Activity-based Regulation (Banks/MFIs/SBLP)

Chapters 2 and 4 highlighted the trend of banks downscaling, to do microlending on their own, or through BCs. This trend is going to accentuate, with the entry of SFBs, and increasing use of MFIs as BCs. All these channels lend to the same clients as that of MFIs and SBLP. However, at present, the regulations on microlending for NBFC-MFIs are far more stringent than others. For example, no other channel is subject to two-lender restriction, interest rate cap, or loan tenure linked to loan size and income level of client household. This has led to a situation of regulatory arbitrage in the same market, with lending to same clients being at higher rate from BCs than NBFC-MFIs, as well as the ability of banks to provide higher sized loans. This also has implications at client level as clients availing loans of ₹25,000 have now the option to get much higher loans from banks, as well as not fall under two-lender regulation applicable to NBFC-MFIs.

The RBI, as the regulator of banks and NBFCs, needs to ensure that lending to microfinance clients remains entity-neutral with respect to compliance, given the various conditionalities imposed in the case of NBFC-MFIs. These conditionalities have created quite a positive impact for clients, and this should not be allowed to be diluted with the prevalent regulatory arbitrage. If not addressed in time, it will lead to multiple lending, indebtedness of clients, higher cost to clients, and narrowing of the market for MFIs. It needs to be emphasized that the argument of competitive markets, wherein clients can choose, does not stand the test of field realities. Field reality shows that microfinance clients are cash deficient, and they would often opt for a bigger loan even if it is higher priced. While this may require lot of deliberations on defining microfinance clients, and evolving consensus across channels, to begin with, the norm on indebtedness and maximum lenders should be applied across all microlenders.

Reporting on Responsible Finance Parameters (MFIs and SBLP)

The data reported for MFIs and SBLP is mainly operational and financial. Although in the case of MFIs, social-performance data is available with many MFIs at institutional level, it does not get disseminated publicly, which makes it difficult to assess the double bottom line performance of MFIs. As discussed in Chapter-3, MFIN has dome commendable work in data dissemination, and having taken the lead in publishing sector-level operational and financial data, time is now ripe for it to expand to collecting key social-performance data. This is doable, as the industry has been able to evolve globally accepted social-performance metrics so, to begin with, key data points can be captured and expanded later. However, to be credible, it also needs to be checked by external agencies. This can be done by MFIN by integrating it with the third-party evaluations being conducted by it. Self-reported data on social aspects is better than no data, but leaves a lot of questions on validity, and a third party validated data will add much credence. This can be used for defining the social metrics/value creation for a possible shared value approach.

The reporting of social performance in the case of SBLP is nonexistent, and one has to depend on periodic studies. However, the digitization project has opened up new possibilities, and possibly a leapfrogging by SBLP. As the digitization program is being piloted, and likely to be scaled up soon, the reporting parameters can be added now. The reporting under SBLP, considering a multi-stakeholder environment, has to be kept simple to start with. As mentioned in last year's report, to begin with, poverty outreach and client-level outcomes can be the key indicators. Both these aspects can be covered through introduction of Progress out of Poverty Index (PPI), which is a simple ten-point questionnaire. The PPI scores of each group member will reflect the poverty outreach, and the analysis of PPI scores over time will provide a reasonably accurate picture of client-level outcome.

Reducing Regional/State/District Concentration (MFIs/SBLP)

Chapters 5 and 6 clearly bring out the fact that both MFIs and SBLP have highly concentrated outreach, which makes the impressive outreach lopsided.

There is no problem with growth, but growing in few pockets exposes clients to overindebtedness, and ultimately affects institutions, in the form of high, nonperforming loans. The data from CBs show that top 80 districts have, on an average, presence of 20 microlenders, and top 30 districts account for one-third of microfinance portfolio—this excludes SBLP, on account of unavailability of data with the CB. This situation, of saturated growth pockets, is causing a lot of concern, with some going to the extent of saying that the sector is approaching the V.2 of 2010 crisis.

Nudging MFIs toward less-penetrated and excluded regions has to be done either by regulation or by investors/lenders. More importantly, this has to be backed by incentives, as mandating MFIs to expand to excluded areas and thereby increase their operational costs, can be counterproductive in the existing tight-margin regime. At present, there is little leeway available on cost front, to incur additional costs. While as recipient of priority sector funding, there can be an argument to require NBFC-MFIs to demonstrate a certain part of their outreach in excluded regions by regulation, it will lead to viability issues. The suggested path is to back such regulatory requirement with incentives. The most tangible incentive could be interest-rate reduction on bank lending, and allowing a higher margin cap, to enable institutions to cover the additional cost. The margin flexibility can be done away with, once the operations reach scale in those areas. The interest-rate reduction and margin flexibility has to be worked out in consultation with MFIs and SROs, in place of being an arbitrary figure. A phased approach needs to be adopted, like requiring MFIs to show 10% of portfolio in earmarked districts by end of the first year, and increasing it progressively.

The approach in the case of SBLP has to be different, as the causes of regional skew there are different. The major reason seems to be support from state governments to SHPAs, by way of funding as well as prioritizing SHGs' agenda. Both NABARD and NRLM need to build strong SHPAs in states with much lower penetration, with adequate funding support. It is acknowledged that many of these areas have negligible, or no presence of suitable SHPAs, and to overcome this, strong SHPAs from other states should be incentivized to start operations there—the concept of building resource SHPAs has been advocated for long, as the quality of

SHPAs affects the group quality. Community mobilization, and making them ready for financial intermediation, is specialized work, and not every NGO or CBO is suited to do this. The nature of funding support also needs to be enhanced, and made front-ended, thereby incentivizing group quality and savings over credit. This has cost implications, but public policy has to incur this for the sake of inclusive development, and this is far more efficient than providing interest-rate subvention in saturated areas.

Prevention of Overindebtedness—Need to Implement E-KYC (Banks/SBLP/MFI)

The regulation has now plugged the gap in CB reporting, by requiring all lenders including SBLP to report to CBs. While this is effective for others at present, in the case of SBLP it will take three–five years, going by the scale of work required in digitizing SHG records. But even in the case of other lenders such as banks and MFIs, the issue of client identification can be improved with the adoption of Aadhaar (which is nearing universal coverage). MFIN members have decided voluntarily to move toward Aadhaar, and its utility is being seen in the field, with MFIs reporting higher rejections from CB checks due to violation of the two-lender norm. At present, a client can provide different IDs to different institutions, and trick the CB system by not getting rejected. Making Aadhaar compulsory across all lenders being the first step, it has to be followed up by moving the sector toward e-verification of Aadhaar through biometrics. This will make the system foolproof, and allow for proper assessment of an individual's credit history. The point about e-KYC is critical as field experience shows that mere capture of the Aadhaar number is not enough, as often typographical mistakes, and sometimes intentional mistakes, keep the system prone to manipulation. This move, by bringing in all lenders under a robust CB ecosystem, supplemented by foolproof client verification, will foster responsible finance, and instances of client distress due to excessive credit can be checked.

Need for Patient Equity (MFIs)

The MFI sector is going through a phenomenal growth, clocking 90% annual growth during 2015–16, despite the noninclusion of Bandhan Bank's figures—which was the largest MFI. The concerns emerging out of this growth, in terms of saturated markets, multiple loans, and incidences of distress have been discussed in Chapter 5. The concern is not only with the growth, but with the quality of growth, as institutions with similar offerings are competing in similar markets. Though it is opined by many that commencement of operations as SFBs by the leading NBFC-MFIs in the near future will temper growth, the moot thing is that as the primary client segment of these banks will remain same, not much is expected to change. Bandhan Bank's example is there: Its transformation has only changed the data for NBFC-MFIs, but in field similar situation prevails—in fact, more concerning is the issue that these transformed MFIs will not be subject to regulations applicable to NBFC-MFIs.

While, the measures outlined above, such as requiring MFIs to go to unserved areas and activity-based regulation, will bring some semblance of order, it is imperative to work on the source of high growth. MFIs have little negotiating room with private equity investors, who expect a minimum return, and are faced with constrictions on both sides—return expectation of investors, and interest-rate-cap regulation, the option available is to grow and reduce costs. The sector has seen that, in 2010, as growth requirements led to cuts in investment in staff training and capacity building, the same situation is prevailing now with staff attrition rate in the sector touching ~25%. In this situation, the critical thing to do is to create sources of domestic patient capital, and substitute return maximizing capital. NABBARD's Microfinance Development Equity Fund (MFDEF) is now closed and even when it was there, it was conservative and accounted for a negligible share. SIDBI is the only existing source of publicly owned, domestic equity for MFIs. SIDBI's total support through equity, subordinate debt, and optionally convertible cumulative preference shares stood at ₹468 crore as on March 31, 2016. However, much of this assistance is for smaller MFIs. The concern of stakeholders and policy makers on high growth needs to be backed by providing sources of patient capital. The role of debt funders is also significant. Banks need to consider a deeper dive into operational performance rather than relying solely on financial numbers. Their reliance on ratings also does not help much, as the ratings are financial and do not provide a deep-dive double bottom line analysis. Banks also do not make use of CPP certifications, CoC assessments, and so on, as regulation requires only one set of financial ratings for their risk assessment, coupled with the fact that bankers are not fully informed about the other assessments. The multiplicity of assessments existing in the market is partly to blame for this. While the lending decisions of banks also depend on financial performance and compliance with guidelines, there is hardly any difference in interest rates charged to different MFIs. For facilitating responsible microfinance, this needs to change, and banks need to take responsibility.

High Time to Collate Multiple Assessments (MFIs)

As mentioned above, the MFIs currently go through multiple assessments and ratings. Before 2010, only financial rating or performance assessment was in vogue, but the crisis, as well as new regulatory requirement for capital adequacy, has led to a situation wherein an institution has to undergo (a) bank loan ratings from RBI accredited rating agencies, (b) securitization ratings, in the case of securitization deals, (c) NCD ratings, (d) performance rating/ microfinance grading for institutional performance assessment, (e) social rating, in case social investors demand it, or if the institution wants to measure its social performance, (f) CoC assessment, (g) CPP certification, and (h) third-party evaluation of MFIN. Although the last one is applicable only for NBFC-MFIs, these multiple assessments consume both time and resources of MFIs.

More important is the fact that similar information is analyzed through different frameworks not adding incremental value, and the net result is ineffective use of these multiple assessments. It is high time that the two issues. that is, bankers' focus on financial performance ratings and existence of multiple ratings/assessments, is dealt with. This issue was covered in *Social Performance Report, 2012*, as well as last year's report wherein it was suggested that there is an urgent need to collate all narrow-focused assessments under one comprehensive framework. Though it will lead to some loss of granular information, but for the higher gains this needs to be accepted. Moreover, there is little use of assessments which are not used actively, as also they fail to provide accurate state of the institution. The ratings being awarded currently, the surge in CPP certifications and high marks under COC assessments sit uneasily with the concerns in the sector. MFIN and SIDBI should take a lead in this—the current initiative on harmonizing CoC and TPE of MFIN is too limited in scope. Once the framework

is developed in consultation with all stakeholders, it will require policy work at the RBI level. This will not only reduce the burden of assessments for MFIs but provide a comprehensive picture at one place, and can be used by bankers easily.

Need for Product Diversity and Robust Measures to Prevent Client Distress (MFIs/SBLP)

As discussed in Chapter 2, while MFIs have achieved significant progress under transparency in communication with clients, establishing grievance redressal systems, and lowering rates of interest, the area which has lagged behind is product diversity. During the last one year, the RBI has relaxed much of operational norms on products, thereby taking away the constraint that would push microlenders for product innovation. The diversity of products seen in the sector is limited to individual loans, emergency loans, housing loans, and sanitation loans, but even these products are not much different, except the loan amount and periodicity of repayment. Further, their share in total portfolio is minimal. It seems that in the rush for growth, there is little time available for products based on specific livelihoods, and its associated cash flow. This requires seeking client feedback, designing livelihood-based products, piloting them, and then scaling up. On the other hand, the movement toward higher repayment frequency based on efficiency requirements, and the practice of cross-selling consumer goods has started in a big way. The repayment frequency needs to be dictated by the client, and not by the institutional requirements. On cross-selling, while certain products such as solar lights and smokeless challahs create value for the client and society, cross-selling of pure consumer durables such as television, phones and so on needs to be relooked. Related to products is the issue of near absence of loan rescheduling policies in the sector. Even with that, the sector reporting a near-zero delinquency rate sits oddly with pockets of saturated markets, drought impacted rural distress, multiple loans, increasing loan size, and higher repayment amounts, with increase in repayment frequency. This seems to be too good to be true, and is quite troubling actually. The recent study on SBLP reported that the maximum number of clients in arrears were on account of genuine problems. MFIs, along with creating product diversity, need to build tolerance for genuine repayment problems, and not be fixated on zero delinquency. The study conducted for this report[18] found that 33% of clients had to contribute for joint liability. This clearly shows that higher loan size is putting repayment capacity under strain.

The movement toward NBFC-MFIs acting as BC to offer to offer deposit services has also not seen much movement, but the provision of credit as BC has seen high growth. This clearly shows that the decision is guided by profit consideration over client needs. Though providing deposit services as BC may not be financially attractive for MFIs, it benefits clients immensely by having access to both credit and savings from one provider. The Voices study conducted for this report found that 80% of clients would like to save with MFIs over banks, on account of their doorstep service and familiarity. This will not only benefit the clients but also help the MFIs to face the competition in near future from SFBs, who will be able to provide both credit and savings.

Lack of product diversity also extends to SBLP, where except the nature of credit facility, not much has changed. Though the traditional argument is that group takes care of individual requirement based on needs, studies show that in most cases, the amount is equally divided among group members. The progress on capturing individual member records under digitization opens up new possibilities for product diversity. A bold rethink on member-based lending, using the group as a cohesive social structure is needed.

SRO: Need for Public Funding and Avoiding Regulatory Arbitrage (MFIs)

Chapter 3 detailed the impressive work done by MFIN in promoting responsible finance, as well as in keeping a tight watch over market practices. However, it needs to be acknowledged that the SRO function sits oddly with a member-funded organization, which also has its primary role of advocacy, and building a conducive ecosystem for its members. It has been able to balance the two roles in recent times due to good leadership and governance systems, but the tenuous line between advocacy, dependence on member funding, and SRO role always has a possibility of being breach. This can be due to various factors, such as members not agreeing with a particular rule or change in leadership. Placing importance on institutional mechanisms over persons is needed, and that will need reducing the dependence of SRO on member funds, as

well as a stricter firewall between SRO, apart from other parts of MFIN's association-related work. Public funding is needed to protect the neutrality, and the fund requirement is meagre, as compared to the benefits.

Another issue relates to SRO roles and check on their functioning. The RBI has recognized MFIN and Sa-Dhan as the SROs, and MFIs can opt for membership of any one or both. This gives the option to MFIs to choose which SRO is more accommodating to their needs, and opens up regulatory arbitrage, as SRO enforcing stricter discipline may not be favored by many. To prevent this, the regulation should ensure that both SROs follow similar rules and procedures, at least on core issues. The present regulatory guidelines on SRO are broad/generic and leave room for SRO's functioning as "light touch." With experience of nearly three years, a more detailed guideline on SRO roles and functioning is required.

Investment in Staff Needs Attention (MFIs)

Responsibility to staff is an important piece of social performance, as motivated and trained staff is an asset in delivering financial service in a responsible manner: Field staff under pressure on account of productivity targets or to maintain zero delinquency are more likely to short circuit processes, as well as deviate from norms of appropriate behavior with clients. Moreover, unsatisfied staff leads to higher attrition, increasing the operational cost. The worrying trend in the sector highlighted last year continues with high staff attrition, field staff remuneration veering toward minimum required under law, increasing productivity, and use of field staff to provide other services like cross-selling. The sector is seeing an average 25% annual staff turnover at field staff level. Tough working conditions in the field, coupled with increasing workload, leads to higher attrition. MFIs need to find creative ways to address these issues, by providing better wages and more capacity building, as well as innovative options like having a less layered structure, but more skilled and better-paid staff. Field staff is the foundation on which the structure has been built, and to continue treating it as business as usual in the name of low-cost model will lead to adverse consequences. Low-cost principle should be applicable across the hierarchy, and not be applicable only to field staff. Adequate compensation, investment in training, and balanced work load are key parameters for keeping staff motivated.

7.5 CONCLUDING NOTES

The financial inclusion sector is seeing paradigm changes. New institutions, new programs, banks downscaling, technology, and favorable ecosystem in terms of digital initiatives, electronic KYC, and almost universal coverage of Aadhaar have strengthened the belief that inclusion of all is a distinct possibility in near future. Apart from these supply-side innovations, demand side has seen coverage of all households under PMJDY, raising expectations and initiatives such as Udyami Mitra and Stand-Up India portal have given hope to micro- and small entrepreneurs of access to financial services. Work on both demand and supply side is in line with the empirically proven link between inclusive growth, and depth of financial access. In this era of possibility, it needs to be ensured that the new players and initiatives remain committed to responsible finance, by meeting the needs of clients in a cost effective, transparent, and responsible manner. While the new initiatives like SFBs and PBs have yet to commence operations, the report analyzed the role of other new initiatives such as MUDRA, PMJDY, and P2P lenders and, based on that, has suggested a responsible agenda for them. Technology, in the form of connectivity or cloud-based big data analytics, is going to be a game changer. This combination of finance and technology termed as FINTECH or Digital Financial Services, needs to adopt global best practices in responsible finance from the start. Along with these new trends, significant progress has been made by both MFIs and SBLP, by bringing nearly 100 million clients to the fold of financial inclusion. Both channels account for dominant share in credit side inclusion of poor borrowers. While the progress is commendable, several issues have emerged across both channels, which reduce their effectiveness and client centricity. It is hoped that the policy and operational action points detailed in this chapter—if actioned—can strengthen their client centricity, as well as ensure that they continue to grow sustainably.

Dr. Martin Luther King Jr. said, "[T]he arc of the moral universe is long, but it bends towards justice."

For too long the public policy has tried to achieve universal financial inclusion, but the environment has never been so favorable as it is currently. The link between inclusive growth and depth of financial services makes it a moral duty for all stakeholders to collectively work toward the goal of universal financial inclusion. Availability of financial resources, tools, infrastructure, technology, and ecosystem-including policy has never been better, and it gives hope that all stakeholders will harness these elements to achieve the goal, making India a more inclusive India and a land of opportunities for all.

NOTES AND REFERENCES

1. Budget speech of the finance minister in 2014.
2. http://pib.nic.in/newsite/PrintRelease.aspx?relid=116209, accessed on October 6, 2016.
3. http://www.smechamberofindia.com/about_msmes.aspx, accessed on October 6, 2016.
4. *Improving Access to Finance for Women Owned Businesses in India*, IFC in partnership with Government of Japan.
5. https://www.standupmitra.in, accessed on October 6, 2016.
6. http://www.mudra.org.in/Offerings, accessed on September 2, 2016.
7. Misra, Alok. 2015. Chapter 6 "Strengthening Responsible Finance for the Excluded." In *Responsible Finance India Report*.
8. Shankar, Savita. 2016, July. "Bridging the 'Missing Middle' between Microfinance and Small and Medium-Sized Enterprise Finance in South Asia". ADB Institute Working Paper No. 587. The working paper also says a similar thing: *"While recently the upper limit of microfinance loans has been increased to ₹100,000, the lower limit for SME financing by commercial banks is usually around 10 times this amount (₹1 million). There is therefore a considerable gap between these two sectors".*
9. MicroSave. 2016. *PMJDY Wave III Assessment*. Lucknow: MicroSave.
10. Compilation of drill down case studies of existing BCs and BC models in MP, 2015, PwC.
11. http://pmjdy.gov.in/files/od/od/od.pdf, accessed on October 6, 2016.
12. National poverty line as per Rangarajan panel considered people living on less than ₹32 a day in rural areas and ₹47 a day in urban areas as poor.
13. BMs with no transaction for last 90 days have been defined as dormant.
14. http://www.cgap.org/sites/default/files/CGAP-Technical-Guide-Agent-Management-Toolkit-Building-a-Viable-Network-of-Branchless-Banking-Agents-Feb-2011.pdf, accessed on October 6, 2016.
15. https://rbidocs.rbi.org.in/rdocs/content/pdfs/CPERR280416.pdf, accessed on October 6, 2016.
16. www.rangde.org; www.micrograam.com, accessed on October 6, 2016.
17. As on March 31, 2015, *Banking & Statistical Returns*, RBI.
18. M2i. 2016. *Voice of Clients Study*. Access Development Services.

About the Author

Alok Misra, PhD in Development Studies from Victoria University of Wellington, Master in Development Management (Gold Medallist) from Asian Institute of Management, Manila, is currently Professor, Public Policy and Governance Area at Management Development Institute, Gurgaon. He is also a member of the Strategic Advisory Board on Microfinance constituted by NABARD, member of MFIN SRO committee, Board member of Rang De, member of Inclusive Finance India Group of Advisors, and member of Digital Finance working group constituted by ITU, Geneva. He has been trained at Harvard Business School in 'Strategic Leadership for Microfinance' and was a Fellow, Fletcher Leadership Program for Financial Inclusion at Tufts University.

Dr Misra has 24 years of professional experience in international development, rural finance/microfinance/inclusive finance, and research at both policy and implementation levels. He has written numerous articles and reports, and last year he authored *Responsible Finance India Report 2015* commissioned by ACCESS Development Services and published by SAGE Publications. His teaching, research, and consulting interests are in development policy analysis, poverty and rural finance, design and evaluation of development projects, inclusive finance, digital finance, impact investment, social entrepreneurship, and risk mitigation.